ॐ

BHAGAVAD GITA APPLIED WISDOM

Ashwini Kumar Aggarwal

जय गुरुदेव

ISBN13: 9781722213657 Paperback Edition
ISBN13: 9798726640921 Hardbound Edition
ISBN13: 9789353001186 Digital Edition

Title Bhagavad Gita Applied Wisdom

Printed and Published by Ashwini Kumar Aggarwal
The Art of Living Centre
147 Punjabi Bagh, Patiala 147001
Punjab, India

Website https://advaita56.weebly.com/
Devotees of Sri Sri Ravi Shankar Ashram

2nd January 2018, Paush Poornima
Ardra Nakshatra, Devi Shakambari Jayanti, Charita Puja
Vikrami Samvat 2074 Sadharana, Saka Era 1939 Hemalambi

1st Edition January 2018

जय गुरुदेव

Dedication

H H Sri Sri Ravi Shankar
the Master of YOGA, JNANA and BHAKTI

An offering at His Lotus feet

A bold and fresh perspective for the modern reader
These verses came to me in meditative states or during silence. I simply penned them down in my free time, when i was relaxed, unhurried.

HISTORIAN / SCRIBE / WRITTEN at
Vyasa / Ganesha / Badrinath

CAST of CHARACTERS

Krishna तत्

Arjuna त्वम्

Sanjaya असि

Dhritarashtra I

Duryodhana II

PLACE of ACTION
Thought, Mind, Heart, Brain, Nervous System, Hands & Feet, Eyes Ears Speech

The TIME
A Critical Juncture, Of paramount importance, NOW

जय गुरुदेव

Gita Dhyanam

A simple means of remembering the celestial beings.

ॐ पार्थाय प्रतिबोधितां भगवता नारायणेन स्वयम् , व्यासेन ग्रथितां पुराणमुनिना मध्येमहाभारतम् ।
अद्वैतामृतवर्षिणीं भगवतीम् अष्टादशाध्यायिनीम् अम्ब त्वाम् अनुसन्दधामि भगवद्गीते भवद्वेषिणीम् ॥ १

नमोऽस्तु ते व्यास विशालबुद्धे , फुल्लारविन्दायतपत्रनेत्र ।
येन त्वया भारततैलपूर्णः , प्रज्वालितो ज्ञानमय1 प्रदीपः ॥ २

प्रपन्नपारिजाताय तोत्रवेत्रैकपाणये । ज्ञानमुद्राय कृष्णाय गीतामृतदुहे नमः ॥ ३

सर्वोपनिषदो गावो दोग्धा गोपालनन्दनः । पार्थो वत्सः सुधीर्भोक्ता दुग्धं गीतामृतं महत् ॥ ४

वसुदेवसुतं देवं कंसचाणूरमर्दनम् । देवकीपरमानन्दं कृष्णं वन्दे जगद्गुरुम् ॥ ५

भीष्मद्रोणतटा जयद्रथजला गान्धारनीलोत्पला शल्यग्राहवती कृपेण वहनी कर्णेन वेलाकुला ।
अश्वत्थामविकर्णघोरमकरा दुर्योधनावर्त्तिनी सोत्तीर्णा खलु पाण्डवै रणनदी कैवर्तकः केशवः ॥ ६

पाराशर्यवचः सरोजममलं गीतार्थगन्धोत्कटं नानाख्यानककेसरं हरिकथा सम्बोधनाबोधितम् ।
लोके सज्जनषट्पदैरहरहः , पेपीयमानं मुदा भूयाद्भारतपङ्कजं कलिमलप्रध्वंसि नः श्रेयसे ॥ ७

मूकं करोति वाचालं पङ्गुं लङ्घयते गिरिम् । यत्कृपा तमहं वन्दे परमानन्दमाधवम् ॥ ८

यं ब्रह्मा वरुणेन्द्ररुद्रमरुतः , स्तुन्वन्ति दिव्यैः स्तवैः वेदैः साङ्गपदक्रमोपनिषदैः , गायन्ति यं सामगाः ।
ध्यानावस्थिततद्गतेन मनसा , पश्यन्ति यं योगिनः यस्यान्तं न विदुः सुरासुरगणाः , देवाय तस्मै नमः ॥ ९ ॥

शान्ताकारं भुजगशयनं पद्मनाभं सुरेशम् , विश्वाधारं गगनसदृशं मेघवर्णं शुभाङ्गम् ।
लक्ष्मीकान्तं कमलनयनं योगिभिर् ध्यानगम्यम्,वन्दे विष्णुं भवभयहरं सर्वलोकैकनाथम् ॥

Table of Contents

GITA DHYANAM 4
BLESSING 6
PRAYER 6
1 YOGA OF MEETING ONESELF 7
2 YOGA OF LORD'S INTERVENTION 21
3 YOGA OF STEERING LIFE 37
4 YOGA OF INTENTION 46
5 YOGA OF CALMNESS 55
6 YOGA OF SELF CONTROL 61
7 YOGA OF DIVINE QUALITIES 75
8 YOGA OF DEMYSTIFYING DEATH 82
9 YOGA OF ROYAL SECRETS 89
10 YOGA OF DIVINE MANIFESTATIONS 97
11 YOGA OF COSMIC PERSONALITY 107
12 YOGA OF DEVOTION 122
13 YOGA OF MATTER & CONSCIOUSNESS 128
14 YOGA OF TRICREATIVE ENERGIES 139
15 YOGA OF THE IDEAL MAN 146
16 YOGA OF GOOD AND BAD HABITS 152
17 YOGA OF SATTVIC RAJASIC TAMASIC WORSHIPS 158
18 YOGA OF LIBERATION BY LETTING GO 165
ENDING PRAYER 182
PARDON SHLOKAS 183
GITA MAHATMYAM 183
DEVANAGARI LATIN VELTHUIS TRANSLITERATION CHART 184
OM JAI JAGADISH HARE 185
EPILOGUE 186

Blessing

A yogi considers even his work as a game, so be a yogi. Yogi means ‘one who does things in perfection.’ Every little thing he does will be perfect because he has that equanimity of mind. Only when you consider your work as a game can you ever be detached about whether it is going to be successful or not. It doesn’t matter anyway.

H H Sri Sri Ravi Shankar

Prayer

ॐ नमो भगवते वासुदेवाय

ॐ नमो भगवते वासुदेवाय

ॐ नमो भगवते वासुदेवाय

ॐ नमो भगवते वासुदेवाय

o.m namo bhagavate vaasudevaaya
o.m namo bhagavate vaasudevaaya
o.m namo bhagavate vaasudevaaya
o.m namo bhagavate vaasudevaaya

1 Yoga of Meeting Oneself

ॐ श्री परमात्मने नमः । अथ प्रथमोऽध्यायः

oṁ śrī paramātmane namaḥ । atha prathamo'dhyāyaḥ

धृतराष्ट्र उवाच

धर्मक्षेत्रे कुरुक्षेत्रे , समवेता युयुत्सवः । मामकाः पाण्डवाश्चैव , किम् अकुर्वत सञ्जय ॥ १.१

dhṛtarāṣṭra uvāca

dharmakṣetre kurukṣetre , samavetā yuyutsavaḥ ।

māmakāḥ pāṇḍavāścaiva , kim akurvata sañjaya ॥ 1.1

Dhritarashtra asked

1.1 In the game of life and death, viewed in the backdrop of self-discipline and a value system, how does it fare between my pleasure wants and my righteous wants? I wish to know because my tendency is slightly off center. So please tell me what (will) happen, what happens when i go after pleasure?

Have you ever wondered as to how does the Gita begin?
It gives a great clue to the seeker - to one wanting freedom.

A blind man, who is a King, is posing a question. The question is addressed in his palace to his charioteer. And it is being asked in a relaxed setting. And it is about the most direct straight forward truth.

Notice that:
- the Q is asked by a King, i.e. one very well off materially. Blindness refers to being off-center or biased, hence unable to decide wisely.
- the Q is asked in his palace, i.e. in a comfort zone.
like we say AC hall or comfy environs for Part2 course is a must.
like we say go to temple only after bath and breakfast.

We started to receive from Guruji because he befriended us, because he dropped to our level and kept no gap.

सञ्जय उवाच

दृष्ट्वा तु पाण्डवानीकम् , व्यूढं दुर्योधनस् तदा । आचार्यम् उपसङ्गम्य , राजा वचनम् अब्रवीत् ॥ १.२

sañjaya uvāca

dṛṣṭvā tu pāṇḍavānīkam , vyūḍhaṁ duryodhanas tadā ।

ācāryam upasaṅgamya , rājā vacanam abravīt ॥ 1.2

Sanjaya said

1.2 Having seen the Pandava army arrayed for battle, the King Duryodhana approached his Teacher up close, and spoke the words...

The king's charioteer responds instantly. There is no delay in the reply. Does this give you any hint? Do you know the value of time? Wake up and start observing the discipline of timeliness.

Right after laying down the parameters and governing codes for attainment of Truth, observance of TIME is displayed upfront.

Highlights of Sanjaya's answer.

He begins with the questioner's son. He begins the narration with a topic that is most dear to the questioner.

Consider for a moment that you ask someone something. How shall the reply be of any use to you if it doesn't immediately catch your attention? Can a bare Truth be spoken if it is irrelevant? Can a lecture be started if it begins uninterestingly, dully, or out of context? Can education be imparted without engaging the student?

पश्यैतां पाण्डुपुत्राणाम् , आचार्य महतीं चमूम् । व्यूढां द्रुपदपुत्रेण , तव शिष्येण धीमता ॥ १.३

paśyaitāṁ pāṇḍuputrāṇām , ācārya mahatīṁ camūm ।

vyūḍhāṁ drupadaputreṇa , tava śiṣyeṇa dhīmatā ॥ 1.3

1.3 Look at the sons of Pandu, O Teacher! Admire the great team, see the most skilled of all you have trained. How your intelligent pupil, the son of Drupad, has arrayed the resources in a manner that can be used flawlessly.

One of the earliest marketing forays by man. This verse is a direct advertisement. Marketing. Advertisement. Sales pitch. What is it? Why is it needed? Can we live without it? This verse gives a fundamental ingredient of marketing. Praise the client first and then the product. Wondrous, isn't it?

अत्र शूरा महेष्वासाः , भीमार्जुनसमा युधि । युयुधानो विराटश्च , द्रुपदश्च महारथः ॥ १.४

atra śūrā maheṣvāsāḥ , bhīmārjunasamā yudhi ।

yuyudhāno virāṭaśca , drupadaśca mahārathaḥ ॥ 1.4

1.4 Skilled and Talented are the great archers, players, administrators, celebrities and scientists. Equal to the mighty Bhima and Arjuna. Filled with cosmic energy, firm as a pillar.

We get vicarious pleasure in watching and reading about someone else. This fact is highlighted and the virtues we all love are listed, so that we can identify with some and enhance some and aim for some.

धृष्टकेतुश् चेकितानः , काशिराजश्च वीर्यवान् । पुरुजित् कुन्तिभोजश्च , शैब्यश्च नरपुङ्गवः ॥ १.५

dhr̥ṣṭaketuś cekitānaḥ , kāśirājaśca vīryavān ।

purujit kuntibhojaśca , śaibyaśca narapuṅgavaḥ ॥ 1.5

1.5 Whose actions are proven and certified, endowed with sharp intellect, splendorous, brave, all-conquering. Well washed, manicured, emitting fragrance and royally dressed, with ice-cool nerves.

युधामन्युश्च विक्रान्तः , उत्तमौजाश्च वीर्यवान् । सौभद्रो द्रौपदेयाश्च , सर्व एव महारथाः ॥ १.६

yudhāmanyuśca vikrāntaḥ , uttamaujāśca vīryavān ।

saubhadro draupadeyāśca , sarva eva mahārathāḥ ॥ 1.6

1.6 Valiant, valorous, with high self-esteem, close-knit brothers, sociable and extrovert.

Apart from listing other peoples aspects and objects that are worthy of my admiration, i forthwith turn to my own inherent traits.

अस्माकं तु विशिष्टा ये , तान् निबोध द्विजोत्तम । नायका मम सैन्यस्य , सञ्ज्ञार्थं तान् ब्रवीमि ते ॥ १.७

asmākaṁ tu viśiṣṭā ye , tān nibodha dvijottama ।

nāyakā mama sainyasya , sañjñārthaṁ tān bravīmi te ॥ 1.7

1.7 I now express my own virtues and skillsets, an outline of my curriculum vitae O all knowing Master!

भवान् भीष्मश्च कर्णश्च , कृपश्च समितिञ्जयः । अश्वत्थामा विकर्णश्च , सौमदत्तिस् तथैव च ॥ १.८

bhavān bhīṣmaśca karṇaśca , kr̥paśca samitiñjayaḥ ।

aśvatthāmā vikarṇaśca , saumadattis tathaiva ca ॥ 1.8

1.8 Myself and some of my remarkable traits consist of terrible and extreme vows taking, absolute servitude, lithesomeness, not taking no for an answer, ample horsepower, omnidirectional hearing and also capacity for drink.

अन्ये च बहवश् शूराः , मदर्थे त्यक्तजीविताः । नानाशस्त्रप्रहरणाः , सर्वे युद्धविशारदाः ॥ १.९

anye ca bahavaś śūrāḥ , madarthe tyaktajīvitāḥ ।

nānāśastrapraharaṇāḥ , sarve yuddhaviśāradāḥ ॥ 1.9

1.9 Other points include a capacity to endear the rich and famous, die for rewards, swiss army knife type skillset, jack of all trades.

अपर्याप्तं तद् अस्माकम् , बलं भीष्माभिरक्षितम् । पर्याप्तं त्विदम् एतेषाम् , बलं भीमाभिरक्षितम् ॥ १.१०

aparyāptaṁ tad asmākam , balaṁ bhīṣmābhirakṣitam ।

paryāptaṁ tvidam eteṣām , balaṁ bhīmābhirakṣitam ॥ 1.10

1.10 Know that our strength is insufficient – our product is inferior, and theirs is superior. The competitor's product shall do your job.

A most fatal error of over smart advertisement, when one acts with greed or feverish ambition, then one's conscience sitting within can no longer take it. And one utters something that is directly detrimental to us, that doesn't go unnoticed by the client, that lays the seed for one's eventual downfall.

अयनेषु च सर्वेषु , यथाभागम् अवस्थिताः । भीष्मम् एवाभिरक्षन्तु , भवन्तस् सर्व एव हि ॥ १.११

ayaneṣu ca sarveṣu , yathābhāgam avasthitāḥ ।

bhīṣmam evābhirakṣantu , bhavantas sarva eva hi ॥ 1.11

1.11 Having established that Bhishma is the most valuable player on our team, we must care, protect, nurture, follow and maintain him to the best of our ability.

This is a king's dictum. It is a law made by the highest authority and needs to be followed in its entirety.

तस्य सञ्जनयन् हर्षम् , कुरुवृद्धः पितामहः । सिंहनादं विनद्योच्चैः , शङ्खं दध्मौ प्रतापवान् ॥ १.१२

tasya sañjanayan harṣam , kuruvṛddhaḥ pitāmahaḥ ।

siṁhanādaṁ vinadyoccaiḥ , śaṅkhaṁ dadhmau pratāpavān ॥ 1.12

1.12 The famous figurehead responded by giving a superlative performance - the Saint's blessings drenched us, to uplift us.

and my friend, do you have any idea what happens when you give proper respect and praise to an esteemed personality?
or when you offer a high seat to the saint? to the master?
or when you take good care of your son or home or car?

Your son or home or car runs to its fullest potential.

Your practice or Sadhana or spiritual discipline gives you untold benefits.

Didn't you know blaring one's trumpet is a direct symbol of pride, wellness and jubilation?

ततश् शङ्खाश्च भेर्यश्च , पणवानकगोमुखाः । सहसैवाभ्यहन्यन्त , स शब्दस् तुमुलोऽभवत् ॥ १.१३

tataś śaṅkhāśca bheryaśca , paṇavānakagomukhāḥ ।

sahasaivābhyahanyanta , sa śabdas tumulo'bhavat ॥ 1.13

1.13 When the Lord is happy, then all of us, you and me and they and it, all flora and fauna, all items, objects and parts of matter get to experience it.

And what does it signify when all blow? When all Cheer? simple - it means a Win Win situation. Here in Verse 1.13 of the Gita is this supreme message of the Lord. Freedom of Expression. Freedom of Communication, of Loud Proclamation. The thrill runs down one's spine, one feels rock solid, brave, bold and joyous.

ततः श्वेतैर् हयैर्युक्ते , महति स्यन्दने स्थितौ । माधवः पाण्डवश्चैव , दिव्यौ शङ्खौ प्रदध्मतुः ॥ १.१४

tataḥ śvetair hayairyukte , mahati syandane sthitau ।

mādhavaḥ pāṇḍavaścaiva , divyau śaṅkhau pradadhmatuḥ ॥ 1.14

1.14 Then the sweet like honey Lord Madhava and the Pandava who had the capability of receiving-learning-soaking, well ensconced in their magnificent, sparkling and luminous chariot-automobile-ferrari-folkswagon-bike or Jet, blew their divine conches...

Ain't it such a joy...To do the same thing as the Lord does...and to be with Him.

Notice a fine sculpting here. A beautiful verse. Handcrafted with care. Full of aesthetic charm. the breath is divine. blowing is divine.

Sri Sri says do your breath practice so that your vision becomes divine.
Tulsidas says Hanuman is the strong wind that can lay the foundation for victory.

All of us are today familiar with Pranayama. A way of practicing the breath to achieve strength and fitness of mind and body. The starting step in the path of achieving freedom for the soul.

The Bhagavad Gita expresses this fluidly. Smoothly it tells about blowing strongly, about breathing deeply. Such a beautiful verse on Pranayama. On Sudarshan Kriya. On two most divine beings practicing breath control.

Another unnoticed point here is the emphasis on the vehicle. Today we recognize someone by looking at the model of their car, or hold someone in esteem just by their car. This verse lays the fascination for cars and vehicles that has continued to this day!

पाञ्चजन्यं हृषीकेशः , देवदत्तं धनञ्जयः । पौण्ड्रं दध्मौ महाशङ्खम् , भीमकर्मा वृकोदरः ॥ १.१५

pāñcajanyaṁ hṛṣīkeśaḥ , devadattaṁ dhanañjayaḥ ।

pauṇḍraṁ dadhmau mahāśaṅkham , bhīmakarmā vṛkodaraḥ ॥ 1.15

1.15 Similarly the obsession with smartphones aka conches – Lord's FiveMetal conch, Dhananjaya's Signature phone, Bhima muscleman's Fullscreen display loudest phone, all rang.

अनन्तविजयं राजा , कुन्तीपुत्रो युधिष्ठिरः । नकुलस् सहदेवश्च , सुघोषमणिपुष्पकौ ॥ १.१६

anantavijayaṁ rājā , kuntīputro yudhiṣṭhiraḥ ।

nakulas sahadevaśca , sughoṣamaṇipuṣpakau ॥ 1.16

1.16 The Steadfast king's all apps inbuilt phone, Nakula's music loaded phone, Sahadeva's diamond studded twin camera phone.

काश्यश्च परमेष्वासः , शिखण्डी च महारथः । धृष्टद्युम्नो विराटश्च , सात्यकिश् चापराजितः ॥ १.१७

kāśyaśca parameṣvāsaḥ , śikhaṇḍī ca mahārathaḥ ।

dhṛṣṭadyumno virāṭaśca , sātyakiś cāparājitaḥ ॥ 1.17

1.17 The king of Kashi – Varanasi the oldest inhabited city, Shikhandi the transgender sporting a gorgeous car. The Farsighted, the Giant and the undaunted Bold; all sounded their conches.

द्रुपदो द्रौपदेयाश्च , सर्वशᳶ पृथिवीपते । सौभद्रश्च महाबाहुः , शङ्खान् दध्मुᳶ पृथक् पृथक् ॥ १.१८

drupado draupadeyāśca , sarvaśaᳶ pṛthivīpate ।

saubhadraśca mahābāhuḥ , śaṅkhān dadhmuᳶ pṛthak pṛthak ॥ 1.18

1.18 O Ruler! Drupada – Draupadi's father, Draupadi's five sons, Subhadra's son Abhimanyu the strong willed, sounded their varied conches from all directions.

स घोषो धार्तराष्ट्राणाम् , हृदयानि व्यदारयत् । नभश्च पृथिवीं चैव , तुमुलो व्यनुनादयन् ॥ १.१९

sa ghoṣo dhārtarāṣṭrāṇām , hṛdayāni vyadārayat ।

nabhaśca pṛthivīṁ caiva , tumulo vyanunādayan ॥ 1.19

1.19 When creation itself began to sound in unison, when "Sound" himself began to speak, his word blasted away the hearts of the wicked. It tore open the stony hearts and paved the way for a spring to burst forth.

Sound is that which can well up a fountain of love. That can make the juices flow.

Sound being an attribute of the Space element, is the most potent of all sensations. Space is far superior to anything else in creation.

अथ व्यवस्थितान् दृष्ट्वा , धार्तराष्ट्रान् कपिध्वजः । प्रवृत्ते शस्त्रसम्पाते , धनुरुद्यम्य पाण्डवः ॥ १.२०

atha vyavasthitān dṛṣṭvā , dhārtarāṣṭrān kapidhvajaḥ ।

pravṛtte śastrasampāte , dhanurudyamya pāṇḍavaḥ ॥ 1.20

1.20 NOW, when the questions were going to be fired, when the dilemma was at its peak, sought very carefully, the Seeking soul, having the stamp of the fair wind.

Now drop what you are doing. Clear your mind of plans and projections.
To Hear what? Hear whom? Your own self buddy.
Your own heart's yearning. Your own deep aspiration. Your own true desire.
Really. is there such a thing? i never did know or maybe i forgot.

Where is the time? Where is the money? Where are the resources? And anyway i am busy. i am earning my bread and butter. I have duties and responsibilities. I have projects and deadlines. I am taking care of a family. I am doing something terribly important. Where is the half chance to listen to my heart?

And then one day the Lord lends a hand. You become aware of the murmur of your heart. A unique and rare happening.

हृषीकेशं तदा वाक्यम् , इदम् आह महीपते ।

hṛṣīkeśaṁ tadā vākyam , idam āha mahīpate ।

Then to Hrishikesha = master of the senses = who has reigned in the senses of touch taste sight speaking; the foremost disciple spoke thus the words...

Only a Topper listens to his heart.

अर्जुन उवाच

सेनयोरुभयोर् मध्ये , रथं स्थापय मेऽच्युत ॥ १.२१

arjuna uvāca

senayorubhayor madhye , rathaṁ sthāpaya me'cyuta ॥ 1.21

Arjuna spoke

1.21 Place me between Left & Right - Between the Opposites - Make my bodyMind Balanced, O Unshakeable One!

the word Arjun begins with the letter A, it means by default the entire alphabet.

Notice that Sanskrit alphabet is अ आ इ etc., English alphabet is A B C etc.

Here it is significant to understand that Arjun refers to you or me, he or she.

the classic yearning of a pure heart.
the direct demand of Spontaneity.
the first wish of Innocence.

When a heart becomes pure, when the mind becomes clear, then
It calls Steadfastness
and
Prays to grant it Centeredness.

यावद् एतान् निरीक्षेऽहम् , योद्धुकामान् अवस्थितान् । कैर्मया सह योद्धव्यम् , अस्मिन् रणसमुद्यमे । १.२२

yāvad etān nirīkṣe'ham , yoddhukāmān avasthitān ।

kairmayā saha yoddhavyam , asmin raṇasamudyame । 1.22

1.22 So that I can clearly analyze my leanings and tendencies, their influence on me, and their potential attack and stress causing capability, that will have to be faced soon.

योत्स्यमानान् अवेक्षेऽहम् , य एतेऽत्र समागताः । धार्तराष्ट्रस्य दुर्बुद्धेः , युद्धे प्रियचिकीर्षवः ॥ १.२३

yotsyamānān avekṣe'ham , ya ete'tra samāgatāḥ ।

dhārtarāṣṭrasya durbuddheḥ , yuddhe priyacikīrṣavaḥ ॥ 1.23

1.23 And survey all instincts and senses together – ready to engage me and draw my attention, just for the sake of their stubborn polarized drives.

सञ्जय उवाच

एवम् उक्तो हृषीकेशः , गुडाकेशेन भारत । सेनयोरुभयोर् मध्ये , स्थापयित्वा रथोत्तमम् ॥ १.२४

sañjaya uvāca

evam ukto hṛṣīkeśaḥ , guḍākeśena bhārata ।

senayorubhayor madhye , sthāpayitvā rathottamam ॥ 1.24

Sanjaya reports

1.24 O Ruler, Hrishikesha – the one who has mastered senses and faculties, being addressed thus by Gudakesha – the thick and curly haired one, drove and stopped the magnificent chariot right in between the opposing teams.

भीष्मद्रोणप्रमुखतः , सर्वेषां च महीक्षिताम् । उवाच पार्थ पश्यैतान् , समवेतान् कुरूनिति ॥ १.२५

bhīṣmadroṇapramukhataḥ , sarveṣāṁ ca mahīkṣitām ।

uvāca pārtha paśyaitān , samavetān kurūniti ॥ 1.25

1.25 He placed me right in front of those who had the biggest pull on me - my grandfather and my guru...and softly stated, how's all the mental flutterings O Partha?

The Lord is no ordinary being.
One who is steadfast, solid, pure and wise,
has intelligence far far beyond our wildest imagination.
When i asked the Steadfast One, to keep me between the center of the Opposing forces,
to make me calm...

He placed me right next to the possessions that were most dear...
Possessions unlike my iphone or macbook air or my merc, replaceable fellows.
Possessions unlike my favourite labrador or my magnificent house, their lifetime is not more than 20 years.
Possessions unlike spouse or son...they may not hold respect for many.

Right in the first step, in the first operation, in the first project, in the first game, the Lord's extraordinary brilliance shines forth.

तत्रापश्यत् स्थितान् पार्थः , पितॄनथ पितामहान् । आचार्यान् मातुलान् भ्रातॄन् , पुत्रान् पौत्रान् सखींस् तथा ॥ १.२६

tatrāpaśyat sthitān pārthaḥ , pitr̥̄natha pitāmahān ।

ācāryān mātulān bhrātr̥̄n , putrān pautrān sakhīṁs tathā ॥ 1.26

श्वशुरान् सुहृदश् चैव , सेनयोरुभयोरपि । तान् समीक्ष्य स कौन्तेयः , सर्वान् बन्धून् अवस्थितान् ॥ १.२७

śvaśurān suhr̥daś caiva , senayorubhayorapi ।

tān samīkṣya sa kaunteyaḥ , sarvān bandhūn avasthitān ॥ 1.27

1.26, 1.27 i see my names, fames and connections. all my facebook friends and more. And my bank balances, properties, assets and networks.

Then. I see all my precious possessions.
i see my clothes and ornaments and things.
i see my ducati and merc and galaxy note.
i see my books and albums and manuscripts.
i see my prizes and medals and trophies. even my certificates insignias and badges...
my mind runs through all the sentiments. my memory arranges all in sequence.
my intellect recalls the connected experiences. my ego aligns my identity and attachments.

कृपया परयाविष्टः , विषीदन्निदम् अब्रवीत् ।

kr̥payā parayāviṣṭaḥ , viṣīdannidam abravīt ।

the intellect simply caved in. i crumpled on the spot. despondency ruled.
and thus tongue burst out...

as the mind surveyed all the possessions and the intellect grappled with the disturbing idea of losing all.

Speech. Retained its functionality. It cried for help.
This verse 1.28a underlines a fundamental design principle. In any product, the scientist must add a SEEK HELP mechanism. A good car will activate alarm sensors when it stalls. Smartphones and Laptops blink – PLEASE CHARGE.

And a sensible human seeks advice when he realizes the challenge is beyond him. The huge plethora of your networks, families, duties or responsibilities is in no way an obstacle to seek fitness of mind and body. A human life ain't to be made devoid of joy, good cheer or good health.

अर्जुन उवाच

दृष्ट्वेमं स्वजनं कृष्ण , युयुत्सुं समुपस्थितम् ॥ १.२८

arjuna uvāca

dr̥ṣṭvemaṁ svajanaṁ kr̥ṣṇa , yuyutsuṁ samupasthitam ॥ 1.28

1.28 My sight wires up to my mind and creates a strong attachment. everything to hook me is right here. i might lose my identity. i may give in to the external environs and temptations and end up effaced.

सीदन्ति मम गात्राणि , मुखं च परिशुष्यति । वेपथुश्च शरीरे मे , रोमहर्षश् च जायते ॥ १.२९

sīdanti mama gātrāṇi , mukhaṁ ca pariśuṣyati ।

vepathuśca śarīre me , romaharṣaś ca jāyate ॥ 1.29

गाण्डीवं स्रम्सते हस्तात् , त्वक्चैव परिदह्यते । न च शक्नोम्यवस्थातुम् , भ्रमतीव च मे मनः ॥ १.३०

gāṇḍīvaṁ sramsate hastāt , tvakcaiva paridahyate ।

na ca śaknomyavasthātum , bhramatīva ca me manaḥ ॥ 1.30

1.29, 1.30 My Mouth is parched. Hair are standing on end. An electric current jolts my Anatomy. The steering wheel slips from my hands. My intellect and skillset are dysfunctional, forgotten. Brain spins uncontrollably. Dizziness overtakes me.
All Alarms go off. Control Panel starts beeping like crazy. HELP. SOS. Help.

निमित्तानि च पश्यामि , विपरीतानि केशव । न च श्रेयोऽनुपश्यामि , हत्वा स्वजनमाहवे ॥ १.३१

nimittāni ca paśyāmi , viparītāni keśava ।

na ca śreyo'nupaśyāmi , hatvā svajanamāhave ॥ 1.31

1.31 And my guts tell me of impending disaster, and moreover it ain't right to dismantle the castle and everything in it that has given me comforts and coexistence. Why to lose relations?

The mind goes into a dizzy spin and starts mumbling incoherently.

न काङ्क्षे विजयं कृष्ण , न च राज्यं सुखानि च । किं नो राज्येन गोविन्द , किं भोगैर् जीवितेन वा ॥ १.३२

na kāṅkṣe vijayaṁ kr̥ṣṇa , na ca rājyaṁ sukhāni ca ।

kiṁ no rājyena govinda , kiṁ bhogair jīvitena vā ॥ 1.32

1.32 We do not expect triumph O Krishna! Not nobility nor comforts either. Of what use is vain glory, why to get mesmerized by senses, or drawn apart by passionate forces?

येषाम् अर्थे काङ्क्षितं नः , राज्यं भोगास् सुखानि च । त इमेऽवस्थिता युद्धे , प्राणांस्त्यक्त्वा धनानि च ॥ १.३३

yeṣām arthe kāṅkṣitaṁ naḥ , rājyaṁ bhogās sukhāni ca ।

ta ime'vasthitā yuddhe , prāṇāṁstyaktvā dhanāni ca ॥ 1.33

1.33 For whose sake will we enjoy the comforts and pleasures? All senses and faculties are assembled to engage and do or die.

And now the emotional outburst, when the faculties get aligned to speak logic that is devoid of relevance, self-defeatist and humungous. However this is a sincere seeker's rambling, so truth and cutting edge facts will also tumble out.

आचार्याः पितरः पुत्राः,तथैव च पितामहाः । मातुलाः श्वशुराः पौत्राः , श्यालास् सम्बन्धिनस् तथा ॥ १.३४

ācāryāḫ pitaraḫ putrāḥ , tathaiva ca pitāmahāḥ ।

mātulāḥ śvaśurāḫ pautrāḥ , śyālās sambandhinas tathā ॥ 1.34

1.34 Thoughts and emotions tingling of teachers, elders, youngsters and grandparents. Memories filled with mother's relatives, in-laws, children and childhood.

एतान् न हन्तुम् इच्छामि , घ्नतोऽपि मधुसूदन । अपि त्रैलोक्यराज्यस्य , हेतोः किं नु महीकृते ॥ १.३५

etān na hantum icchāmi , ghnato'pi madhusūdana ।

api trailokyarājyasya , hetoḫ kiṁ nu mahīkr̥te ॥ 1.35

1.35 There is no spirit to engage O Madhusudana! Nay even if I go down fighting. The three continents I have no wish for, then why bother with a trifling piece of land?

निहत्य धार्तराष्ट्रान् नः , का प्रीतिस् स्याज्जनार्दन । पापमेवाश्रयेद् अस्मान् , हत्वैतान् आततायिनः ॥ १.३६

nihatya dhārtarāṣṭrān naḥ , kā prītis syājjanārdana ।

pāpamevāśrayed asmān , hatvaitān ātatāyinaḥ ॥ 1.36

1.36 Shouldn't we refrain from wrong against wrong O Janardana? Erroneous judgments are culpable isn't it? What pleasures may we derive by shooing off the wicked?

तस्मान् नार्हा वयं हन्तुम् , धार्तराष्ट्रान् स्वबान्धवान् । स्वजनं हि कथं हत्वा , सुखिनस् स्याम माधव ॥ १.३७

tasmān nārhā vayaṁ hantum , dhārtarāṣṭrān svabāndhavān ।

svajanaṁ hi kathaṁ hatvā , sukhinas syāma mādhava ॥ 1.37

1.37 Therefore we should let go of this craziness, that distances our relations. How can we enjoy the leftovers O Madhava?

यद्यप्येते न पश्यन्ति , लोभोपहतचेतसः । कुलक्षयकृतं दोषम् , मित्रद्रोहे च पातकम् ॥ १.३८

yadyapyete na paśyanti , lobhopahatacetasaḥ ।

kulakṣayakr̥taṁ doṣam , mitradrohe ca pātakam ॥ 1.38

1.38 Their intellect is corrupted by greed, they do not mind getting separated from family and friends...

कथं न ज्ञेयम् अस्माभिः , पापाद् अस्मान् निवर्तितुम् । कुलक्षयकृतं दोषम् , प्रपश्यद्भिर् जनार्दन ॥ १.३९

kathaṁ na jñeyam asmābhiḥ , pāpād asmān nivartitum ।

kulakṣayakr̥taṁ doṣam , prapaśyadbhir janārdana ॥ 1.39

1.39 Why shouldn't it strike us not to prevent damage? O Janardana! At least we can withdraw from the calamitous, having sensed it in advance.

कुलक्षये प्रणश्यन्ति , कुलधर्मास् सनातनाः । धर्मे नष्टे कुलं कृत्स्नम् , अधर्मोऽभिभवत्युत ॥ १.४०

kulakṣaye praṇaśyanti , kuladharmās sanātanāḥ ।

dharme naṣṭe kulaṁ kr̥tsnam ,adharmo'bhibhavatyuta ॥ 1.40

1.40 In the separation of families, the traditions also get lost; breaking the joint system destroys the fabric of society, leading to large scale lawlessness.

अधर्माभिभवात् कृष्ण , प्रदुष्यन्ति कुलस्त्रियः । स्त्रीषु दुष्टासु वार्ष्णेय , जायते वर्णसङ्करः ॥ १.४१

adharmābhibhavāt kr̥ṣṇa , praduṣyanti kulastriyaḥ ।

strīṣu duṣṭāsu vārṣṇeya , jāyate varṇasaṅkaraḥ ॥ 1.41

1.41 When lawlessness turns rampant, adultery becomes common O Krishna! Then one loses the purity of family trees, and it becomes very difficult to determine matches and partners in marriage.

सङ्करो नरकायैव , कुलघ्नानां कुलस्य च । पतन्ति पितरो ह्येषाम् , लुप्तपिण्डोदकक्रियाः ॥ १.४२

saṅkaro narakāyaiva , kulaghnānāṁ kulasya ca ।

patanti pitaro hyeṣām , luptapiṇḍodakakriyāḥ ॥ 1.42

1.42 Such a state of affairs surely creates havoc in all layers of society and all systems of governance.

दोषैरेतैः कुलघ्नानाम् , वर्णसङ्करकारकैः । उत्साद्यन्ते जातिधर्माः , कुलधर्माश्च शाश्वताः ॥ १.४३

doṣairetaiḥ kulaghnānām , varṇasaṅkarakārakaiḥ ।

utsādyante jātidharmāḥ , kuladharmāśca śāśvatāḥ ॥ 1.43

1.43 In due course the destruction of a society's fabric gives birth to various illnesses, handicapped children, malformed bodies, retarded minds.

उत्सन्नकुलधर्माणाम् , मनुष्याणां जनार्दन । नरकेऽनियतं वासः , भवतीत्यनुशुश्रुम ॥ १.४४

utsannakuladharmāṇām , manuṣyāṇāṁ janārdana ।

narake'niyataṁ vāsaḥ , bhavatītyanuśuśruma ॥ 1.44

1.44 Haven't we all heard the repercussions of destroying family traditions O Janardana? Society becomes hellish and barbaric.

अहो बत महत् पापम् , कर्तुं व्यवसिता वयम् । यद् राज्यसुखलोभेन , हन्तुं स्वजनमुद्यताः ॥ १.४५

aho bata mahat pāpam , kartuṁ vyavasitā vayam ।

yad rājyasukhalobhena , hantuṁ svajanamudyatāḥ ॥ 1.45

1.45 Alas! It is so unfortunate that we are on the brink of committing a disaster. When greed takes over the mental faculties, man becomes a criminal for lordly gains.
Blurting forth, one reaches the point of no return, the mind has deserted oneself.

यदि मामप्रतीकारम् , अशस्त्रं शस्त्रपाणयः । धार्तराष्ट्रा रणे हन्युः , तन्मे क्षेमतरं भवेत् ॥ १.४६

yadi māmapratīkāram , aśastraṁ śastrapāṇayaḥ ।

dhārtarāṣṭrā raṇe hanyuḥ , tanme kṣemataraṁ bhavet ॥ 1.46

1.46 I prefer to surrender, to be robbed and smashed without resisting !

सञ्जय उवाच

एवम् उक्त्वार्जुनस् सङ्ख्ये , रथोपस्थ उपाविशत् । विसृज्य सशरं चापम् , शोकसंविग्नमानसः ॥ १.४७

sañjaya uvāca

evam uktvārjunas saṅkhye , rathopastha upāviśat ।

visṛjya saśaraṁ cāpam , śokasaṁvignamānasaḥ ॥ 1.47

a reporter saw me thus. and reported that

1.47 Sorrowing and miserable, i relinquished my wits and sank down, hiding from mySelf, towards the far end of my being. i folded myself into a corner of this world, as if lost, as if defeated.

Unable to resist the emotional fancies, unable to withstand the enormous pulls of raaga and dvesha. Unable to overcome the ambitious mental currents. Unable to see through the complex lattices, arrays and matrices conjured up by my super phenomenal brain. Thus ends Chapter 1 of the Bhagavad Gita. A chapter of high Contrast. Of brilliant hues and shades of Creation. Offering a most extraordinary description of the range of virtues, abilities, strengths and desires of this infinite Universe.

AND the 1st chapter of the Bhagavad Gita gives a guideline for anyone wanting Freedom. It simply, directly, effortlessly spells out the correct situation for the one wishing to meet the Self. For the one wanting to meet the Lord.

ॐ तत् सत् । इति श्रीमद्भगवद्गीतासु , उपनिषत्सु , ब्रह्मविद्यायां योगशास्त्रे श्रीकृष्णार्जुनसंवादे

अर्जुन-विषाद्-योगो नाम , प्रथमोऽध्यायः ॥ १ ॥

oṁ tat sat । iti śrīmadbhagavadgītāsu , upaniṣatsu , brahmavidyāyāṁ yogaśāstre śrīkṛṣṇārjunasaṁvāde arjuna-viṣāda-yogo nāma , prathamo'dhyāyaḥ

॥ 1 ॥

2 Yoga of Lord's Intervention

ॐ श्री परमात्मने नमः । अथ द्वितीयोऽध्यायः

oṁ śrī paramātmane namaḥ I atha dvitīyo'dhyāyaḥ

सञ्जय उवाच

तं तथा कृपयाविष्टम् , अश्रुपूर्णाकुलेक्षणम् । विषीदन्तम् इदं वाक्यम् , उवाच मधुसूदनः ॥ २.१

sañjaya uvāca

taṁ tathā kr̥payāviṣṭam , aśrupūrṇākulekṣaṇam I

viṣīdantam idaṁ vākyam , uvāca madhusūdanaḥ II 2.1

Sanjaya relates

2.1 Lord looked at the tear filled cloudy countenance, taking in the devastating impact of senses, a crumpled heart, and said...

श्री भगवान् उवाच

कुतस् त्वा कश्मलम् इदम् , विषमे समुपस्थितम् । अनार्यजुष्टम् अस्वर्ग्यम् , अकीर्तिकरमर्जुन ॥ २.२

śrī bhagavān uvāca

kutas tvā kaśmalam idam , viṣame samupasthitam I

anāryajuṣṭam asvargyam , akīrtikaramarjuna II 2.2

2.2 How come a moody sullen attitude at this critical juncture? It cannot activate your defense mechanisms, nor can it trigger inborn talents nor prevent any harmful tendencies.

क्लैब्यं मा स्म गमः पार्थ , नैतत्त्वय्युपपद्यते । क्षुद्रं हृदयदौर्बल्यम् , त्यक्त्वोत्तिष्ठ परन्तप ॥ २.३

klaibyaṁ mā sma gamaḥ pārtha , naitattvayyupapadyate I

kṣudraṁ hr̥dayadaurbalyam , tyaktvottiṣṭha parantapa II 2.3

2.3 O Partha! Be manly, face up to the challenge, act according to your status. Get up and going O Parantapa!

अर्जुन उवाच

कथं भीष्ममहं सङ्ख्ये , द्रोणं च मधुसूदन । इषुभिः प्रति योत्स्यामि , पूजार्हावरिसूदन ॥ २.४

arjuna uvāca

kathaṁ bhīṣmamahaṁ saṅkhye,droṇaṁ ca madhusūdana I

iṣubhiḥ prati yotsyāmi , pūjārhāvarisūdana II 2.4

Arjuna blusters

2.4 O Madhusudana! How can one antagonize one's kith and kin who are old and respectable too? Must not we condone the errors and commissions of our own family, company and government?

गुरूनहत्वा हि महानुभावान् , श्रेयो भोक्तुं भैक्ष्यम् अपीह लोके ।

हत्वार्थकामांस्तु गुरूनिहैव , भुञ्जीय भोगान् रुधिरप्रदिग्धान् ॥ २.५

gurūnahatvā hi mahānubhāvān , śreyo bhoktuṁ bhaikṣyam apīha loke ।

hatvārthakāmāṁstu gurūnihaiva ,bhuñjīya bhogān rudhirapradigdhān ॥ 2.5

2.5 Shouldn't anyone be judged by their past performance alone? May not we give more weight to earlier achievements? Is not animosity towards the high and mighty detrimental to one's well-being?

न चैतद् विद्मः कतरन्नो गरीयः , यद्वा जयेम यदि वा नो जयेयुः ।

यानेव हत्वा न जिजीविषामः , तेऽवस्थिताः प्रमुखे धार्तराष्ट्राः ॥ २.६

na caitadvidmaḥ kataranno garīyaḥ , yadvā jayema yadi vā no jayeyuḥ ।

yāneva hatvā na jijīviṣāmaḥ , te'vasthitāḥ pramukhe dhārtarāṣṭrāḥ ॥ 2.6

2.6 I do not fathom the path i must choose that will lead me to certain success. I am wary of engaging my strength in efforts that deplete my vitality.

कार्पण्यदोषोपहतस्वभावः , पृच्छामि त्वां धर्मसम्मूढचेताः ।

यच्छ्रेयस् स्यान्निश्चितं ब्रूहि तन्मे , शिष्यस्तेऽहं शाधि मां त्वां प्रपन्नम् ॥ २.७

kārpaṇyadoṣopahatasvabhāvaḥ , pṛcchāmi tvāṁ dharmasammūḍhacetāḥ ।
yacchreyas syānniścitaṁ brūhi tanme ,

śiṣyaste'haṁ śādhi māṁ tvāṁ prapannam ॥ 2.7

2.7 The weakness of my mind makes me helpless. The delusion of my senses makes my intellect indecisive. In this moment i surrender myself. I seek moral guidance, as a child seeks his parent's protection to tide over a trying hour. Nay tide over a lifetime. Give me instruction O Lord, i wish to learn what is right and i wish to tread that path.

न हि प्रपश्यामि ममापनुद्याद् , यच्छोकमुच्छोषणम् इन्द्रियाणाम् ।

अवाप्य भूमावसपत्नमृद्धम् , राज्यम् सुराणाम् अपि चाधिपत्यम् ॥ २.८

na hi prapaśyāmi mamāpanudyād , yacchokamucchoṣaṇam indriyāṇām ।

avāpya bhūmāvasapatnamṛddham,rājyam surāṇām api cādhipatyam ॥ 2.8

2.8 Instruct me to decide consciously, to move alertly, to overcome confusion. This clarity is beyond my capability right now. My mission and vision are all mixed up.

सञ्जय उवाच

एवम् उक्त्वा हृषीकेशम् , गुडाकेशः परन्तपः । न योत्स्य इति गोविन्दम् , उक्त्वा तूष्णीं बभूव ह ॥ २.९

sañjaya uvāca

evam uktvā hṛṣīkeśam , guḍākeśa× parantapaḥ ।

na yotsya iti govindam , uktvā tūṣṇīṁ babhūva ha ॥ 2.9

Sanjaya reported
2.9 Having thus said his piece, the disciple Gudakesha added - i shall not move an inch without your input O Govinda! And became sullen and silent.

तमुवाच हृषीकेशः , प्रहसन्निव भारत । सेनयोरुभयोर् मध्ये , विषीदन्तम् इदं वचः ॥ २.१०

tamuvāca hṛṣīkeśaḥ , prahasanniva bhārata ।

senayorubhayor madhye , viṣīdantam idaṁ vacaḥ ॥ 2.10

2.10 Amused as it were, the Lord spoke calmly to him who was caught up in internal conflict, O Dhritarashtra!

श्री भगवान् उवाच

अशोच्यान् अन्वशोचस्त्वम् , प्रज्ञावादांश्च भाषसे । गतासून् अगतासूंश्च , नानुशोचन्ति पण्डिताः ॥ २.११

śrī bhagavān uvāca
aśocyān anvaśocastvam , prajñāvādāṁśca bhāṣase ।

gatāsūn agatāsūṁśca , nānuśocanti paṇḍitāḥ ॥ 2.11

the good Lord said soothingly
2.11 You are worrying over trifles. At the same time you are posing as a mature adult. The wise don't grieve over the past that is gone nor do they get anxious about the future that is yet to come.

न त्वेवाहं जातु नासम् , न त्वं नेमे जनाधिपाः । न चैव न भविष्यामः , सर्वे वयमतः परम् ॥ २.१२

na tvevāhaṁ jātu nasam , na tvaṁ neme janādhipāḥ ।

na caiva na bhaviṣyāmaḥ , sarve vayamata× param ॥ 2.12

2.12 "So many valuable possessions i didn't have earlier, i may lose all my wealth and skillset in the future", all such notions are erroneous.

देहिनोऽस्मिन् यथा देहे , कौमारं यौवनं जरा । तथा देहान्तरप्राप्तिः , धीरस्तत्र न मुह्यति ॥ २.१३

dehino'smin yathā dehe , kaumāraṁ yauvanaṁ jarā ।

tathā dehāntaraprāptiḥ , dhīrastatra na muhyati ॥ 2.13

2.13 A man moves through boyhood, youth and old age. He makes and breaks various networks and connections. A mature adult is least bothered with such natural changes in the course of life.

मात्रास्पर्शास् तु कौन्तेय , शीतोष्णसुखदुःखदाः । आगमापायिनोऽनित्याः , तांस्तितिक्षस्व भारत ॥ २.१४

mātrāsparśās tu kaunteya , śītoṣṇasukhaduḥkhadāḥ ।

āgamāpāyino'nityāḥ , tāṁstitikṣasva bhārata ॥ 2.14

2.14 Senses and their objects of contact give rise to sensations of cooling and heating, likeable or irritable, and all for a short while O Kaunteya. Such fleeting excitements are like the movement of traffic, some going and others arriving O Bharata! No need to get flustered, rather be placid and tolerant of them.

यं हि न व्यथयन्त्येते , पुरुषं पुरुषर्षभ । समदुःखसुखं धीरम् , सोऽमृतत्वाय कल्पते ॥ २.१५

yaṁ hi na vyathayantyete , puruṣaṁ puruṣarṣabha ।

samaduḥkhasukhaṁ dhīram , so'mṛtatvāya kalpate ॥ 2.15

2.15 O Purusharshabha! That brave one who is not bewildered by these flitting sense movements, who faces petty losses and gains with fortitude, he qualifies to rise to the next level and undertake great works.

नासतो विद्यते भावः , नाभावो विद्यते सतः । उभयोरपि दृष्टोऽन्तः , त्वनयोस् तत्त्वदर्शिभिः ॥ २.१६

nāsato vidyate bhāvaḥ , nābhāvo vidyate sataḥ ।

ubhayorapi dṛṣṭo'ntaḥ , tvanayos tattvadarśibhiḥ ॥ 2.16

2.16 Individual fancies have little scope of manifestation, while collective energies can produce wonders. This inherent truth is clearly perceived by able administrators and statesmen.

अविनाशि तु तद् विद्धि , येन सर्वम् इदं ततम् । विनाशम् अव्ययस्यास्य , न कश्चित् कर्तुमर्हति ॥ २.१७

avināśi tu tad viddhi , yena sarvam idaṁ tatam ।

vināśam avyayasyāsya , na kaścit kartumarhati ॥ 2.17

2.17 Understand that the Truth is universal, Truth is inherent in all. Truth may become veiled or muddy, but it can never be avoided nor surpassed.

Truth alone Triumphs.

अन्तवन्त इमे देहाः , नित्यस्योक्ताश् शरीरिणः । अनाशिनोऽप्रमेयस्य , तस्माद् युध्यस्व भारत ॥ २.१८

antavanta ime dehāḥ , nityasyoktāś śarīriṇaḥ ।

anāśino'prameyasya , tasmād yudhyasva bhārata ॥ 2.18

2.18 Objects, bodies and things are all time bound, they will pass without negating or

lessening the inherent Truth. Truth cannot be objectified or quantified. Do not duck your responsibility in the light of this wisdom.

य एनं वेत्ति हन्तारम् , यश्चैनं मन्यते हतम् । उभौ तौ न विजानीतः , नायं हन्ति न हन्यते ॥ २.१९

ya enaṁ vetti hantāram , yaścainaṁ manyate hatam ।

ubhau tau na vijānītaḥ , nāyaṁ hanti na hanyate ॥ 2.19

2.19 The one who considers that Truth can be bent or used for malpractice, and the one who thinks Truth can be wiped out or hid, both are confused and uneducated. Truth cannot harm, nor can Truth be overshadowed.

न जायते म्रियते वा कदाचित् , नायं भूत्वा भविता वा न भूयः ।

अजो नित्यश् शाश्वतोऽयं पुराणः , न हन्यते हन्यमाने शरीरे ॥ २.२०

na jāyate mriyate vā kadācit , nāyaṁ bhūtvā bhavitā vā na bhūyaḥ ।

ajo nityaś śāśvato'yaṁ purāṇaḥ , na hanyate hanyamāne śarīre ॥ 2.20

2.20 Truth is unborn and unconditioned by time. There is no death for Truth. Truth is not a theatre projection that can be turned off. The screening of movies and the happenings to the actors and buildings in the movies in no way affects the screen or the movie hall.

वेदाविनाशिनं नित्यम् , य एनम् अजम् अव्ययम् । कथं स पुरुषᳵ पार्थ , कं घातयति हन्ति कम् ॥ २.२१

vedāvināśinaṁ nityam , ya enam ajam avyayam ।

kathaṁ sa puruṣaᳵ pārtha ,kaṁ ghātayati hanti kam ॥ 2.21

2.21 The knower of this profound wisdom is himself Truth, his ideas move towards the sublime, his concepts mature, his undertakings become successful and his fame spreads far and wide. Such a one has risen above uninformed and half-baked acts.

वासांसि जीर्णानि यथा विहाय , नवानि *गृह्णाति* नरोऽपराणि ।

तथा शरीराणि विहाय जीर्णानि , अन्यानि संयाति नवानि देही ॥ २.२२

vāsāṁsi jīrṇāni yathā vihāya ,navāni gṛhṇāti naro'parāṇi ।

tathā śarīrāṇi vihāya jīrṇāni , anyāni saṁyāti navāni dehī ॥ 2.22

2.22 Just as you wear fresh clothes after a shower or discard those tattered, the Soul moves on without being bound by events. Events extinguish but life goes on. The Truth stands.

नैनं छिन्दन्ति शस्त्राणि , नैनं दहति पावकः । न चैनं क्लेदयन्त्यापः , न शोषयति मारुतः ॥ २.२३

nainaṁ chindanti śastrāṇi , nainaṁ dahati pāvakaḥ ।

na cainaṁ kledayantyāpaḥ , na śoṣayati mārutaḥ ॥ 2.23

2.23 Weapons cannot blunt the Truth. Fires cannot incinerate the Truth. Waters cannot drown the Truth. Storms leave Truth untouched.

अच्छेद्योऽयम् अदाह्योऽयम् ,अक्लेद्योऽशोष्य एव च । नित्यस् सर्वगतस् स्थाणुः, अचलोऽयं सनातनः ॥ २.२४

acchedyo'yam adāhyo'yam , akledyo'śoṣya eva ca ।

nityas sarvagatas sthāṇuḥ , acalo'yaṁ sanātanaḥ ॥ 2.24

2.24 So also the Soul cannot be blunted, incinerated, drowned or harmed. The Soul has the qualities of Truth, namely unbound by time, all-pervading in space, untarnished, unyielding and ancient.

अव्यक्तोऽयम् अचिन्त्योऽयम् , अविकार्योऽयम् उच्यते । तस्मादेवं विदित्वैनम् , नानुशोचितुम् अर्हसि ॥ २.२५

avyakto'yam acintyo'yam , avikāryo'yam ucyate ।

tasmādevaṁ viditvainam , nānuśocitum arhasi ॥ 2.25

2.25 Truth is subtle. Imperceptible and Unblemished. All the scriptures and wise men say the same. Having understood this uncompromising fact, boldly overcome any fears and misgivings.

It is as it is. It will not change. Advance Meditation Course lion process.

अथ चैनं नित्यजातम् , नित्यं वा मन्यसे मृतम् । तथापि त्वं महाबाहो , नैवं शोचितुम् अर्हसि ॥ २.२६

atha cainaṁ nityajātam , nityaṁ vā manyase mr̥tam ।

tathāpi tvaṁ mahābāho , naivaṁ śocitum arhasi ॥ 2.26

2.26 On the other hand since appearances are deceptive, since it is hard to understand something subtle that doesn't get born nor does die O Mahabaho, so you might as well accept the passing phases too.

जातस्य हि ध्रुवो मृत्युः , ध्रुवं जन्म मृतस्य च । तस्माद् अपरिहार्येऽर्थे , न त्वं शोचितुम् अर्हसि ॥ २.२७

jātasya hi dhruvo mr̥tyuḥ , dhruvaṁ janma mr̥tasya ca ।

tasmād aparihārye'rthe , na tvaṁ śocitum arhasi ॥ 2.27

2.27 Since what manifests disappears after a while. Events bubble forth and float away. So why not accept this inevitable phenomenon of transitoriness?

Everything changes. This will also change. Advance Meditation Course lion process.

अव्यक्तादीनि भूतानि , व्यक्तमध्यानि भारत । अव्यक्तनिधनान्येव , तत्र का परिदेवना ॥ २.२८

avyaktādīni bhūtāni , vyaktamadhyāni bhārata ।

avyaktanidhanānyeva , tatra kā paridevanā ॥ 2.28

2.28 All processes and projects, trades and deals heat up and reach the critical stage, then surely get addressed or completed or shelved and thus become insignificant. O Bharata! Events move from insignificance to significance and then again to insignificance, take this reality in your stride.

आश्चर्यवत् पश्यति कश्चिद् एनम् , आश्चर्यवद् वदति तथैव चान्यः ।

आश्चर्यवच्चैनमन्यश् शृणोति , श्रुत्वाप्येनं वेद न चैव कश्चित् ॥ २.२९

āścaryavat paśyati kaścid enam , āścaryavad vadati tathaiva cānyaḥ ।

āścaryavaccainamanyaś śṛṇoti,śrutvāpyenaṁ veda na caiva kaścit ॥ 2.29

2.29 Some look upon the Soul with wonder, others hold animated discussions on the Soul, yet others hear marvellous stories regarding the Soul. However none of these understand the Soul correctly.
All of us form some opinion regarding divinity, and otherwise engage in benchmarking and quantifying the Guru, obviously such judgments fall far short of the real.

देही नित्यम् अवध्योऽयम् , देहे सर्वस्य भारत । तस्मात् सर्वाणि भूतानि , न त्वं शोचितुम् अर्हसि ॥ २.३०

dehī nityam avadhyo'yam , dehe sarvasya bhārata ।

tasmāt sarvāṇi bhūtāni , na tvaṁ śocitum arhasi ॥ 2.30

2.30 The Soul that dwells in everyone's body cannot be harmed O Bharata! Therefore how can you think in reality that anyone can suffer a loss?

स्वधर्मम् अपि चावेक्ष्य, न विकम्पितुम् अर्हसि । धर्म्याद्धि युद्धाच्छ्रेयोऽन्यत् , क्षत्रियस्य न विद्यते ॥ २.३१

svadharmam api cāvekṣya , na vikampitum arhasi ।

dharmyāddhi yuddhācchreyo'nyat , kṣatriyasya na vidyate ॥ 2.31

2.31 Moreover, for the ruler of a state, it is his bounden duty to protect the citizens and ensure their welfare.

यदृच्छया चोपपन्नम् , स्वर्गद्वारम् अपावृतम् । सुखिनः क्षत्रियाः पार्थ , लभन्ते युद्धमीदृशम् ॥ २.३२

yadṛcchayā copapannam , svargadvāram apāvṛtam ।

sukhinaḥ kṣatriyāḥ pārtha , labhante yuddhamīdṛśam ॥ 2.32

2.32 Blessed are those rulers who take the liberty of safeguarding their state with realistic technology and appropriate strategy.

अथ चेत् त्वमिमं धर्म्यम् , सङ्ग्रामं न करिष्यसि । ततस् स्वधर्मं कीर्तिं च , हित्वा पापम् अवाप्स्यसि ॥ २.३३

atha cet tvamimaṁ dharmyam , saṅgrāmaṁ na kariṣyasi ।

tatas svadharmaṁ kīrtiṁ ca , hitvā pāpam avāpsyasi ॥ 2.33

2.33 Now if someone forsakes his responsibility of defending his country, he not only loses his honour but also invites guilt and blame.

अकीर्तिं चापि भूतानि , कथयिष्यन्ति तेऽव्ययाम् । सम्भावितस्य चाकीर्तिः , मरणादतिरिच्यते ॥ २.३४

akīrtiṁ cāpi bhūtāni , kathayiṣyanti te'vyayām ।

sambhāvitasya cākīrtiḥ , maraṇādatiricyate ॥ 2.34

2.34 Gossip mongers will recount endless tales of dishonour, for a king or a gentleman, shame is much more painful than death.

भयाद् रणाद् उपरतम् , मंस्यन्ते त्वां महारथाः । येषां च त्वं बहुमतः , भूत्वा यास्यसि लाघवम् ॥ २.३५

bhayād raṇād uparatam , maṁsyante tvāṁ mahārathāḥ ।

yeṣāṁ ca tvaṁ bahumataḥ ,bhūtvā yāsyasi lāghavam ॥ 2.35

2.35 The adversaries and other statesmen will form the notion that he fled due to fear. Such ignominy will reduce his stature mightily and the embarrassment would be intolerable.

अवाच्यवादांश्च बहून् , वदिष्यन्ति तवाहिताः । निन्दन्तस् तव सामर्थ्यम् , ततो दुःखतरं नु किम् ॥ २.३६

avācyavādāṁśca bahūn , vadiṣyanti tavāhitāḥ ।

nindantas tava sāmarthyam,tato duḥkhataraṁ nu kim ॥ 2.36

2.36 The words passed in resulting chatters will be cutting, critical and extremely abusive. When a king's capability gets defamed, it is most painful to bear.

हतो वा प्राप्स्यसि स्वर्गम् , जित्वा वा भोक्ष्यसे महीम् । तस्माद् उत्तिष्ठ कौन्तेय , युद्धाय कृतनिश्चयः ॥ २.३७

hato vā prāpsyasi svargam , jitvā vā bhokṣyase mahīm ।

tasmād uttiṣṭha kaunteya , yuddhāya kr̥taniścayaḥ ॥ 2.37

2.37 Losing a well fought match earns huge applause and raises all round esteem. On the other hand being victorious catapults one to euphoric stardom. Therefore stand up O Kaunteya, determined to play.

सुखदुःखे समे कृत्वा , लाभालाभौ जयाजयौ । ततो युद्धाय युज्यस्व , नैवं पापम् अवाप्स्यसि ॥ २.३८

sukhaduḥkhe same kr̥tvā , lābhālābhau jayājayau ।

tato yuddhāya yujyasva , naivaṁ pāpam avāpsyasi ॥ 2.38

2.38 Take favourable and unfavourable circumstances in your stride. Accept gains

and losses as stepping stones to success. Let victory and defeat enhance your strength and broaden your vision. Bring such a temperament to your work and play and that's what makes life blossom.

एषा तेऽभिहिता साङ्ख्ये , बुद्धिर् योगे त्विमां श्रृणु । बुद्ध्या युक्तो यया पार्थ , कर्मबन्धं प्रहास्यसि ॥ २.३९

eṣā te'bhihitā sāṅkhye , buddhir yoge tvimāṁ śr̥ṇu ।

buddhyā yukto yayā pārtha , karmabandhaṁ prahāsyasi ॥ 2.39

2.39 Thus has the teaching been enumerated from the perspective of JNANA. Now hear how life is to be lived in the context of KARMA. By either method you shall arrive at the final destination of attaining liberation.

नेहाभिक्रमनाशोऽस्ति , प्रत्यवायो न विद्यते । स्वल्पम् अप्यस्य धर्मस्य , त्रायते महतो भयात् ॥ २.४०

nehābhikramanāśo'sti , pratyavāyo na vidyate ।

svalpam apyasya dharmasya , trāyate mahato bhayāt ॥ 2.40

2.40 In the practice of discipline as outlined in the Scriptures and learnt from a Guru, there is no scope for failure. Adversity and grief bid adieu forthwith. Even adhering to and incorporating 20% of the wisdom shields one and one's family from the greatest storm.

Look between the lines and notice that the saints and honest commoners enjoy the maximum security and live smoothly and peacefully.

Look at it from another angle. To ensure success in any material field all laws of physics and chemistry and society apply and need to be addressed adequately with huge expenditure of resources. But to ensure physical strength, mental fitness and emotional purity some few scriptural guidelines and the Master's word is ample.

When one takes the path to self-purification and inner fitness, both success and failure help immensely. This is not the case for one aiming to win laurels in worldly matters.

व्यवसायात्मिका बुद्धिः , एकेह कुरुनन्दन । बहुशाखा ह्यनन्ताश्च , बुद्धयोऽव्यवसायिनाम् ॥ २.४१

vyavasāyātmikā buddhiḥ , ekeha kurunandana ।

bahuśākhā hyanantāśca , buddhayo'vyavasāyinām ॥ 2.41

2.41 The high goals are achieved through single minded effort O Kurunandana! That is why big success eludes those engaged in multitasking and dabbling away their energies in many directions.

याम् इमां पुष्पितां वाचम् , प्रवदन्त्यविपश्चितः । वेदवादरताः पार्थ , नान्यदस्तीति वादिनः ॥ २.४२

yām imāṁ puṣpitāṁ vācam , pravadantyavipaścitaḥ ।

vedavādaratāḥ pārtha , nānyadastīti vādinaḥ ॥ 2.42

2.42 Guard yourself from half-knowledge and incomplete skillsets. Fancy oratory leads nowhere and becomes a stumbling block.

"Half-Knowledge is dangerous". नीम हकीम खतरे जान ।

कामात्मानस् स्वर्गपराः , जन्मकर्मफलप्रदाम् । क्रियाविशेषबहुलाम् , भोगैश्वर्यगतिं प्रति ॥ २.४३

kāmātmānas svargaparāḥ , janmakarmaphalapradām ।

kriyāviśeṣabahulām , bhogaiśvaryagatiṁ prati ॥ 2.43

2.43 Those waylaid by half-baked measures always fall short of any attainment. Malpractices and superstitions rule the roost of those held up by quacks.

भोगैश्वर्यप्रसक्तानाम् , तयापहृतचेतसाम् । व्यवसायात्मिका बुद्धिः , समाधौ न विधीयते ॥ २.४४

bhogaiśvaryaprasaktānām , tayāpahṛtacetasām ।

vyavasāyātmikā buddhiḥ , samādhau na vidhīyate ॥ 2.44

2.44 Those seeking quick gains and enamoured by crash courses and shortcuts end up in null and void.

त्रैगुण्यविषया वेदाः , निस्त्रैगुण्यो भवार्जुन । निर्द्वन्द्वो नित्यसत्त्वस्थः , निर्योगक्षेम आत्मवान् ॥ २.४५

traiguṇyaviṣayā vedāḥ , nistraiguṇyo bhavārjuna ।

nirdvandvo nityasattvasthaḥ ,niryogakṣema ātmavān ॥ 2.45

2.45 Short term material goals weaken the integrity by splitting the mind towards three aspects of wine, woman and song. Rise above such disturbing lures. Free your mind from conflicting desires and become steadfast in long term goals with total commitment.

यावानर्थ उदपाने , सर्वतस् सम्प्लुतोदके । तावान् सर्वेषु वेदेषु , ब्राह्मणस्य विजानतः ॥ २.४६

yāvānartha udapāne , sarvatas samplutodake ।

tāvān sarveṣu vedeṣu , brāhmaṇasya vijānataḥ ॥ 2.46

2.46 Silly advice from many quarters is akin to too many cooks spoil the broth. Bragging your aim and broadcasting your strategy will result in a flood of failure.

कर्मण्येवाधिकारस्ते , मा फलेषु कदाचन । मा कर्मफलहेतुर् भूः , मा ते सङ्गोऽस्त्वकर्मणि ॥ २.४७

karmaṇyevādhikāraste , mā phaleṣu kadācana ।

mā karmaphalahetur bhūḥ ,mā te saṅgo'stvakarmaṇi ॥ 2.47

2.47 Desires and efforts and aims should align properly. Mission and vision should be streamlined. In work or play give your 100% surrendering the results to the divine. Be not greedy for accolade. Be not blocked by gloomy foreboding. All have been blessed by a free will to choose and act for the greatest good.

योगस्थ× कुरु कर्माणि , सङ्गं त्यक्त्वा धनञ्जय । सिद्ध्यसिद्ध्योस् समो भूत्वा , समत्वं योग उच्यते ॥ २.४८

yogastha× kuru karmāṇi , saṅgaṁ tyaktvā dhanañjaya ।

siddhyasiddhyos samo bhūtvā , samatvaṁ yoga ucyate ॥ 2.48

2.48 Being integrated in body-mind-soul, not polarized nor unduly influenced, work and play to your heart's content O Dhananjaya! Equanimity in action is called Yoga.

दूरेण ह्यवरं कर्म , बुद्धियोगाद् धनञ्जय । बुद्धौ शरणम् अन्विच्छ , कृपणा× फलहेतवः ॥ २.४९

dūreṇa hyavaraṁ karma , buddhiyogād dhanañjaya ।

buddhau śaraṇam anviccha , kr̥paṇā× phalahetavaḥ ॥ 2.49

2.49 Working with ulterior motives and playing with match fixing is a poverty riddled inferior living. Unfortunate indeed are such men. You must shun these at all cost.

बुद्धियुक्तो जहातीह , उभे सुकृतदुष्कृते । तस्माद् योगाय युज्यस्व , योग× कर्मसु कौशलम् ॥ २.५०

buddhiyukto jahātīha , ubhe sukr̥taduṣkr̥te ।

tasmād yogāya yujyasva , yoga× karmasu kauśalam ॥ 2.50

2.50 The one who gives his 100% gets rid of all bias and temptation. Therefore put your heart and soul in your deeds. Skill in Action is called Yoga. Dexterity is another name for yogic living.

कर्मजं बुद्धियुक्ता हि , फलं त्यक्त्वा मनीषिणः । जन्मबन्धविनिर्मुक्ताः , पदं गच्छन्त्यनामयम् ॥ २.५१

karmajaṁ buddhiyuktā hi , phalaṁ tyaktvā manīṣiṇaḥ ।

janmabandhavinirmuktāḥ , padaṁ gacchantyanāmayam ॥ 2.51

2.51 Yogis work with a clarity of the intellect, thus they overcome hurdles and temptations. Freed from anxieties and guilts they race to their goals easily.

यदा ते मोहकलिलम् , बुद्धिर् व्यतितरिष्यति । तदा गन्तासि निर्वेदम् , श्रोतव्यस्य श्रुतस्य च ॥ २.५२

yadā te mohakalilam , buddhir vyatitariṣyati ।

tadā gantāsi nirvedam , śrotavyasya śrutasya ca ॥ 2.52

2.52 When discipline and sanyam lead to clarity of intellect, then one becomes steadfast in one's pursuit and is not hijacked by the multiplicity of advertisements that lead one astray.

श्रुतिविप्रतिपन्ना ते , यदा स्थास्यति निश्चला । समाधावचला बुद्धिः , तदा योगम् अवाप्स्यसि ॥ २.५३

śrutivipratipannā te , yadā sthāsyati niścalā ।

samādhāvacalā buddhiḥ , tadā yogam avāpsyasi ॥ 2.53

2.53 Rumors and titillating news no longer hold sway when the intellect becomes determined and focussed. Steadily and with surety then one becomes a Yogi.

NOW THE FAMOUS 18 VERSES THAT ENCOMPASS THE GITA PHILOSOPHY IN TOTALITY, KNOWN AS STITHA-PRAGNA DARSHAN

अर्जुन उवाच

स्थितप्रज्ञस्य का भाषा , समाधिस्थस्य केशव । स्थितधीः किं प्रभाषेत , किम् आसीत व्रजेत किम् ॥ २.५४

arjuna uvāca

sthitaprajñasya kā bhāṣā , samādhisthasya keśava ।

sthitadhīḥ kiṁ prabhāṣeta , kim āsīta vrajeta kim ॥ 2.54

The awakened Aspirant asks

2.54 I wish to know the description of the Wise O Keshava! I wish to draw from the qualities of the Successful. I wish to learn to speak like the Great, to conduct myself accordingly, and to solve challenges and face situations as a Master would.

श्री भगवान् उवाच

प्रजहाति यदा कामान् , सर्वान् पार्थ मनोगतान् । आत्मन्येवात्मना तुष्टः , स्थितप्रज्ञस् तदोच्यते ॥ २.५५

śrī bhagavān uvāca

prajahāti yadā kāmān , sarvān pārtha manogatān ।

ātmanyevātmanā tuṣṭaḥ , sthitaprajñas tadocyate ॥ 2.55

Supremely satisfied at this noble quest, happily the Guru replies

2.55 The wise radiates a cheery contentment, since he has no conflicting aims, nor aims that are beyond his resources.

दुःखेष्वनुद् विग्नमनाः , सुखेषु विगतस्पृहः । वीतरागभयक्रोधः , स्थितधीर् मुनिर् उच्यते ॥ २.५६

duḥkheṣvanud vignamanāḥ , sukheṣu vigataspṛhaḥ ।

vītarāgabhayakrodhaḥ , sthitadhīr munir ucyate ॥ 2.56

2.56 The intelligent is not at all anxious about duties, nor is he over awed by successes. The heat of passions, the nameless fears, and the burning hates of whose have departed becomes sturdy and secure.

यस् सर्वत्रानभिस्नेहः , तत् तत् प्राप्य शुभाशुभम् । नाभिनन्दति न द्वेष्टि , तस्य प्रज्ञा प्रतिष्ठिता ॥ २.५७

yas sarvatrānabhisnehaḥ , tat tat prāpya śubhāśubham ।

nābhinandati na dveṣṭi , tasya prajñā pratiṣṭhitā ॥ 2.57

2.57 The great does not get pricked often by thorny people. He does not get embroiled in controversy. He maintains a safe distance from flashy allurements.

यदा संहरते चायम् , कूर्मोऽङ्गानीव सर्वशः । इन्द्रियाणीन्द्रियार्थेभ्यः , तस्य प्रज्ञा प्रतिष्ठिता ॥ २.५८

yadā saṁharate cāyam , kūrmo'ṅgānīva sarvaśaḥ ।

indriyāṇīndriyārthebhyaḥ , tasya prajñā pratiṣṭhitā ॥ 2.58

2.58 Just as a tortoise retracts its limbs sensing danger, the mature maintains his cool amidst dangerous situations and does not over react or get unnecessarily entangled.

विषया विनिवर्तन्ते , निराहारस्य देहिनः । रसवर्जं रसोऽप्यस्य , परं दृष्ट्वा निवर्तते ॥ २.५९

viṣayā vinivartante , nirāhārasya dehinaḥ ।

rasavarjaṁ raso'pyasya , paraṁ dr̥ṣṭvā nivartate ॥ 2.59

2.59 Lures and temptations are ever hiding in a man's heart even though he may pretend otherwise. However when the noble final goal is accomplished, then the greed snaps and weakens.

यततो ह्यपि कौन्तेय , पुरुषस्य विपश्चितः । इन्द्रियाणि प्रमाथीनि , हरन्ति प्रसभं मनः ॥ २.६०

yatato hyapi kaunteya , puruṣasya vipaścitaḥ ।

indriyāṇi pramāthīni , haranti prasabhaṁ manaḥ ॥ 2.60

2.60 Know the tremendous enticing power of liqueur, wealth and fame; do not underestimate or invite bad company; refrain from tempting nature, since these are known to smash even the stoutest.

तानि सर्वाणि संयम्य , युक्त आसीत मत्परः । वशे हि यस्येन्द्रियाणि , तस्य प्रज्ञा प्रतिष्ठिता ॥ २.६१

tāni sarvāṇi saṁyamya , yukta āsīta matparaḥ ।

vaśe hi yasyendriyāṇi , tasya prajñā pratiṣṭhitā ॥ 2.61

2.61 Having kept greed, guilt and fantasy at bay, the one determined to succeed should persevere in his commitments. Such a persevering soul is a noble one.

ध्यायतो विषयान् पुंसः , सङ्गस्तेषूपजायते । सङ्गात् सञ्जायते कामः , कामात् क्रोधोऽभिजायते ॥ २.६२

dhyāyato viṣayān puṁsaḥ , saṅgasteṣūpajāyate ।

saṅgāt sañjāyate kāmaḥ , kāmat krodho'bhijāyate ॥ 2.62

2.62 Be very clear of the workings of the mind. By repeatedly getting attracted and allured to the sense objects that give pleasure, sex or pomposity, one develops an addiction for them that is hard to overcome later. This obsession gives rise to lust and craving, which if repressed, thwarted or disappointed gives birth to venomous anger.

क्रोधाद् भवति सम्मोहः , सम्मोहात् स्मृतिविभ्रमः । स्मृतिभ्रंशाद् बुद्धिनाशः , बुद्धिनाशात् प्रणश्यति ॥ २.६३

krodhād bhavati sammohaḥ , sammohāt smr̥tivibhramaḥ ı

smr̥tibhraṁśād buddhināśaḥ ,buddhināśāt praṇaśyati ll 2.63

2.63 Anger that is bitter and vengeful foments to obscure the functioning of the senses. That soon leads to erratic, confused and suspicious memory. Without a good working memory, the intellect gets damaged and reason and caution is thrown to the wind. That is the shortest path to self destruction, irreversible and permanent.

रागद्वेषवियुक्तैस् तु , विषयान् इन्द्रियैश्चरन् । आत्मवश्यैर् विधेयात्मा , प्रसादम् अधिगच्छति ॥ २.६४

rāgadveṣaviyuktais tu , viṣayān indriyaiścaran ı

ātmavaśyair vidheyātmā , prasādam adhigacchati ll 2.64

2.64 The smart one who nips the evil in the bud, who uses Pratyahara to make a U-turn from his tendencies, achieves self-restraint leading to a soothing tranquility.

The Gita is not just teaching optimism or pragmatism nor advocating rebellion or escapism. It is laying threadbare the workings of the mind and brain and memory. It is teaching how to carefully, sensibly, cleverly handle the mind and senses, nurture the brain, and lay the wide road leading to positive success.

प्रसादे सर्वदुःखानाम् , हानिरस्योपजायते । प्रसन्नचेतसो ह्याशु , बुद्धिः पर्यवतिष्ठते ॥ २.६५

prasāde sarvaduḥkhānām , hānirasyopajāyate ı

prasannacetaso hyāśu , buddhiḥ paryavatiṣṭhate ll 2.65

2.65 When tranquility settles in the memory it wipes out earlier impressions of attractions and revulsions. Such peace is the foundation for a robust intelligence that leads to great success in life.

नास्ति बुद्धिर् अयुक्तस्य , न चायुक्तस्य भावना । न चाभावयतश् शान्तिः , अशान्तस्य कुतस् सुखम् ॥ २.६६

nāsti buddhir ayuktasya , na cāyuktasya bhāvanā ı

na cābhāvayataś śāntiḥ , aśāntasya kutas sukham ll 2.66

2.66 Real intelligence eludes the undisciplined man who is not practicing Sanyam. Emotional purity and guts are also not possible for he who skips Sadhana. How can such a person even think of long term prosperity or any attainment?

इन्द्रियाणां हि चरताम् , यन् मनोऽनुविधीयते । तदस्य हरति प्रज्ञाम् , वायुर् नावमिवाम्भसि ॥ २.६७

indriyāṇāṁ hi caratām , yan mano'nuvidhīyate ı

tadasya harati prajñām , vāyur nāvamivāmbhasi ll 2.67

2.67 Verily the roving and lustful eyes and ears destroy reason and intellect, just as a gale tsunami smashes boats away.

तस्माद् यस्य महाबाहो , निगृहीतानि सर्वशः । इन्द्रियाणीन्द्रियार्थेभ्यः , तस्य प्रज्ञा प्रतिष्ठिता ॥ २.६८

tasmād yasya mahābāho , nigṛhītāni sarvaśaḥ ।

indriyāṇīndriyārthebhyaḥ , tasya prajñā pratiṣṭhitā ॥ 2.68

2.68 Hence O Mahabaho! Keeping eyes, ears and mouth in check, nay particularly shielded from all temptation, is the deep rooted quality of a super soul.

The Gita prescribes neither suppression nor expressing desires uncontrollably, it rather gives tools and lays emphasis on intelligently guiding and loving regulating one's wishes and faculties.

या निशा सर्वभूतानाम् , तस्यां जागर्ति संयमी । यस्यां जाग्रति भूतानि , सा निशा पश्यतो मुनेः ॥ २.६९

yā niśā sarvabhūtānām , tasyāṁ jāgarti saṁyamī ।

yasyāṁ jāgrati bhūtāni , sā niśā paśyato muneḥ ॥ 2.69

2.69 That is a time of unconsciousness for the lay person immersed in intoxication of any kind, and it is a serious matter that leaks and wipes out his merits and skills. The Yogi never has a moment of such depravation, being wide awake and resilient to pitfalls and hurdles.

A man just busy, just clever in handling news and information, is of a very inferior order; his orbit actually is susceptible to all kinds of shocks and insecurities.

A Yogi however is far beyond in a totally different zone, in a completely protected Space Time environ, his orbit is beautiful, graceful and secure.
Physically both are seemingly "together", but the subtle and causal energy of both is entirely distinct.
For e.g. Vimal keeps spinning in waves of deceit and conceit, Willy enjoys not a moment of peace even though reading gutka after gutka, rolling in wealth JagjitMom relates endless stories of mishaps and troubles.
It is the same world, the same planet, the contemporary time, birds everywhere are tweeting, sun is radiant, skies are benevolent, there is bliss.

आपूर्यमाणम् अचलप्रतिष्ठम् , समुद्रमापॾ प्रविशन्ति यद्वत् ।

तद्वत् कामा यं प्रविशन्ति सर्वे , स शान्तिम् आप्नोति न कामकामी ॥ २.७०

āpūryamāṇam acalapratiṣṭham , samudramāpaॾ praviśanti yadvat ।

tadvat kāmā yaṁ praviśanti sarve , sa śāntim āpnoti na kāmakāmī ॥ 2.70

2.70 Waters and Storms and Tsunamis play n frolic n jostle in a serene Ocean. The innards and guts and faith and attitude of one whose mirror is clean, who reflects deeply and with clarity, are the choicest heavens worth aspiring for and attaining.

विहाय कामान् यस् सर्वान् , पुमांश्चरति निःस्पृहः । निर्ममो निरहङ्कारः , स शान्तिम् अधिगच्छति ॥ २.७१

vihāya kāmān yas sarvān , pumāṁścarati niḥspṛhaḥ ।

nirmamo nirahaṅkāraḥ , sa śāntim adhigacchati ॥ 2.71

2.71 Drop this befuddling i-sense that separates you from godliness and divinity. Wake up and see, all is Satyam Shivam Sundaram. Practice PadmaSadhana, Sudarshan Kriya, Sanyam to achieve all round well-being.

एषा ब्राह्मी स्थितिः पार्थ, नैनां प्राप्य विमुह्यति । स्थित्वास्याम् अन्तकालेऽपि, ब्रह्मनिर्वाणम् ऋच्छति ॥ २.७२

eṣā brāhmī sthitiḥ pārtha , naināṁ prāpya vimuhyati ।

sthitvāsyām antakāle'pi , brahmanirvāṇam ṛcchati ॥ 2.72

2.72 O Partha! This is the state known as Brahman the eternal blissful. It has been achieved by millions, it is achievable by you too.

ॐ तत् सत् । इति श्रीमद्भगवद्गीतासु उपनिषत्सु ब्रह्मविद्यायां योगशास्त्रे श्रीकृष्णार्जुनसंवादे

साङ्ख्य-योगो नाम द्वितीयोऽध्यायः ॥ २॥

oṁ tat sat । iti śrīmadbhagavadgītāsu upaniṣatsu brahmavidyāyāṁ yogaśāstre śrīkṛṣṇārjunasaṁvāde sāṅkhya-yogo nāma dvitīyo'dhyāyaḥ

॥ 2 ॥

3 Yoga of Steering Life

Yoga of Taking Responsibility

ॐ श्री परमात्मने नमः । अथ तृतीयोऽध्यायः

oṁ śrī paramātmane namaḥ । atha tṛtīyo'dhyāyaḥ

अर्जुन उवाच

ज्यायसी चेत् कर्मणस् ते , मता बुद्धिर् जनार्दन । तत्किं कर्मणि घोरे माम् , नियोजयसि केशव ॥ ३.१

arjuna uvāca

jyāyasī cet karmaṇas te , matā buddhir janārdana ।

tatkiṁ karmaṇi ghore mām , niyojayasi keśava ॥ 3.1

Arjuna despairingly queried

3.1 Is it that knowing is better than performing? If so why am i being asked to do a distasteful deed?

व्यामिश्रेणेव वाक्येन , बुद्धिं मोहयसीव मे । तदेकं वद निश्चित्य , येन श्रेयोऽहम् आप्नुयाम् ॥ ३.२

vyāmiśreṇeva vākyena , buddhiṁ mohayasīva me ।

tadekaṁ vada niścitya , yena śreyo'ham āpnuyām ॥ 3.2

3.2 with your apparently contradictory directives, my intellect is sorely confused. Please tell me clearly the one objective that is appropriate and best for me.

श्री भगवान् उवाच

लोकेऽस्मिन् द्विविधा निष्ठा , पुरा प्रोक्ता मयानघ । ज्ञानयोगेन साङ्ख्यानाम् , कर्मयोगेन योगिनाम् ॥ ३.३

śrī bhagavān uvāca

loke'smin dvividhā niṣṭhā , purā proktā mayānagha ।

jñānayogena sāṅkhyanam , karmayogena yoginām ॥ 3.3

Bhagawan replied

3.3 in the world two types of objectives were previously ordained by me. the way of knowledge for the thoughtful reserved ones, and the way of performing actions for those so inclined.

न कर्मणामनारम्भात् , नैष्कर्म्यं पुरुषोऽश्नुते । न च संन्यसनादेव , सिद्धिं समधिगच्छति ॥ ३.४

na karmaṇāmanārambhāt , naiṣkarmyaṁ puruṣo'śnute ।

na ca saṁnyasanādeva , siddhiṁ samadhigacchati ॥ 3.4

3.4 by not shouldering one's responsibility, none gets free of obligations. Likewise, nor by merely being inactive does anyone attain to greatness.

न हि कश्चित् क्षणम् अपि , जातु तिष्ठत्यकर्मकृत् । कार्यते ह्यवशᳵ कर्म , सर्वᳶ प्रकृतिजैर् गुणैः ॥ ३.५

na hi kaścit kṣaṇam api , jātu tiṣṭhatyakarmakṛt ।

kāryate hyavaśa× karma , sarva× prakṛtijair guṇaiḥ ॥ 3.5

3.5 Certainly, none can be inactive for any length of time; since the nature of this body impels it to be helplessly doing some action or another.

कर्मेन्द्रियाणि संयम्य , य आस्ते मनसा स्मरन् । इन्द्रियार्थान् विमूढात्मा , मिथ्याचारस् स उच्यते ॥ ३.६

karmendriyāṇi saṁyamya , ya āste manasā smaran ।

indriyārthān vimūḍhātmā , mithyācāras sa ucyate ॥ 3.6

3.6 The one who broods over misgivings and mulls over various desires in the mind while keeping the mouth shut and hands actionless, is a fool and has been called a hypocrite.

यस्त्विन्द्रियाणि मनसा , नियम्यारभतेऽर्जुन । कर्मेन्द्रियैᳵ कर्मयोगम् , असक्तस् स विशिष्यते ॥ ३.७

yastvindriyāṇi manasā , niyamyārabhate'rjuna ।

karmendriyai× karmayogam , asaktas sa viśiṣyate ॥ 3.7

3.7 But, the man who judiciously regulates his sensory impulses while performing his duties honestly is praised by all.

नियतं कुरु कर्म त्वम् , कर्म ज्यायो ह्यकर्मणः । शरीरयात्रापि च ते , न प्रसिद्ध्येद् अकर्मणः ॥ ३.८

niyataṁ kuru karma tvam , karma jyāyo hyakarmaṇaḥ ।

śarīrayātrāpi ca te , na prasiddhyed akarmaṇaḥ ॥ 3.8

3.8 Hence you must always rise up to responsibility. Performing is clearly better than non-performance. Moreover your body cannot be supported by being idle.

यज्ञार्थात् कर्मणोऽन्यत्र , लोकोऽयं कर्मबन्धनः । तदर्थं कर्म कौन्तेय , मुक्तसङ्गस् समाचर ॥ ३.९

yajñārthāt karmaṇo'nyatra , loko'yaṁ karmabandhanaḥ ।

tadarthaṁ karma kaunteya , muktasaṅgas samācara ॥ 3.9

3.9 Selfish actions are prohibited while Selfless service is eulogized. Hence O son of Kunti, do your work without greed.

सहयज्ञाᳶ प्रजास् सृष्ट्वा , पुरोवाच प्रजापतिः । अनेन प्रसविष्यध्वम् , एष वोऽस्त्विष्टकामधुक् ॥ ३.१०

sahayajñā× prajās sṛṣṭvā , purovāca prajāpatiḥ ।

anena prasaviṣyadhvam , eṣa vo'stviṣṭakāmadhuk ॥ 3.10

3.10 This world has been built by great administrators who worked ceaselessly with a sense of nurturing. Their blessings are always with us in our activities.

देवान् भावयतानेन , ते देवा भावयन्तु वः । परस्परं भावयन्तः , श्रेयऽ परम् अवाप्स्यथ ॥ ३.११

devān bhāvayatānena , te devā bhāvayantu vaḥ ।

parasparaṁ bhāvayantaḥ , śreyaऽ param avāpsyatha ॥ 3.11

3.11 In turn help those great beings who maintain the mighty laws and govern the lands. Thus working together you shall attain all success.

इष्टान् भोगान् हि वो देवाः , दास्यन्ते यज्ञभाविताः । तैर्दत्तानप्रदायैभ्यः , यो भुङ्क्ते स्तेन एव सः ॥ ३.१२

iṣṭān bhogān hi vo devāḥ , dāsyante yajñabhāvitāḥ ।

tairdattānapradāyaibhyaḥ , yo bhuṅkte stena eva saḥ ॥ 3.12

3.12 The rulers are supremely pleased with honest works by the populace and bestow upon all many rewards. Thus those who abstain from working are indeed thieves.

यज्ञशिष्टाशिनस् सन्तः , मुच्यन्ते सर्वकिल्बिषैः । भुञ्जते ते त्वघं पापाः , ये पचन्त्यात्मकारणात् ॥ ३.१३

yajñaśiṣṭāśinas santaḥ , mucyante sarvakilbiṣaiḥ ।

bhuñjate te tvaghaṁ pāpāḥ , ye pacantyātmakāraṇāt ॥ 3.13

3.13 A man who earns his bread honestly and donates a share for social welfare is devoid of all penalty. While the cruel and miserly are sooner or later aptly punished.

अन्नाद्भवन्ति भूतानि , पर्जन्याद् अन्नसम्भवः । यज्ञाद्भवति पर्जन्यः , यज्ञऽ कर्मसमुद्भवः ॥ ३.१४

annādbhavanti bhūtāni , parjanyād annasambhavaḥ ।

yajñādbhavati parjanyaḥ , yajñaऽ karmasamudbhavaḥ ॥ 3.14

3.14 The ecosystem is supported by honest work, that in turn ensures food and livelihood for all. Even the natural forces and seasons respond favourably to the righteous deeds.

कर्म ब्रह्मोद्भवं विद्धि , ब्रह्माक्षरसमुद्भवम् । तस्मात् सर्वगतं ब्रह्म , नित्यं यज्ञे प्रतिष्ठितम् ॥ ३.१५

karma brahmodbhavaṁ viddhi , brahmākṣarasamudbhavam ।

tasmāt sarvagataṁ brahma , nityaṁ yajñe pratiṣṭhitam ॥ 3.15

3.15 Our planet has been created by the mighty primeval forces which are eternal. And all here is sustained by hard work and judicious action.

एवं प्रवर्तितं चक्रम् , नानुवर्तयतीह यः । अघायुरिन्द्रियारामः , मोघं पार्थ स जीवति ॥ ३.१६

evaṁ pravartitaṁ cakram , nānuvartayatīha yaḥ ।

aghāyurindriyārāmaḥ , moghaṁ pārtha sa jīvati ॥ 3.16

3.16 Whosoever does not contribute to this cycle of sustenance and growth, lives in vain infatuated by his senses and reaps the punishment due to him.

यस्त्वात्मरतिरेव स्यात् , आत्मतृप्तश्च मानवः । आत्मन्येव च सन्तुष्टः , तस्य कार्यं न विद्यते ॥ ३.१७

yastvātmaratireva syāt , ātmatr̥ptaśca mānavaḥ ।

ātmanyeva ca santuṣṭaḥ , tasya kāryaṁ na vidyate ॥ 3.17

3.17 Only for a confirmed Renunciate who is ever absorbed in a contemplative lifestyle is there no need to perform physical labour.

नैव तस्य कृतेनार्थः , नाकृतेनेह कश्चन । न चास्य सर्वभूतेषु , कश्चिद् अर्थव्यपाश्रयः ॥ ३.१८

naiva tasya kr̥tenārthaḥ , nākr̥teneha kaścana ।

na cāsya sarvabhūteṣu , kaścid arthavyapāśrayaḥ ॥ 3.18

3.18 Such a Sadhu is not dependent on maintaining his body, albeit living on alms or forest fruits. Nor does he actively seek anything else from the world.

तस्माद् असक्तस् सततम् , कार्यं कर्म समाचर । असक्तो ह्याचरन् कर्म , परम् आप्नोति पूरुषः ॥ ३.१९

tasmād asaktas satatam , kāryaṁ karma samācara ।

asakto hyācaran karma , param āpnoti pūruṣaḥ ॥ 3.19

3.19 Hence, Always rise up to shoulder Responsibility. Perform your duty honestly and attain eternal greatness.

कर्मणैव हि संसिद्धिम् , आस्थिता जनकादयः । लोकसङ्ग्रहमेवापि , सम्पश्यन् कर्तुमर्हसि ॥ ३.२०

karmaṇaiva hi saṁsiddhim , āsthitā janakādayaḥ ।

lokasaṅgrahamevāpi , sampaśyan kartumarhasi ॥ 3.20

3.20 The men and women of yore too attained greatness only by selfless Action. With a view to protect and nurture the masses also you must do your duty.

यद् यदाचरति श्रेष्ठः , तत् तदेवेतरो जनः । स यत् प्रमाणं कुरुते , लोकस् तद् अनुवर्तते ॥ ३.२१

yad yadācarati śreṣṭhaḥ , tat tadevetaro janaḥ ।

sa yat pramāṇaṁ kurute , lokas tad anuvartate ॥ 3.21

3.21 Whatever a great soul does is adhered to by the commoner. The high standards set by the wise are followed to this day by mankind.

न मे पार्थास्ति कर्तव्यम् , त्रिषु लोकेषु किञ्चन । नानवाप्तम् अवाप्तव्यम् , वर्त एव च कर्मणि ॥ ३.२२

na me pārthāsti kartavyam , triṣu lokeṣu kiñcana ।

nānavāptam avāptavyam , varta eva ca karmaṇi ॥ 3.22

3.22 Even the good Lord is always at work in the form of sun and moon, breeze and rains, having nothing to gain whatsoever from anyone.

यदि ह्यहं न वर्तेयम् , जातु कर्मण्यतन्द्रितः । मम वर्त्मानुवर्तन्ते , मनुष्याᳶ पार्थ सर्वशः ॥ ३.२३

yadi hyahaṁ na varteyam , jātu karmaṇyatandritaḥ ।

mama vartmānuvartante , manuṣyāᳶ pārtha sarvaśaḥ ॥ 3.23

3.23 Know that mankind imitates and follows the proactive nature at all times.

उत्सीदेयुरिमे लोकाः , न कुर्यां कर्म चेदहम् । सङ्करस्य च कर्ता स्याम् , उपहन्यामिमाᳶ प्रजाः ॥ ३.२४

utsīdeyurime lokāḥ , na kuryāṁ karma cedaham ।

saṅkarasya ca kartā syām , upahanyāmimāᳶ prajāḥ ॥ 3.24

3.24 If nature came to a standstill, if the seasons stopped, it would result in chaos and destruction.

सक्ताᳶ कर्मण्यविद्वांसः , यथा कुर्वन्ति भारत । कुर्याद् विद्वांस्तथासक्तः , चिकीर्षुर् लोकसङ्ग्रहम् ॥ ३.२५

saktāᳶ karmaṇyavidvāṁsaḥ , yathā kurvanti bhārata ।

kuryād vidvāṁstathāsaktaḥ , cikīrṣur lokasaṅgraham ॥ 3.25

3.25 The cruel and ignorant may act for petty motives, but the wise and caring act for the welfare of the world.

न बुद्धिभेदं जनयेत् , अज्ञानां कर्मसङ्गिनाम् । जोषयेत् सर्वकर्माणि , विद्वान् युक्तस् समाचरन् ॥ ३.२६

na buddhibhedaṁ janayet , ajñānāṁ karmasaṅginām ।

joṣayet sarvakarmāṇi , vidvān yuktas samācaran ॥ 3.26

3.26 The wise do their bounden duty silently, side-stepping the ways of the foolish, not locking horns with them.

प्रकृतेᳶ क्रियमाणानि , गुणैᳶ कर्माणि सर्वशः । अहङ्कारविमूढात्मा , कर्ताहम् इति मन्यते ॥ ३.२७

prakṛteᳶ kriyamāṇāni , guṇaiᳶ karmāṇi sarvaśaḥ ।

ahaṅkāravimūḍhātmā , kartāham iti manyate ॥ 3.27

3.27 The real doership is in the ceaseless activity of primeval nature. It alone inspires the intelligence to act, whereas the false egoist takes undue credit.

तत्त्ववित् तु महाबाहो , गुणकर्मविभागयोः । गुणा गुणेषु वर्तन्ते , इति मत्वा न सज्जते ॥ ३.२८

tattvavit tu mahābāho , guṇakarmavibhāgayoḥ ।

guṇā guṇeṣu vartante , iti matvā na sajjate ॥ 3.28

3.28 The discerning individual who intuitively senses a higher power directing his actions does not fall prey to petty pompousness.

प्रकृतेर् गुणसम्मूढाः , सज्जन्ते गुणकर्मसु । तान् अकृत्स्नविदो मन्दान् , कृत्स्नविन् न विचालयेत् ॥ ३.२९

prakr̥ter guṇasammūḍhāḥ , sajjante guṇakarmasu ।

tān akr̥tsnavido mandān , kr̥tsnavinna vicālayet ॥ 3.29

3.29 Those attracted by the sensual forces delude themselves in wrong notions. The pragmatic person should not get bowled over nor interfere nor try to direct such lowly people.

मयि सर्वाणि कर्माणि , सन्न्यस्याध्यात्मचेतसा । निराशीर् निर्ममो भूत्वा , युध्यस्व विगतज्वरः ॥ ३.३०

mayi sarvāṇi karmāṇi , sannyasyādhyātmacetasā ।

nirāśīr nirmamo bhūtvā , yudhyasva vigatajvaraḥ ॥ 3.30

3.30 Free from false ego and feverishness, Trusting the Lord to be with you, with the mind focussed on your duty, perform righteous action.

ये मे मतम् इदं नित्यम् , अनुतिष्ठन्ति मानवाः । श्रद्धावन्तोऽनसूयन्तः , मुच्यन्ते तेऽपि कर्मभिः ॥ ३.३१

ye me matam idaṁ nityam , anutiṣṭhanti mānavāḥ ।

śraddhāvanto'nasūyantaḥ , mucyante te'pi karmabhiḥ ॥ 3.31

3.31 Liberated are those who thus go about their work uncomplainingly with full faith in the Divine.

ये त्वेतद् अभ्यसूयन्तः , नानुतिष्ठन्ति मे मतम् । सर्वज्ञानविमूढांस्तान् , विद्धि नष्टान् अचेतसः ॥ ३.३२

ye tvetad abhyasūyantaḥ , nānutiṣṭhanti me matam ।

sarvajñānavimūḍhāṁstān , viddhi naṣṭān acetasaḥ ॥ 3.32

3.32 Doomed are those who grumble and complain, lacking faith in the nature of righteous deeds and scriptures.

सदृशं चेष्टते स्वस्याः , प्रकृतेर् ज्ञानवानपि । प्रकृतिं यान्ति भूतानि , निग्रहः किं करिष्यति ॥ ३.३३

sadr̥śaṁ ceṣṭate svasyāḥ , prakr̥ter jñānavānapi ।

prakr̥tiṁ yānti bhūtāni , nigrahaḥ kiṁ kariṣyati ॥ 3.33

3.33 Any sensible person will be guided by the intellect to take appropriate action. What can mere rumination do?

इन्द्रियस्येन्द्रियस्यार्थे , रागद्वेषौ व्यवस्थितौ । तयोर्न वशम् आगच्छेत् , तौ ह्यस्य परिपन्थिनौ ॥ ३.३४

indriyasyendriyasyārthe , rāgadveṣau vyavasthitau ।

tayorna vaśam āgacchet , tau hyasya paripanthinau ॥ 3.34

3.34 Each sense and its sensory object has a corresponding relationship of like or dislike varying for each individual temperament. Let that not obstruct the discerning fellow from performance of duty.

श्रेयान् स्वधर्मो विगुणः , परधर्मात् स्वनुष्ठितात् । स्वधर्मे निधनं श्रेयः , परधर्मो भयावहः ॥ ३.३५

śreyān svadharmo viguṇaḥ , paradharmāt svanuṣṭhitāt ।

svadharme nidhanaṁ śreyaḥ , paradharmo bhayāvahaḥ ॥ 3.35

3.35 Each of us has a defined set of duties in a current frame of time. Better to earnestly discharge that rather than look over the shoulder at what others are doing. There is great risk in being tempted to do something else.

अर्जुन उवाच

अथ केन प्रयुक्तोऽयम् , पापं चरति पूरुषः । अनिच्छन्नपि वार्ष्णेय , बलादिव नियोजितः ॥ ३.३६

arjuna uvāca

atha kena prayukto'yam , pāpaṁ carati pūruṣaḥ ।

anicchannapi vārṣṇeya , balādiva niyojitaḥ ॥ 3.36

Arjuna has a curiosity

3.36 How come an individual commits blunders or unforced errors?

श्री भगवान् उवाच

काम एष क्रोध एषः , रजोगुणसमुद्भवः । महाशनो महापाप्मा , विद्ध्येनम् इह वैरिणम् ॥ ३.३७

śrī bhagavān uvāca

kāma eṣa krodha eṣaḥ , rajoguṇasamudbhavaḥ ।

mahāśano mahāpāpmā , viddhyenam iha vairiṇam ॥ 3.37

The gracious Lord replies

3.37 It is due to blinding desire and wrath born of feverishness.

धूमेनाव्रियते *वह्निः* , यथादर्शो मलेन च । यथोल्बेनावृतो गर्भः , तथा तेनेदमावृतम् ॥ ३.३८

dhūmenāvriyate vahniḥ , yathādarśo malena ca ।

yatholbenāvr̥to garbhaḥ , tathā tenedamāvr̥tam ॥ 3.38

3.38 Just as fire is obscured by smoke, a mirror by dust, and an embryo is covered by its womb, so is the intellect wrapped up in desires.

आवृतं ज्ञानम् एतेन , ज्ञानिनो नित्यवैरिणा । कामरूपेण कौन्तेय , दुष्पूरेणानलेन च ॥ ३.३९

āvr̥taṁ jñānam etena , jñānino nityavairiṇā ।

kāmarūpeṇa kaunteya , duṣpūreṇānalena ca ॥ 3.39

3.39 O Kaunteya ! Unappeasable as fire, the feverish desire in one's heart is one's main enemy, since it clouds the intellect.

इन्द्रियाणि मनो बुद्धिः , अस्याधिष्ठानम् उच्यते । एतैर् विमोहयत्येषः , ज्ञानम् आवृत्य देहिनम् ॥ ३.४०

indriyāṇi mano buddhiḥ , asyādhiṣṭhānam ucyate ।

etair vimohayatyeṣaḥ , jñānam āvr̥tya dehinam ॥ 3.40

3.40 Seated within, It gnaws through a man's senses, blows away his reason, and deludes him completely.

तस्मात् त्वमिन्द्रियाण्यादौ , नियम्य भरतर्षभ । पाप्मानं प्रजहि ह्येनम् , ज्ञानविज्ञाननाशनम् ॥ ३.४१

tasmāt tvamindriyāṇyādau , niyamya bharatarṣabha ।

pāpmānaṁ prajahi hyenam , jñānavijñānanāśanam ॥ 3.41

3.41 O Best of all Citizens ! With slow, systematic and careful examination of each wish, separate and throw out the tendency that is harmful and that goes against pragmatic understanding.

इन्द्रियाणि पराण्याहुः , इन्द्रियेभ्यः परं मनः । मनसस्तु परा बुद्धिः , यो बुद्धेः परतस्तु सः ॥ ३.४२

indriyāṇi parāṇyāhuḥ , indriyebhyaḥ paraṁ manaḥ ।

manasastu parā buddhiḥ , yo buddheḥ paratastu saḥ ॥ 3.42

3.42 The wise say that the senses have a great say on the body, the intellect can sway the senses, the contained experiences in memory can overcome the intellect. However the Divine dwells in every heart, and its nobility is supreme.

एवं बुद्धेः परं बुद्ध्वा , संस्तभ्यात्मानम् आत्मना । जहि शत्रुं महाबाहो , कामरूपं दुरासदम् ॥ ३.४३

evaṁ buddheḥ paraṁ buddhvā , saṁstabhyātmānam ātmanā ।

jahi śatruṁ mahābāho , kāmarūpaṁ durāsadam ॥ 3.43

3.43 Recognize that noblest virtue within, and being guided by it, correct the reasoning brain, O mighty Hero ! Thereby may you weed out the destructive thorny infatuation.

ॐ तत् सत् । इति श्रीमद्भगवद्गीतासु उपनिषत्सु ब्रह्मविद्यायां योगशास्त्रे श्रीकृष्णार्जुनसंवादे

कर्म-योगो नाम तृतीयोऽध्यायः ॥ ३॥

oṁ tat sat । iti śrīmadbhagavadgītāsu upaniṣatsu brahmavidyāyām̐ yogaśāstre śrīkr̥ṣṇārjunasaṁvāde karma-yogo nāma tr̥tīyo'dhyāyaḥ

॥ 3 ॥

4 Yoga of Intention

Yoga of Intent in Performing Work. In continuation of emphasizing Karma Yoga in 3rd Chapter, specific mention of how should one's INTENT be while performing duty. The quality of thoughts in the mind and emotion in the heart while doing action is stated with great clarity.

ॐ श्री परमात्मने नमः । अथ चतुर्थोऽध्यायः

oṁ śrī paramātmane namaḥ । atha caturtho'dhyāyaḥ

श्री भगवान् उवाच

इमं विवस्वते योगम् , प्रोक्तवान् अहम् अव्ययम् । विवस्वान् मनवे प्राह , मनुर् इक्ष्वाकवेऽब्रवीत् ॥ ४.१

śrī bhagavān uvāca

imaṁ vivasvate yogam , proktavān aham avyayam ।

vivasvān manave prāha , manur ikṣvākave'bravīt ॥ 4.1

The timeless Lord stated

4.1 I taught this perfect teaching to Vivasvan the Sun, who in turn imparted it to Manu the law giver, and Manu proclaimed the same to Ikshvaku his son, the illustrious ancestor of Lord Ram.

एवं परम्पराप्राप्तम् , इमं राजर्षयो विदुः । स कालेनेह महता , योगो नष्टः परन्तप ॥ ४.२

evaṁ paramparāprāptam , imaṁ rājarṣayo viduḥ ।

sa kāleneha mahatā , yogo naṣṭaẖ parantapa ॥ 4.2

4.2 Likewise the Knowledge had flourished in successive empires ruled by wise kings. By a long lapse of intervening time it had lost its core essence in the current context.

स एवायं मया तेऽद्य , योगः प्रोक्तः पुरातनः । भक्तोऽसि मे सखा चेति , रहस्यं ह्येतद् उत्तमम् ॥ ४.३

sa evāyaṁ mayā te'dya , yogaẖ proktaẖ purātanaḥ ।

bhakto'si me sakhā ceti , rahasyaṁ hyetad uttamam ॥ 4.3

4.3 The same precious teaching has been revived today for the sake of the sincere seeker, the ardent aspirant for truth, and one who places absolute trust in Divine.

अर्जुन उवाच

अपरं भवतो जन्म , परं जन्म विवस्वतः । कथम् एतद् विजानीयाम् , त्वम् आदौ प्रोक्तवान् इति ॥ ४.४

arjuna uvāca

aparaṁ bhavato janma , paraṁ janma vivasvataḥ ।

katham etad vijānīyām , tvam ādau proktavān iti II 4.4

Arjuna is flabbergasted

4.4 Dear Friend, we are contemporaries here and now, how come it got imparted to the ancients who came before us?

श्री भगवान् उवाच

बहूनि मे व्यतीतानि , जन्मानि तव चार्जुन । तान्यहं वेद सर्वाणि , न त्वं वेत्थ परन्तप ॥ ४.५

śrī bhagavān uvāca

bahūni me vyatītāni , janmāni tava cārjuna ।

tānyahaṁ veda sarvāṇi , na tvaṁ vettha parantapa II 4.5

The kind Lord resolves

4.5 This creation is ageless, the same wisdom dawns again and again in purified temperaments that have a thirst for the ultimate.

अजोऽपि सन्नव्ययात्मा , भूतानाम् ईश्वरोऽपि सन् । प्रकृतिं स्वाम् अधिष्ठाय , सम्भवाम्यात्ममायया ॥ ४.६

ajo'pi sannavyayātmā , bhūtānām īśvaro'pi san ।

prakr̥tiṁ svām adhiṣṭhāya , sambhavāmyātmamāyayā II 4.6

4.6 Ideas are imperishable, eternal and recursive. They blossom in the one with a clear mind by the general laws of nature.

यदा यदा हि धर्मस्य , ग्लानिर् भवति भारत । अभ्युत्थानम् अधर्मस्य , तदात्मानं सृजाम्यहम् ॥ ४.७

yadā yadā hi dharmasya , glānir bhavati bhārata ।

abhyutthānam adharmasya , tadātmānaṁ sr̥jāmyaham II 4.7

4.7 Whenever a heart cries out for help, whenever the situation becomes overpowering, the forces of nature move swiftly to lend a hand. This we have all experienced in moments of extreme danger, when somehow our willpower surges up and our body braces to quell the difficulty. Likewise a nation responds as one in the face of an emergency.

परित्राणाय साधूनाम् , विनाशाय च दुष्कृताम् । धर्मसंस्थापनार्थाय , सम्भवामि युगे युगे ॥ ४.८

paritrāṇāya sādhūnām , vināśāya ca duṣkr̥tām ।

dharmasaṁsthāpanārthāya , sambhavāmi yuge yuge II 4.8

4.8 For the protection of the righteous, for the destruction of the wicked, and for the establishment of law and order, noble souls and saints take birth in every hamlet from time to time.

जन्म कर्म च मे दिव्यम् , एवं यो वेत्ति तत्त्वतः । त्यक्त्वा देहं पुनर्जन्म , नैति मामेति सोऽर्जुन ॥ ४.९

janma karma ca me divyam , evaṁ yo vetti tattvataḥ ।

tyaktvā dehaṁ punarjanma , naiti māmeti so'rjuna ॥ 4.9

4.9 He who relates to the truth and derives sustenance by divine works is always protected.

वीतरागभयक्रोधाः , मन्मया माम् उपाश्रिताः । बहवो ज्ञानतपसा , पूता मद्भावम् आगताः ॥ ४.१०

vītarāgabhayakrodhāḥ , manmayā mām upāśritāḥ ।

bahavo jñānatapasā , pūtā madbhāvam āgatāḥ ॥ 4.10

4.10 The shackles of infatuation, fear and anger do not touch those who repeat the Divine name. Their souls are purified in the fire of sincerity and they attain the poise and equanimity of a peaceful existence.

ये यथा मां प्रपद्यन्ते , तांस्तथैव भजाम्यहम् । मम वर्त्मानुवर्तन्ते , मनुष्याः पार्थ सर्वशः ॥ ४.११

ye yathā māṁ prapadyante , tāṁstathaiva bhajāmyaham ।

mama vartmānuvartante , manuṣyā× pārtha sarvaśaḥ ॥ 4.11

4.11 Many are the differing paths to salvation. Diverse paths lead to the divine, each to its own merit is justified.

काङ्क्षन्तः कर्मणां सिद्धिम् , यजन्त इह देवताः । क्षिप्रं हि मानुषे लोके , सिद्धिर् भवति कर्मजा ॥ ४.१२

kāṅkṣanta× karmaṇāṁ siddhim , yajanta iha devatāḥ ।

kṣipraṁ hi mānuṣe loke , siddhir bhavati karmajā ॥ 4.12

4.12 Those longing for success in any field do rigorous and systematic practice. It is a sure sign for being victorious in the chosen domain.

चातुर्वर्ण्यं मया सृष्टम् , गुणकर्मविभागशः । तस्य कर्तारम् अपि माम् , विद्ध्यकर्तारम् अव्ययम् ॥ ४.१३

cāturvarṇyaṁ mayā sṛṣṭam , guṇakarmavibhāgaśaḥ ।

tasya kartāram api mām , viddhyakartāram avyayam ॥ 4.13

4.13 The various temperaments and talents have been infused appropriately by the Divine in different men and women. Nature imparts such variations across regions, races and cultures. Similar to roses in Punjab, Lotuses in Bangalore, Mountains in Himalayas, Polar Bears in Siberia.

न मां कर्माणि लिम्पन्ति , न मे कर्मफले स्पृहा । इति मां योऽभिजानाति , कर्मभिर् न स बध्यते ॥ ४.१४

na māṁ karmāṇi limpanti , na me karmaphale spṛhā ।

iti māṁ yo'bhijānāti , karmabhir na sa badhyate ॥ 4.14

4.14 Work and its rewards does not color Nature. Tigers, Trees, Rivers, Birds, Fruits and

Earth remain unblemished by what they do or not do. The man who understands this fact also incorporates it in his thinking, thereby he too is freed from the weight and bondage of taking credit.

एवं ज्ञात्वा कृतं कर्म , पूर्वैरपि मुमुक्षुभिः । कुरु कर्मैव तस्मात् त्वम् , पूर्वैः पूर्वतरं कृतम् ॥ ४.१५

evaṁ jñātvā kr̥taṁ karma , pūrvairapi mumukṣubhiḥ ।

kuru karmaiva tasmāt tvam , pūrvai× pūrvataraṁ kr̥tam ॥ 4.15

4.15 The men long ago had realized this, having identified with Nature; so must You perform work O Seeker desiring Liberation.

किं कर्म किम् अकर्मेति , कवयोऽप्यत्र मोहिताः । तत्ते कर्म प्रवक्ष्यामि , यज्ज्ञात्वा मोक्ष्यसेऽशुभात् ॥ ४.१६

kiṁ karma kim akarmeti , kavayo'pyatra mohitāḥ ।

tatte karma pravakṣyāmi , yajjñātvā mokṣyase'śubhāt ॥ 4.16

4.16 Many are not sure of their duty, even the scholarly get confused and bogged down by wrong notions of Responsibility. I shall teach thee the method of cheerfully attending to work so that it may not become a burden.

कर्मणो ह्यपि बोद्धव्यम् , बोद्धव्यं च विकर्मणः । अकर्मणश्च बोद्धव्यम् , गहना कर्मणो गतिः ॥ ४.१७

karmaṇo hyapi boddhavyam,boddhavyaṁ ca vikarmaṇaḥ ।

akarmaṇaśca boddhavyam , gahanā karmaṇo gatiḥ ॥ 4.17

4.17 A fine intellect is needed to discriminate between right and wrong, since situations present themselves such that what was correct in the first becomes inappropriate in the next. Unpredictable, nay unfathomable are the events across time.

कर्मण्यकर्म यः पश्येत् , अकर्मणि च कर्म यः । स बुद्धिमान् मनुष्येषु , स युक्तः कृत्स्नकर्मकृत् ॥ ४.१८

karmaṇyakarma ya× paśyet , akarmaṇi ca karma yaḥ ।

sa buddhiman manuṣyeṣu ,sa yukta× kr̥tsnakarmakr̥t ॥ 4.18

4.18 The one who remains alert and aware to such seeming contradictions in nature can handle the situations with elan.

यस्य सर्वे समारम्भाः , कामसङ्कल्पवर्जिताः । ज्ञानाग्निदग्धकर्माणम् , तमाहुः पण्डितं बुधाः ॥ ४.१९

yasya sarve samārambhāḥ , kāmasaṅkalpavarjitāḥ ।

jñānāgnidagdhakarmāṇam , tamāhu× paṇḍitaṁ budhāḥ ॥ 4.19

4.19 He whose aspirations are devoid of selfish gains, and whose deeds are illuminated brightly in the world, he is hailed as a great man.

त्यक्त्वा कर्मफलासङ्गम् , नित्यतृप्तो निराश्रयः । कर्मण्यभिप्रवृत्तोऽपि , नैव किञ्चित् करोति सः ॥ ४.२०

tyaktvā karmaphalāsaṅgam , nityatr̥pto nirāśrayaḥ ।

karmaṇyabhipravr̥tto'pi , naiva kiñcit karoti saḥ ॥ 4.20

4.20 Having dropped the burden of royalty-credit-appreciation-intellectual right, deriving all contentment from work alone, such a soul lives free.

निराशीर् यतचित्तात्मा , त्यक्तसर्वपरिग्रहः । शारीरं केवलं कर्म , कुर्वन् नाप्नोति किल्बिषम् ॥ ४.२१

nirāśīr yatacittātmā , tyaktasarvaparigrahaḥ ।

śārīraṁ kevalaṁ karma , kurvan nāpnoti kilbiṣam ॥ 4.21

4.21 Without the cutting excitement of reward or the depressing frustration of punishment, such a one rises above greed - a most potent pitfall.

यदृच्छालाभसन्तुष्टः , द्वन्द्वातीतो विमत्सरः । समस् सिद्धावसिद्धौ च , कृत्वापि न निबध्यते ॥ ४.२२

yadr̥cchālābhasantuṣṭaḥ , dvandvātīto vimatsaraḥ ।

samas siddhāvasiddhau ca , kr̥tvāpi na nibadhyate ॥ 4.22

4.22 Accepting calmly the nature's bounty, unwavering in the face of jealousy, keeping sane through thick and thin - he moves unfettered.

गतसङ्गस्य मुक्तस्य , ज्ञानावस्थितचेतसः । यज्ञायाचरत× कर्म , समग्रं प्रविलीयते ॥ ४.२३

gatasaṅgasya muktasya , jñānāvasthitacetasaḥ ।

yajñāyācarata× karma , samagraṁ pravilīyate ॥ 4.23

4.23 Devoid of burning ambitions, yet acting enthusiastically for the welfare of all - he forms no scars of impressions. His memory remains free and his intellect can work without polarisation.

NOW ANOTHER MIGHTY STATEMENT

ब्रह्मार्पणं ब्रह्म हविः , ब्रह्माग्नौ ब्रह्मणा हुतम् । ब्रह्मैव तेन गन्तव्यम् , ब्रह्मकर्मसमाधिना ॥ ४.२४

brahmārpaṇaṁ brahma haviḥ , brahmāgnau brahmaṇā hutam ।

brahmaiva tena gantavyam , brahmakarmasamādhinā ॥ 4.24

4.24 Regard each and every thought, word and deed as the supreme Lord's will. Calmly notice in all situations and persons his direct presence.

So it is said – एक पत्ता भी नहिं हिलता उनकी मर्जी के बिना - This saying has a meaning that is literal as well as figurative. In many instances it is simply correct to take it literally. However in some cases, there is an element of free-will. The free-will is based on complex laws and varies from person to person and situation to situation. More like the stage boundary allotted to an actor, arena limit for a sportsman, grazing yard for a cow, children to a couple or populace to a state.

दैवम् एवापरे यज्ञम् , योगिनः पर्युपासते । ब्रह्माग्नावपरे यज्ञम् , यज्ञेनैवोपजुह्वति ॥ ४.२५

daivam evāpare yajñam , yoginaḥ paryupāsate ।

brahmāgnāvapare yajñam , yajñenaivopajuhvati ॥ 4.25

4.25 Some great masters work as per the directives of their own tradition only; the brave regard all traditions as equal and with ease perform whatever is expected of them.

श्रोत्रादीनि इन्द्रियाण्यन्ये , संयमाग्निषु जुह्वति । शब्दादीन् विषयान् अन्ये , इन्द्रियाग्निषु जुह्वति ॥ ४.२६

śrotrādīni indriyāṇyanye , saṁyamāgniṣu juhvati ।

śabdādīn viṣayān anye , indriyāgniṣu juhvati ॥ 4.26

4.26 Some become great musicians, others singers, sopranos and divas. Similarly many excel in fine arts and crafts - whether sculpture, painting or dance.

सर्वाणि इन्द्रियकर्माणि , प्राणकर्माणि चापरे । आत्मसंयमयोगाग्नौ , जुह्वति ज्ञानदीपिते ॥ ४.२७

sarvāṇi indriyakarmāṇi , prāṇakarmāṇi cāpare ।

ātmasaṁyamayogāgnau , juhvati jñānadīpite ॥ 4.27

4.27 There are those who rise to just administration and become noble kings.

द्रव्ययज्ञास् तपोयज्ञाः , योगयज्ञास् तथापरे । स्वाध्यायज्ञानयज्ञाश्च , यतयस् संशितव्रताः ॥ ४.२८

dravyayajñās tapoyajñāḥ , yogayajñās tathāpare ।

svādhyāyajñānayajñāśca , yatayas saṁśitavratāḥ ॥ 4.28

4.28 Fine businessmen, philanthropists, ascetics, mystics and martial artists also the world produces.

अपाने जुह्वति प्राणम् , प्राणेऽपानं तथापरे । प्राणापानगती रुद्ध्वा , प्राणायामपरायणाः ॥ ४.२९

apāne juhvati prāṇam , prāṇe'pānaṁ tathāpare ।

prāṇāpānagatī ruddhvā , prāṇāyāmaparāyaṇāḥ ॥ 4.29

4.29 Engineers and Doctors, Scientists and Innovators, Soldiers and Rescue workers - who can keep their cool in the face of calamity, perform their duty under trying circumstances.

अपरे नियताहाराः , प्राणान् प्राणेषु जुह्वति । सर्वेऽप्येते यज्ञविदः , यज्ञक्षपितकल्मषाः ॥ ४.३०

apare niyatāhārāḥ , prāṇān prāṇeṣu juhvati ।

sarve'pyete yajñavidaḥ , yajñakṣapitakalmaṣāḥ ॥ 4.30

4.30 Sportsmen and women, gymnasts and runners, swimmers and athletes - those who can regulate their diet and keep a strict watch over it shine brilliantly in the world.

यज्ञशिष्टामृतभुजः , यान्ति ब्रह्म सनातनम् । नायं लोकोऽस्त्ययज्ञस्य , कुतोऽन्यः कुरुसत्तम ॥ ४.३१

yajñaśiṣṭāmṛtabhujaḥ , yānti brahma sanātanam ।

nāyaṁ loko'styayajñasya , kuto'nyaḥ kurusattama ॥ 4.31

4.31 Lay men and women who eat hard-earned bread after duly sharing with their families and amongst society attain Salvation quickly, how can the thief or miserly even think of it?

एवं बहुविधा यज्ञाः , वितता ब्रह्मणो मुखे । कर्मजान् विद्धि तान् सर्वान् , एवं ज्ञात्वा विमोक्ष्यसे ॥ ४.३२

evaṁ bahuvidhā yajñāḥ , vitatā brahmaṇo mukhe ।

karmajān viddhi tān sarvān ,evaṁ jñātvā vimokṣyase ॥ 4.32

4.32 Such are some of the various means and methods by which mankind makes a respectful living and thereby rises to greatness.

श्रेयान् द्रव्यमयाद् यज्ञात् , ज्ञानयज्ञः परन्तप । सर्वं कर्माखिलं पार्थ , ज्ञाने परिसमाप्यते ॥ ४.३३

śreyān dravyamayād yajñāt , jñānayajñaḥ parantapa ।

sarvaṁ karmākhilaṁ pārtha , jñāne parisamāpyate ॥ 4.33

4.33 Judicious plan based action is superior to direct labour, as envisaged in a societal setup where the more cultured and educated are much revered.

तद् विद्धि प्रणिपातेन , परिप्रश्नेन सेवया । उपदेक्ष्यन्ति ते ज्ञानम् , ज्ञानिनस् तत्त्वदर्शिनः ॥ ४.३४

tad viddhi praṇipātena , paripraśnena sevayā ।

upadekṣyanti te jñānam , jñāninas tattvadarśinaḥ ॥ 4.34

4.34 The teachers and professors and gurus and masters who know their subject thoroughly instruct the sincere student whole heartedly.

यज्ज्ञात्वा न पुनर्मोहम् , एवं यास्यसि पाण्डव । येन भूतान्यशेषेण , द्रक्ष्यस्यात्मन्यथो मयि ॥ ४.३५

yajjñātvā na punarmoham , evaṁ yāsyasi pāṇḍava ।

yena bhūtānyaśeṣeṇa , drakṣyasyātmanyatho mayi ॥ 4.35

4.35 Having received that wisdom you shall not O Ardent disciple again fall prey to delusion. The wisdom shall illumine the goodness in all beings as a common trait of the divine.

अपि चेदसि पापेभ्यः , सर्वेभ्यः पापकृत्तमः । सर्वं ज्ञानप्लवेनैव , वृजिनं सन्तरिष्यसि ॥ ४.३६

api cedasi pāpebhyaḥ , sarvebhyaḥ pāpakṛttamaḥ ।

sarvaṁ jñānaplavenaiva , vṛjinaṁ santariṣyasi ॥ 4.36

4.36 When wisdom dawns it sets right the path of even those prone to terrible mistakes.

यथैधांसि समिद्धोग्निः , भस्मसात् कुरुतेऽर्जुन । ज्ञानाग्निस् सर्वकर्माणि , भस्मसात् कुरुते तथा ॥ ४.३७

yathaidhāṁsi samiddhogniḥ , bhasmasātkurute'rjuna ।

jñānāgnis sarvakarmāṇi , bhasmasātkurute tathā ॥ 4.37

4.37 Just as a blazing fire quickly reduces dry timber to ashes, so is the darkness of ignorance banished at once in the torch-light of wisdom.

न हि ज्ञानेन सदृशम् , पवित्रम् इह विद्यते । तत् स्वयं योगसंसिद्धः , कालेनात्मनि विन्दति ॥ ४.३८

na hi jñānena sadṛśam , pavitram iha vidyate ।

tat svayaṁ yogasaṁsiddhaḥ , kālenātmani vindati ॥ 4.38

4.38 Verily right Knowledge is the perfect cleanser of one's heart and mind. The one living a life of Yoga (disciplined action) ascertains it to be a spark of the divine.

श्रद्धावाँल्लभते ज्ञानम् , तत्परस् संयतेन्द्रियः । ज्ञानं लब्ध्वा परां शान्तिम् , अचिरेणाधिगच्छति ॥ ४.३९

śraddhāvām̐llabhate jñānam , tatparas saṁyatendriyaḥ ।

jñānaṁ labdhvā parāṁ śāntim , acireṇādhigacchati ॥ 4.39

4.39 Knowledge is bestowed on the sincere disciple whose heart is full of steady faith. Knowledge balances the sensual urges and culminates in supreme peace.

अज्ञश् चाश्रद्दधानश्च , संशयात्मा विनश्यति । नायं लोकोऽस्ति न परः , न सुखं संशयात्मनः ॥ ४.४०

ajñaś cāśraddadhānaśca , saṁśayātmā vinaśyati ।

nāyaṁ loko'sti na paraḥ ,na sukhaṁ samśayātmanaḥ ॥ 4.40

4.40 The wavering mind and the doubting intellect take one to ruin. Such a person finds no acceptance at home or in the workplace, and suffers rejection elsewhere.

योगसन्न्यस्तकर्माणम् , ज्ञानसञ्छिन्नसंशयम् । आत्मवन्तं न कर्माणि , निबध्नन्ति धनञ्जय ॥ ४.४१

yogasannyastakarmāṇam , jñānasañchinnasaṁśayam ।

ātmavantaṁ na karmāṇi , nibadhnanti dhanañjaya ॥ 4.41

4.41 He who has banished ignorance through a disciplined lifestyle, whose doubts have evaporated in the sun of knowledge, who reposes faith within, lives a fulsome life worth living.

तस्माद् अज्ञानसम्भूतम् , हृत्स्थं ज्ञानासिनात्मनः । छित्त्वैनं संशयं योगम् , आतिष्ठोत्तिष्ठ भारत ॥ ४.४२

tasmād ajñānasambhūtam , hṛtsthaṁ jñānāsinātmanaḥ ।

chittvainaṁ saṁśayaṁ yogam ,ātiṣṭhottiṣṭha bhārata ॥ 4.42

4.42 Hence with all faculties tuned to receiving fresh knowledge, break apart through the haze of doubts. Implement a Yogic lifestyle, arise O Bharata to righteous action.

ॐ तत् सत् । इति श्रीमद्भगवद्गीतासु उपनिषत्सु ब्रह्मविद्यायां योगशास्त्रे श्रीकृष्णार्जुनसंवादे
ज्ञान-कर्म-सन्न्यास-योगो नाम चतुर्थोऽध्यायः ॥ ४॥ (ज्ञान-विभाग-योगो नाम)

oṁ tat sat । iti śrīmadbhagavadgītāsu upaniṣatsu brahmavidyāyāṁ yogaśāstre śrīkṛṣṇārjunasaṁvāde jñāna-karma-sannyāsa-yogo nāma caturtho'dhyāyaḥ
॥ 4 ॥ jñāna-vibhāga-yogo nāma

5 Yoga of Calmness

Yoga of calm Asceticism

ॐ श्री परमात्मने नमः । अथ पञ्चमोऽध्यायः

oṁ śrī paramātmane namaḥ I atha pañcamo'dhyāyaḥ

अर्जुन उवाच

सन्न्यासं कर्मणां कृष्ण , पुनर् योगं च शंससि । यच्छ्रेय एतयोरेकम् , तन्मे ब्रूहि सुनिश्चितम् ॥ ५.१

arjuna uvāca

sannyāsaṁ karmaṇāṁ kṛṣṇa , punar yogaṁ ca śaṁsasi I

yacchreya etayorekam , tanme brūhi suniścitam II 5.1

Arjuna perplexed queries

5.1 O Krishna ! Thee have stated calm Asceticism as well as righteous Action. How to know which to apply when?

श्री भगवान् उवाच

सन्न्यासः कर्मयोगश्च , निःश्रेयसकरावुभौ । तयोस्तु कर्मसन्न्यासात् , कर्मयोगो विशिष्यते ॥ ५.२

śrī bhagavān uvāca

sannyāsaḥ karmayogaśca , niḥśreyasakarāvubhau I

tayostu karmasannyāsāt , karmayogo viśiṣyate II 5.2

The merciful Lord replies

5.2 Both the paths of calm Asceticism as well as of purposeful Action lead to glory. The path of purposeful Action is the more favourable of the two for thee Arjuna.

ज्ञेयस् स नित्यसन्न्यासी , यो न द्वेष्टि न काङ्क्षति । निर्द्वन्द्वो हि महाबाहो , सुखं बन्धात् प्रमुच्यते ॥ ५.३

jñeyas sa nityasannyāsī , yo na dveṣṭi na kāṅkṣati I

nirdvandvo hi mahābāho , sukhaṁ bandhāt pramucyate II 5.3

5.3 An ascetic is clearly known to all as a man of frugal needs. He is one who subsists directly on nature, subsuming the contradictory and varied bodily demands. Such a soul easily reposes in tranquility.

साङ्ख्ययोगौ पृथग्बालाः , प्रवदन्ति न पण्डिताः। एकम् अप्यास्थितस् सम्यक् , उभयोर्विन्दते फलम् ॥ ५.४

sāṅkhyayogau pṛthagbālāḥ , pravadanti na paṇḍitāḥ I

ekam apyāsthitas samyak , ubhayorvindate phalam ॥ 5.4

5.4 It is childish to debate on the superior amongst the two paths. Cheerfulness and tranquility attained by any means amounts to the same bliss.

यत् साङ्ख्यैः प्राप्यते स्थानम् , तद् योगैरपि गम्यते । एकं साङ्ख्यं च योगं च , यः पश्यति स पश्यति ॥ ५.५

yat sāṅkhyaiḥ prāpyate sthānam , tad yogairapi gamyate ।

ekaṁ sāṅkhyaṁ ca yogaṁ ca , yaḥ paśyati sa paśyati ॥ 5.5

5.5 The nectar of a peaceful life that is being enjoyed by an Ascetic is very well enjoyed by a man through righteous Action as well. The wise sees both men as equal in attainment.

सन्न्यासस्तु महाबाहो , दुःखम् आप्तुम् अयोगतः । योगयुक्तो मुनिर् ब्रह्म , नचिरेणाधिगच्छति ॥ ५.६

sannyāsastu mahābāho , duḥkham āptum ayogataḥ ।

yogayukto munir brahma , nacireṇādhigacchati ॥ 5.6

5.6 O Highly Capable ! Asceticism might be devoid of charm for a multitalented personality, for him the charming method is through full exhibition of his skills.

योगयुक्तो विशुद्धात्मा , विजितात्मा जितेन्द्रियः । सर्वभूतात्मभूतात्मा , कुर्वन्नपि न लिप्यते ॥ ५.७

yogayukto viśuddhātmā , vijitātmā jitendriyaḥ ।

sarvabhūtātmabhūtātmā , kurvannapi na lipyate ॥ 5.7

5.7 The talented individual who focusses on his targets with a serene and balanced mindset and with cheerfulness pursues his aim, does not get smeared by societal jabs.

नैव किञ्चित् करोमीति , युक्तो मन्येत तत्त्ववित् । पश्यञ्श्रृण्वन् स्पृशञ्जिघ्रन् , अश्नन् गच्छन् स्वपञ्श्वसन् ॥ ५.८

naiva kiñcit karomīti , yukto manyeta tattvavit ।

paśyañ-śr̥ṇvan spr̥śañ-jighran , aśnan gacchan svapañ-śvasan ॥ 5.8

5.8 The noble personality rises above petty egotism and attributes his success to God, Society and Family. He remains neutral in his sights and senses.

प्रलपन् विसृजन् ***गृह्णन्*** , उन्मिषन् निमिषन्नपि । इन्द्रियाणीन्द्रियार्थेषु , वर्तन्त इति धारयन् ॥ ५.९

pralapan visr̥jan gr̥hṇan , unmiṣan nimiṣannapi ।

indriyāṇīndriyārtheṣu , vartanta iti dhārayan ॥ 5.9

5.9 The noble soul is not entangled in his pursuits, convinced of simply doing his duty.

ब्रह्मण्याधाय कर्माणि , सङ्गं त्यक्त्वा करोति यः । लिप्यते न स पापेन , पद्मपत्रम् इवाम्भसा ॥ ५.१०

brahmaṇyādhāya karmāṇi , saṅgaṁ tyaktvā karoti yaḥ ।

lipyate na sa pāpena , padmapatram ivāmbhasā ॥ 5.10

5.10 He who believes his achievements and rewards to be a fortuitous course of Nature remains untainted, just like a Lotus rising above muddy waters.

कायेन मनसा बुद्ध्या , केवलैर् इन्द्रियैरपि । योगिनः कर्म कुर्वन्ति , सङ्गं त्यक्त्वात्मशुद्धये ॥ ५.११

kāyena manasā buddhyā , kevalair indriyairapi ।

yoginaḥ karma kurvanti , saṅgaṁ tyaktvātmaśuddhaye ॥ 5.11

5.11 Men of Action work single mindedly with one-pointedness of body-intellect-senses. Just so their character remains ever pure.

युक्तः कर्मफलं त्यक्त्वा , शान्तिम् आप्नोति नैष्ठिकीम् । अयुक्तः कामकारेण , फले सक्तो निबध्यते ॥ ५.१२

yuktaḥ karmaphalaṁ tyaktvā , śāntim āpnoti naiṣṭhikīm ।

ayuktaḥ kāmakāreṇa , phale sakto nibadhyate ॥ 5.12

5.12 Thus working devoutedly the Yogi attains to supreme peace. The undevout and unfaithful stumbles clumsily on the path.

सर्वकर्माणि मनसा , सन्न्यस्यास्ते सुखं वशी । नवद्वारे पुरे देही , नैव कुर्वन् न कारयन् ॥ ५.१३

sarvakarmāṇi manasā , sannyasyāste sukhaṁ vaśī ।

navadvāre pure dehī , naiva kurvan na kārayan ॥ 5.13

5.13 The Ascetic on the other hand having marginalized his needs and controlled his wants rests at ease within himself. His actions are quite limited and negligible, being not required in any case.

न कर्तृत्वं न कर्माणि , लोकस्य सृजति प्रभुः । न कर्मफलसंयोगम् , स्वभावस्तु प्रवर्तते ॥ ५.१४

na kartṛtvaṁ na karmāṇi , lokasya sṛjati prabhuḥ ।

na karmaphalasaṁyogam , svabhāvastu pravartate ॥ 5.14

5.14 All Talents, Skillsets and Performances are catalyzed by Nature. The Lord witnesses them fondly.

नादत्ते कस्यचित् पापम् , न चैव सुकृतं विभुः । अज्ञानेनावृतं ज्ञानम् , तेन मुह्यन्ति जन्तवः ॥ ५.१५

nādatte kasyacit pāpam , na caiva sukṛtaṁ vibhuḥ ।

ajñānenāvṛtaṁ jñānam , tena muhyanti jantavaḥ ॥ 5.15

5.15 Even meritorious deeds and the unmeritorious ones are looked upon kindly by the Lord.

Society may get excited or depressed by the same, not so the Lord.

ज्ञानेन तु तद् अज्ञानम् , येषां नाशितमात्मनः । तेषाम् आदित्यवज्ज्ञानम् , प्रकाशयति तत् परम् ॥ ५.१६

jñānena tu tad ajñānam , yeṣāṁ nāśitamātmanaḥ ।

teṣām ādityavajjñānam , prakāśayati tat param ॥ 5.16

5.16 Even to those whose lowly nature has been overcome by noble goals, the sunshine illumines the correct path.

तद्बुद्धयस् तदात्मानः , तन्निष्ठास् तत्परायणाः । गच्छन्त्यपुनरावृत्तिम् , ज्ञाननिर्धूतकल्मषाः ॥ ५.१७

tadbuddhayas tadātmānaḥ , tanniṣṭhās tatparāyaṇāḥ ।

gacchantyapunarāvṛttim , jñānanirdhūtakalmaṣāḥ ॥ 5.17

5.17 Such Ascetics retract their senses and intellect from the world outside to their inner being, and becoming absorbed within reach the highest ideal.

विद्याविनयसम्पन्ने , ब्राह्मणे गवि हस्तिनि । शुनि चैव श्वपाके च , पण्डितास् समदर्शिनः ॥ ५.१८

vidyāvinayasampanne , brāhmaṇe gavi hastini ।

śuni caiva śvapāke ca , paṇḍitās samadarśinaḥ ॥ 5.18

5.18 The great Lord views all happenings, personalities, and flora and fauna with a kind eye. So does an Ascetic established within.

इहैव तैर्जितस् सर्गः , येषां साम्ये स्थितं मनः । निर्दोषं हि समं ब्रह्म , तस्माद् ब्रह्मणि ते स्थिताः ॥ ५.१९

ihaiva tairjitas sargaḥ , yeṣāṁ sāmye sthitaṁ manaḥ ।

nirdoṣaṁ hi samaṁ brahma , tasmād brahmaṇi te sthitāḥ ॥ 5.19

5.19 In this plane of ceaseless activity the Ascetic is a hero having streamlined his movements.

न प्रहृष्येत्प्रियं प्राप्य , नोद्विजेत् प्राप्य चाप्रियम् । स्थिरबुद्धिर् असम्मूढः , ब्रह्मविद् ब्रह्मणि स्थितः ॥ ५.२०

na prahṛṣyetpriyaṁ prāpya , nodvijet prāpya cāpriyam ।

sthirabuddhir asammūḍhaḥ , brahmavid brahmaṇi sthitaḥ ॥ 5.20

5.20 Remaining calm in favourable and unfavourable times, the Renunciate is unaffected.

बाह्यस्पर्शेष्वसक्तात्मा , विन्दत्यात्मनि यत् सुखम् । स ब्रह्मयोगयुक्तात्मा , सुखम् अक्षयम् अश्नुते ॥ ५.२१

bāhyasparśeṣvasaktātmā , vindatyātmani yat sukham ।

sa brahmayogayuktātmā , sukham akṣayam aśnute ॥ 5.21

5.21 Passing his days in the practice of Meditation the Renunciate enjoys supreme bliss.

ये हि संस्पर्शजा भोगाः , दुःखयोनय एव ते । आद्यन्तवन्तः कौन्तेय , न तेषु रमते बुधः ॥ ५.२२
ye hi saṁsparśajā bhogāḥ , duḥkhayonaya eva te ।
ādyantavantaḥ kaunteya , na teṣu ramate budhaḥ ॥ 5.22
5.22 Having known that craving and aversion lead nowhere, the Ascetic rejoices sans both.

शक्नोतीहैव यस् सोढुम् , प्राक् शरीरविमोक्षणात् । कामक्रोधोद्भवं वेगम् , स युक्तस् स सुखी नरः ॥ ५.२३
śaknotīhaiva yas soḍhum , prāk śarīravimokṣaṇāt ।
kāmakrodhodbhavaṁ vegam , sa yuktas sa sukhī naraḥ ॥ 5.23
5.23 Such a noble soul who can ward off the impulses born of desire or of anger is indeed a happy man.

योऽन्तस् सुखोऽन्तरारामः , तथान्तर्ज्योतिरेव यः । स योगी ब्रह्मनिर्वाणम् , ब्रह्मभूतोऽधिगच्छति ॥ ५.२४
yo'ntas sukho'ntarārāmaḥ , tathāntarjyotireva yaḥ ।
sa yogī brahmanirvāṇam , brahmabhūto'dhigacchati ॥ 5.24
5.24 He who experiences inner fulfilment and whose intellect has become non-judgmental, the highest grace is showered upon him.

लभन्ते ब्रह्मनिर्वाणम् , ऋषयः क्षीणकल्मषाः । छिन्नद्वैधा यतात्मानः , सर्वभूतहिते रताः ॥ ५.२५
labhante brahmanirvāṇam , ṛṣayaḥ kṣīṇakalmaṣāḥ ।
chinnadvaidhā yatātmānaḥ , sarvabhūtahite ratāḥ ॥ 5.25

5.25 The Highest Grace is bestowed on the Renunciates whose wants are minimal, who remain strong and stable in the face of pleasantness and harshness, who wish for the benefit of the entire nation.

कामक्रोधवियुक्तानाम् , यतीनां यतचेतसाम् । अभितो ब्रह्मनिर्वाणम् , वर्तते विदितात्मनाम् ॥ ५.२६
kāmakrodhaviyuktānām , yatīnāṁ yatacetasām ।
abhito brahmanirvāṇam , vartate viditātmanām ॥ 5.26
5.26 Such Ascetics to whom lust and anger is alien, live in total freedom; having balanced their needs and expectations, being fully satisfied with themselves.

स्पर्शान् कृत्वा बहिर् बाह्यान् , चक्षुश् चैवान्तरे भ्रुवोः । प्राणापानौ समौ कृत्वा , नासाभ्यन्तरचारिणौ ॥ ५.२७
sparśān kṛtvā bahir bāhyān ,cakṣuś caivāntare bhruvoḥ ।
prāṇāpānau samau kṛtvā , nāsābhyantaracāriṇau ॥ 5.27

5.27 Sitting in a comfortable posture, having closed his eyes, and concentrating on the Ajna Chakra between the eyebrows, the Ascetic regulates the incoming and outgoing breaths.

यतेन्द्रियमनोबुद्धिः , मुनिर् मोक्षपरायणः । विगतेच्छाभयक्रोधः , यस् सदा मुक्त एव सः ॥ ५.२८

yatendriyamanobuddhiḥ , munir mokṣaparāyaṇaḥ I

vigatecchābhayakrodhaḥ , yas sadā mukta eva saḥ II 5.28

5.28 With his goal as liberation free from lust, fear and anger; the Ascetic thus contemplating achieves nirvana.

भोक्तारं यज्ञतपसाम् , सर्वलोकमहेश्वरम् । सुहृदं सर्वभूतानाम् , ज्ञात्वा मां शान्तिम् ऋच्छति ॥ ५.२९

bhoktāraṁ yajñatapasām , sarvalokamaheśvaram I

suhṛdaṁ sarvabhūtānām , jñātvā māṁ śāntim ṛcchati II 5.29

5.29 Anyone who reposes faith in Nature and directs his practices for the sake of the Lord with benevolence towards all, attains nirvana.

ॐ तत् सत् । इति श्रीमद्भगवद्गीतासु उपनिषत्सु ब्रह्मविद्यायां योगशास्त्रे श्रीकृष्णार्जुनसंवादे

कर्म-सन्न्यास-योगो नाम पञ्चमोऽध्यायः ॥ ५॥ (सन्न्यास-योगो नाम)

oṁ tat sat I iti śrīmadbhagavadgītāsu upaniṣatsu brahmavidyāyāṁ yogaśāstre

śrīkṛṣṇārjunasaṁvāde karma-sannyāsa-yogo nāma pañcamo'dhyāyaḥ

II **5** II sannyāsa-yogo nāma

6 Yoga of Self Control

श्री भगवान् उवाच The Good Lord said

अनाश्रितः कर्मफलम् , कार्यं कर्म करोति यः । स सन्न्यासी च योगी च , न निरग्निर्न चाक्रियः ॥ ६.१

"sriibhagavaan uvaaca

anaa"srita× karmaphalam, kaarya.m karma karoti ya.h |

sa sannyaasii ca yogii ca, na niragnirna caakriya.h || 6.1

6.1 The one who performs action that is enjoined, and at the same time is not hankering after its results - that one is a Sannyasin and a Yogin.
Just someone who does not perform rituals, or who is not engaged in day to day duties - is not a sannyasi, nor a yogi.

यं सन्न्यासमिति प्राहुः , योगं तं विद्धि पाण्डव । न ह्यसन्न्यस्तसङ्कल्पः , योगी भवति कश्चन ॥ ६.२

ya.m sannyaasamiti praahu.h, yoga.m ta.m viddhi paa.n.dava |

na hyasannyastasa"nkalpa.h, yogii bhavati ka"scana || 6.2

6.2 O Pandava, know clearly the meaning of sannyasa. It is the state of renunciation. A state of contentment. Of fullness. Know that none qualifies for the doors of yoga-hood without dropping feverish desires.

आरुरुक्षोर्मुनेर्योगम् , कर्म कारणमुच्यते । योगारूढस्य तस्यैव , शमः कारणमुच्यते ॥ ६.३

aaruruk.sormuneryogam, karma kaara.namucyate |

yogaaruu.dhasya tasyaiva, "sama× kaara.namucyate || 6.3

6.3 For the one seeking growth in life, advancement in career, for him strenuous activity and determined efforts are enjoined as the means. Such a one is hailed as a Muni, since the path of growth is attempted only by the focused, committed and devoted individual.

For he who hath already reached the mountain peak, who hath ascended to the pinnacle, who has won the Olympic gold, who has cleared the interview and been selected; for him it is a time for calmness, introspection, serenity.
Opposite values are complementary in nature.

यदा हि नेन्द्रियार्थेषु , न कर्मस्वनुषज्जते । सर्वसङ्कल्पसन्न्यासी , योगारूढस्तदोच्यते ॥ ६.४

yadaa hi nendriyaarthe.su, na karmasvanu.sajjate |

sarvasa"nkalpasannyaasii, yogaaruu.dhastadocyate || 6.4

6.4 One not indulging in senses, nor overtly in actions, and has renounced from the heart the pulls and nudges. Such a one is said to be firmly established in Yoga, in the Oneness, in the Self.

उद्धरेदात्मनात्मानम् , नात्मानमवसादयेत् । आत्मैव ह्यात्मनो बन्धुः , आत्मैव रिपुरात्मनः ॥ ६.५

uddharedaatmanaatmaanam, naatmaanamavasaadayet |

aatmaiva hyaatmano bandhu.h, aatmaiva ripuraatmana.h || 6.5

6.5 Let him lift himself up by all means at his disposal. Let not his spirit be low, let him not be sunk under the pressures. Let him not feel unwelcome or uncared for.

Save the mind at any cost.

बन्धुरात्मात्मनस्तस्य , येनात्मैवात्मना जितः । अनात्मनस्तु शत्रुत्वे , वर्तेतात्मैव शत्रुवत् ॥ ६.६

bandhuraatmaatmanastasya, yenaatmaivaatmanaa jita.h |

anaatmanastu "satrutve, vartetaatmaiva "satruvat || 6.6

6.6 For some of us our body and mind are aligned and disciplined. It is wonderful to have one's own company like the best of friends.
For those without self-control, their life is at civil war, a state of hostility persists within. Boredom rules and they are uneasy with their own company.

जितात्मनः प्रशान्तस्य , परमात्मा समाहितः । शीतोष्णसुखदुःखेषु , तथा मानापमानयोः ॥ ६.७

jitaatmana× pra"saantasya, paramaatmaa samaahita.h |

"siito.s.nasukhadu.hkhe.su, tathaa maanaapamaanayo.h || 6.7

6.7 For one absorbed in the Lord and at ease with his environs, his behavior is affable, gentle and calm. His emotions are not tossed by the vagaries of the weather, and remain neutral in phases of illness or insult.

ज्ञानविज्ञानतृप्तात्मा , कूटस्थो विजितेन्द्रियः । युक्त इत्युच्यते योगी , समलोष्टाश्मकाञ्चनः ॥ ६.८

j~naanavij~naanat.rptaatmaa, kuu.tastho vijitendriya.h |

yukta ityucyate yogii, samalo.s.taa"smakaa~ncana.h || 6.8

6.8 Contented in one's skills, resources, family and work conditions, and steady as a rock, is what defines a Yogi.

He doesn't succumb to property offers, golden bribes or any illegal deals. He neither falls prey to casual vices, nor is he corrupted by huge wealth.

सुहृन्मित्रार्युदासीनमध्यस्थद्वेष्यबन्धुषु । साधुष्वपि च पापेषु , समबुद्धिर्विशिष्यते ॥ ६.९

suh.rnmitraaryudaasiinamadhyasthadve.syabandhu.su |

saadhu.svapi ca paape.su, samabuddhirvi"si.syate || 6.9

6.9 One who can remain focused in the face of hurdles, who can be natural in the company of friends or strangers, who can keep his wits in favourable or dangerous situations, he is the one who goes on to excel.

योगी युञ्जीत सततम् , आत्मानं रहसि स्थितः । एकाकी यतचित्तात्मा , निराशीरपरिग्रहः ॥ ६.१०

yogii yu~njiita satatam, aatmaana.m rahasi sthita.h |

ekaakii yatacittaatmaa, niraa"siiraparigraha.h || 6.10

6.10 By constantly engaging in one's enjoined pursuits. By being alert and awake. By a lot of practice and effort, and stationed in one's place of responsibility.

Responsibility leads to power.

शुचौ देशे प्रतिष्ठाप्य , स्थिरमासनमात्मनः । नात्युच्छ्रितं नातिनीचम् , चैलाजिनकुशोत्तरम् ॥ ६.११

"sucau de"se prati.s.thaapya, sthiramaasanamaatmana.h |

naatyucchrita.m naatiniicam, cailaajinaku"sottaram || 6.11

6.11 Sit in a clean well-ventilated place. Sit steady. Let the posture be erect and the body be comfortable. Use appropriate asana, yoga mat, or backrest. Do not be shivering or sweating.

तत्रैकाग्रं मनः कृत्वा , यतचित्तेन्द्रियक्रियः । उपविश्यासने युञ्ज्यात् , योगमात्मविशुद्धये ॥ ६.१२

tatraikaagra.m mana.h k.rtvaa, yatacittendriyakriya.h |

upavi"syaasane yu~njyaat, yogamaatmavi"suddhaye || 6.12

6.12 Sit having made a strong sankalpa for one-pointedness. Sit having detached the senses for the time-being.

Sit having made the three wills – I want nothing, I do nothing. I am nothing.

Sitting on the yoga mat, free from doubt, let him practice the going inward, taking normal breaths, for the self-purification.

समं कायशिरोग्रीवम् , धारयन्नचलं स्थिरः । सम्प्रेक्ष्य नासिकाग्रं स्वम् , दिशश्चानवलोकयन् ॥ ६.१३

sama.m kaaya"sirogriivam, dhaarayannacala.m sthira.h |

samprek.sya naasikaagra.m svam, di"sa"scaanavalokayan || 6.13

6.13 Sit straight with body, neck and head in one line. Be still and immovable like a statue.

Let the gaze be steady and slightly lowered, inclined at 30° towards the nose tip.

Concentrate at the incoming and outgoing breaths. Let the mind be detached from the eyes and unnoticing any sensation or sound. Unite the mind and body by the breath.

प्रशान्तात्मा विगतभीः , ब्रह्मचारिव्रते स्थितः । मनः संयम्य मच्चित्तः , युक्त आसीत मत्परः ॥ ६.१४

pra"saantaatmaa vigatabhii.h, brahmacaarivrate sthita.h |

mana.h sa.myamya maccitta.h, yukta aasiita matpara.h || 6.14

6.14 On the Supreme. Within. Calm and composed. Guilt free, blame free, without hatred or fear. Keeping distractions and pleasures at bay, with a stillness in the heart, with the thoughts controlled as if putting a toll-gate. Let him sit dwelling on the Highest, In Me.

The Supreme can be the sound Om. It can be one's chosen deity Krishna. It can be the gap between the breaths. It can be the space between two thoughts. It is what one's Master teaches, follow the Guru's advice.

युञ्जन्नेवं सदात्मानम् , योगी नियतमानसः । शान्तिं निर्वाणपरमाम् , मत्संस्थामधिगच्छति ॥ ६.१५

yu~njanneva.m sadaatmaanam, yogii niyatamaanasa.h |

"saanti.m nirvaa.naparamaam, matsa.msthaamadhigacchati || 6.15

6.15 And the fruit of such absolute focus is Samadhi. Nirvana. The mind slips into meditation. The heart attains bliss. The person becomes affable, tranquil, caring.

नात्यश्नतस्तु योगोऽस्ति , न चैकान्तमनश्नतः । न चाति स्वप्नशीलस्य , जाग्रतो नैव चार्जुन ॥ ६.१६

naatya"snatastu yogo'sti , na caikaantamana"snata.h |

na caati svapna"siilasya , jaagrato naiva caarjuna || 6.16

6.16 Balance and discipline in day to day living. Paying attention to body by exercise and food and sleep, to breath by pranayama, and to the mind by sudarshan kriya. Neither be a workaholic nor be a lazy fellow. Do not be prone to fantasy and day dreaming, and do not engage and grapple with each and every situation.

Accept people and situations as they are.

युक्ताहारविहारस्य , युक्तचेष्टस्य कर्मसु । युक्तस्वप्नावबोधस्य , योगो भवति दुःखहा ॥ ६.१७

yuktaahaaravihaarasya, yuktace.s.tasya karmasu |

yuktasvapnaavabodhasya, yogo bhavati du.hkhahaa || 6.17

6.17 Be regulated in food and exercise; be balanced in activity and duty. Take proper sleep and rest, and nurture senses equitably. Such a lifestyle leads to freedom from pain. It frees one from suffering. It extinguishes the pangs of remorse and banishes turmoil from life.

Regulated food includes eating fresh, vegetarian, timely meals while sitting. Regulated exercise includes walking, swimming, sports or gymnasium in a proper environment.

Balance in activity and duty includes having good teamwork, using the right tools, maintaining good posture and taking sufficient breaks for rest and hobby. Proper sleep includes using correct cot and mattress and sleeping with the lights off. Nurturing senses equitably includes paying attention to brushing twice daily, taking care of hair and skin by appropriate massage, taking care of eyes and ears and ensuring correct breathing.

यदा विनियतं चित्तम् , आत्मन्येवावतिष्ठते । निःस्पृहः सर्वकामेभ्यः , युक्त इत्युच्यते तदा ॥ ६.१८

yadaa viniyata.m cittam, aatmanyevaavati.s.thate |

ni.hsp.rha.h sarvakaamebhya.h, yukta ityucyate tadaa || 6.18

6.18 When someone is not scattered by desires at cross purposes, not torn by divergent notions, not attracted to the undesirable facets in life, then he is said to be Enlightened, a Yogi.

यथा दीपो निवातस्थः , नेङ्गते सोपमा स्मृता । योगिनो यतचित्तस्य , युञ्जतो योगमात्मनः ॥ ६.१९

yathaa diipo nivaatastha.h, ne"ngate sopamaa sm.rtaa |

yogino yatacittasya, yu~njato yogamaatmana.h || 6.19

6.19 An unflickering candle light, a steady flame, a lamp placed on a windless, draught free sill. Nearly impossible. A flame can never be still. It catches the faintest breeze and flickers.

Such is a human mind. But that of a Yogi is steady. It is beyond movement, beyond the pulls of temptation or the pushes of irritation. Calm and above the storms of emotions.

यत्रोपरमते चित्तम् , निरुद्धं योगसेवया । यत्र चैवात्मनात्मानम् , पश्यन्नात्मनि तुष्यति ॥ ६.२०

yatroparamate cittam, niruddha.m yogasevayaa |

yatra caivaatmanaatmaanam, pa"syannaatmani tu.syati || 6.20

6.20 Dropping all efforts, repose in the Self, where there is deep rest. A sense of complete satisfaction abounds.

सुखमात्यन्तिकं यत्तत् , बुद्धिग्राह्यमतीन्द्रियम् । वेत्ति यत्र न चैवायम् , स्थितश्चलति तत्त्वतः ॥ ६.२१

sukhamaatyantika.m yattat, buddhigraahyamatiindriyam |

vetti yatra na caivaayam, sthita"scalati tattvata.h || 6.21

6.21 Where the intellect finds a transcendental happiness free of logic, beyond the sensory pleasures. Where a set point prevails, where he moves not from the serenity.

It is a state of living in the present moment, devoid of grief.

यं लब्ध्वा चापरं लाभम् , मन्यते नाधिकं ततः । यस्मिन्स्थितो न दुःखेन , गुरुणापि विचाल्यते ॥ ६.२२

ya.m labdhvaa caapara.m laabham, manyate naadhika.m tata.h |

yasminsthito na du.hkhena, guru.naapi vicaalyate || 6.22

6.22 Obtaining which there is no further yearning. Not like one has won an Olympic gold and still wants another, not like having won the Nobel Prize in medicine one is now hoping to bag the Oscar as well!

In such a state of tranquility, even in the face of a great storm he is unperturbed and uncrushed.

Established firmly in the knowledge that pleasure and pain are what make the shores of life. These touch the body, yet leave the mind unscathed, and the heart unblemished. Such is the state of Yoga. Such is the mind of a Yogi.

तं विद्याद् दुःखसंयोगवियोगं योगसञ्ज्ञितम् । स निश्चयेन योक्तव्यः , योगोऽनिर्विण्णचेतसा ॥ ६.२३

ta.m vidyaad du.hkhasa.myogaviyoga.m yogasa~nj~nitam |

sa ni"scayena yoktavya.h, yogo'nirvi.n.nacetasaa || 6.23

6.23 Let him know. Let the seeker know this state of affairs. Let the aspirant know what life is all about and what a human birth is for. It must be firmly and earnestly put into practice by him.

सङ्कल्पप्रभवान्कामान् , त्यक्त्वा सर्वानशेषतः । मनसैवेन्द्रियग्रामम् , विनियम्य समन्ततः ॥ ६.२४

sa"nkalpaprabhavaankaamaan, tyaktvaa sarvaana"se.sata.h |

manasaivendriyagraamam, viniyamya samantata.h || 6.24

6.24 Rejecting undesirable, vain, foolish notions and cravings without reserve. Discard without harbouring even the slightest hesitation, to plug the leaky thoughts, thoughts that drain the prana.

First stop chasing the wrong notions. Become aware of the improper impulses. Observe, filter and select the thoughts. Put a toll gate in the mind.

शनैः शनैरुपरमेत् , बुद्ध्या धृतिगृहीतया । आत्मसंस्थं मन× कृत्वा , न किञ्चिदपि चिन्तयेत् ॥ ६.२५

"sanai.h "sanairuparamet, buddhyaa dh.rtig.rhiitayaa |

aatmasa.mstha.m mana× k.rtvaa, na ki~ncidapi cintayet || 6.25

6.25 Slowly steadily make the progress towards tranquility. By reason stabilize the mind. Do not waver even a bit and do not give up.

Attend the Advance Meditation Course every year and the Satsang every week!

यतो यतो निश्चरति , मनश्चञ्चलमस्थिरम् । ततस्ततो नियम्यैतत् , आत्मन्येव वशं नयेत् ॥ ६.२६

yato yato ni"scarati, mana"sca~ncalamasthiram |

tatastato niyamyaitat, aatmanyeva va"sa.m nayet || 6.26

6.26 Again and again come back to the center. The mind is tacky, unsteady and wavering, it is simply kiddish by nature. The body grows but the mind remains childish, with loving patience guide it. Be regular and firm in the practice of harnessing the mind.

प्रशान्तमनसं ह्येनम् , योगिनं सुखमुत्तमम् । उपैति शान्तरजसम् , ब्रह्मभूतमकल्मषम् ॥ ६.२७

pra"saantamanasa.m hyenam, yogina.m sukhamuttamam |

upaiti "saantarajasam, brahmabhuutamakalma.sam || 6.27

6.27 Peace dawns, the highest bliss is attained by such a seeker. His identification with Brahman is seamless; he merges into the divinity and is absorbed without a doubt.

युञ्जन्नेवं सदात्मानम् , योगी विगतकल्मषः । सुखेन ब्रह्मसंस्पर्शम् , अत्यन्तं सुखमश्नुते ॥ ६.२८

yu~njanneva.m sadaatmaanam, yogii vigatakalma.sa.h |

sukhena brahmasa.mspar"sam, atyanta.m sukhama"snute || 6.28

6.28 The seeker's doubts, blemishes and imperfections are gone without a trace. His merits overflow to the brim, he enjoys infinite joy.

सर्वभूतस्थमात्मानम् , सर्वभूतानि चात्मनि । ईक्षते योगयुक्तात्मा , सर्वत्र समदर्शनः ॥ ६.२९

sarvabhuutasthamaatmaanam, sarvabhuutaani caatmani |

iik.sate yogayuktaatmaa, sarvatra samadar"sana.h || 6.29

6.29 He sees all beings as part of him, and he sees a bit of himself in all beings. He identifies easily with one and all. His sight sees everything as equitable, none is alien for him.

Now the cream of the Gita. The nectarine words of the benevolent Lord.

यो मां पश्यति सर्वत्र , सर्वं च मयि पश्यति । तस्याहं न प्रणश्यामि , स च मे न प्रणश्यति ॥ ६.३०

yo maa.m pa"syati sarvatra, sarva.m ca mayi pa"syati |

tasyaaha.m na pra.na"syaami, sa ca me na pra.na"syati || 6.30

6.30 He who sees Me everywhere and in all sees Me. Of him I shall not lose hold of, he shall not be separated from Me.

For the one who identifies this creation with the Lord, who sees all peoples, all phenomena, governments, religions, flora and fauna, scientific and material changes, news and entertainments; as part of godliness, as attributes of divinity – He shall not be forsaken.

सर्वभूतस्थितं यो माम् , भजत्येकत्वमास्थितः । सर्वथा वर्तमानोऽपि , स योगी मयि वर्तते ॥ ६.३१

sarvabhuutasthita.m yo maam, bhajatyekatvamaasthita.h |

sarvathaa vartamaano'pi, sa yogii mayi vartate || 6.31

6.31 The one who worships Me, glorifies Me, sings My praises. The one who spends quality time in Satsanga, who talks about Me, telling My stories. The one who is immersed in Me.

आत्मौपम्येन सर्वत्र , समं पश्यति योऽर्जुन । सुखं वा यदि वा दुःखम् , स योगी परमो मतः ॥ ६.३२

aatmaupamyena sarvatra, sama.m pa"syati yo'rjuna |

sukha.m vaa yadi vaa du.hkham, sa yogii paramo mata.h || 6.32

6.32 O Arjuna-the brilliant-the fair-the open minded-the clear hearted-the one who sparkles like silver and is stainless;

In joy as well as in sorrow, in victory as well as in defeat, the one who sees beyond and acknowledges the Oneness, the Divinity, the Mighty Hand rather than the localized tiny event and person;

The one who surrenders every moment, every breath to the divine, who gives credit to the divine for each happening whether pleasurable or traumatic;

Who remembers the Divine come what may,
O Arjuna, O Seeker, O Aspirant, O Student;
Such a one is a perfected soul, a param yogi, an enlightened liberated being.

अर्जुन उवाच The pure aspirant-the ardent devotee-the seeker asked

योऽयं योगस्त्वया प्रोक्तः , साम्येन मधुसूदन । एतस्याहं न पश्यामि , चञ्चलत्वात्स्थितिं स्थिराम् ॥ ६.३३

arjuna uvaaca

yo'ya.m yogastvayaa prokta.h, saamyena madhusuudana |

etasyaaha.m na pa"syaami, ca~ncalatvaatsthiti.m sthiraam || 6.33

6.33 O Madhusudana-O Vanquisher of obscene pleasures-O subduer of lust;

I am unable to comprehend this state of equilibrium that you speak of, due to my restlessness. I am fidgety, my mind is cloudy and your words are not sinking in.

Notice that a pure heart speaks without editing, speaks straight from the core, speaks spontaneously. Such is a sincere devotee and so is the Master pleased with him and grants his wish!

चञ्चलं हि मनः कृष्ण , प्रमाथि बलवद्दृढम् । तस्याहं निग्रहं मन्ये , वायोरिव सुदुष्करम् ॥ ६.३४

ca~ncala.m hi mana× k.r.s.na, pramaathi balavadd.r.dham |

tasyaaha.m nigraha.m manye, vaayoriva sudu.skaram || 6.34

6.34 O Krishna-O the deep blue-O the infinite space-O the absolute joy;

Indeed shaky is my mind. Indeed it vacillates and makes frenzied tyrannical decisions. I think it is overpowering as a tornado.

श्रीभगवान् उवाच The Good Lord replied

असंशयं महाबाहो , मनो दुर्निग्रहं चलम् । अभ्यासेन तु कौन्तेय , वैराग्येण च गृह्यते ॥ ६.३५

"sriibhagavaan uvaaca

asa.m"saya.m mahaabaaho, mano durnigraha.m calam |

abhyaasena tu kaunteya, vairaagye.na ca g.rhyate || 6.35

6.35 Doubtless, O Mighty armed! O Well prepared! O Highly skilled! What you say is certainly correct.
But, O Kaunteya! O son of the noble Kunti! O son of the fair maiden! By repeated practice, by constant alertness, by detached thoughtful planning the mind can be mastered. By dispassionately delving into the nature of things and peoples the mind is steadied.

असंयतात्मना योगः , दुष्प्राप इति मे मतिः । वश्यात्मना तु यतता , शक्योऽवाप्तुमुपायतः ॥ ६.३६

asa.myataatmanaa yoga.h, du.spraapa iti me mati.h |

va"syaatmanaa tu yatataa, "sakyo'vaaptumupaayata.h || 6.36

6.36 Yes, for the undisciplined person, for the wayward character, for the indifferent student; Yoga is well-nigh impossible. Achievement of aims or success in life is quite difficult, rather out of the question.

Yet, for the one who endeavours, who is sincere and earnest, who invests appropriate, timely and skillful efforts and goes about in a determined fashion; all is within reach. Success is ensured, thus have I fashioned the laws.

Such are the rules of nature; such are the fundamental laws governing the creation.

अर्जुन उवाच Arjuna-the Aspirant queried

अयतिः श्रद्धयोपेतः , योगाच्चलितमानसः । अप्राप्य योगसंसिद्धिम् , कां गतिं कृष्ण गच्छति ॥ ६.३७

arjuna uvaaca

ayati.h "sraddhayopeta.h, yogaaccalitamaanasa.h |

apraapya yogasa.msiddhim, kaa.m gati.m k.r.s.na gacchati || 6.37

6.37 What if my efforts do not yield the desired results well in time? What if my task remains unfinished in this lifetime? What if I didn't make it?

Then what happens to me? Where do I go, where do I reach? How does such a situation fare? Please tell me O Krishna, O dear Lord, O most Benevolent!

कच्चिन्नोभयविभ्रष्टः , छिन्नाभ्रमिव नश्यति । अप्रतिष्ठो महाबाहो , विमूढो ब्रह्मणः पथि ॥ ६.३८

kaccinnobhayavibhra.s.ta.h, chinnaabhramiva na"syati |

aprati.s.tho mahaabaaho, vimuu.dho brahma.na.h pathi || 6.38

6.38 Like a rent cloud spilling all its water, aren't both worlds lost then?
Aren't all resources exhausted, efforts expended; facing failure; isn't the mind and body irrecoverably damaged?
O Mighty Armed, O All Knowing! Wouldn't he then lose all faith and strength?
Wouldn't his mind become blocked from hope or progress?

एतन्मे संशयं कृष्ण , छेत्तुमर्हस्यशेषतः । त्वदन्यः संशयस्यास्य , छेत्ता न ह्युपपद्यते ॥ ६.३९

etanme sa.m"saya.m k.r.s.na, chettumarhasya"se.sata.h |

tvadanya.h sa.m"sayasyaasya, chettaa na hyupapadyate || 6.39

6.39 This is my big fear, my stumbling block, the doubt that gnaws at my heart. Please resolve this dilemma completely, without any shade remaining, you must; O Krishna!

श्रीभगवान् उवाच The Good Lord answered

पार्थ नैवेह नामुत्र , विनाशस्तस्य विद्यते । न हि कल्याणकृत्कश्चित् , दुर्गतिं तात गच्छति ॥ ६.४०

"sriibhagavaan uvaaca

paartha naiveha naamutra, vinaa"sastasya vidyate |

na hi kalyaa.nak.rtka"scit, durgati.m taata gacchati || 6.40

6.40 Indeed O Partha! O Prince of Prithu country! Not here in the present circumstances, neither in the foreseeable future, nor in the next birth is there any lasting defeat. There is no long term effect of such failure. There is no harm accrued to the one engaged in righteous action.

There is no serious damage befallen to him who endeavored but didn't make it, didn't complete the task in time, or it rained and washed away his effort.

The laws of nature are sensible, tolerant and benign. The laws of physics are very broad in every respect. The supreme consciousness restores grace for the honest individual in due course.

प्राप्य पुण्यकृतां लोकान् , उषित्वा शाश्वतीः समाः । शुचीनां श्रीमतां गेहे , योगभ्रष्टोऽभिजायते ॥ ६.४१

praapya pu.nyak.rtaa.m lokaan, u.sitvaa "saa"svatii.h samaa.h |

"suciinaa.m "sriimataa.m gehe, yogabhra.s.to'bhijaayate || 6.41

6.41 The merit of honest effort is well acknowledged by near and dear ones. Society respects such individuals. Their failures are erased and efforts are rewarded over due course of time. A failed attempt does not lead to destruction. Rather it is a stepping stone to success.

Even the said individual who gave his 100% knows it very well in the core of his heart and escapes trauma of any kind in case of disappointment. ***Do not be a football of others opinion.***

अथवा योगिनामेव , कुले भवति धीमताम् । एतद्धि दुर्लभतरम् , लोके जन्म यदीदृशम् ॥ ६.४२

athavaa yoginaameva, kule bhavati dhiimataam |

etaddhi durlabhataram, loke janma yadiid.r"sam || 6.42

6.42 Or he progresses to even greater heights.

Being chucked out of school or failure in exams or in marriage; for a true soul opens up avenues of far greater merit.

तत्र तं बुद्धिसंयोगम् , लभते पौर्वदेहिकम् । यतते च ततो भूयः , संसिद्धौ कुरुनन्दन ॥ ६.४३

tatra ta.m buddhisa.myogam, labhate paurvadehikam |

yatate ca tato bhuuya.h, sa.msiddhau kurunandana || 6.43

6.43 And he strives again for perfection. He gets up and picks up the thread yet again. Such an individual labours further, does not give up in the face of failure, and surely obtains success.

पूर्वाभ्यासेन तेनैव , ह्रियते ह्यवशोऽपि सः । जिज्ञासुरपि योगस्य , शब्दब्रह्मातिवर्तते ॥ ६.४४

puurvaabhyaasena tenaiva, hriyate hyava"so'pi sa.h |

jij~naasurapi yogasya, "sabdabrahmaativartate || 6.44

6.44 By one's practices when young, by one's responsibilities and good performance in an earlier job, by one's **random acts of kindness**, by one's tapas and merit from earlier lifetimes;
One has the divine force with us. One is filled with a divine aura that is irresistible. When one begins early, wakes up before dawn, reaches office or the interview or the Advance Meditation Course before time, then the supreme consciousness grabs hold. It pushes us over and across the sound barrier like an electron tunneling through in quantum mechanics.

असङ्गोऽहम् पुनः पुनः Detach Again and Again. Practice again and again.
There is so much emphasis on repetition. On practice. On striving again and again.

प्रयत्नाद्यतमानस्तु , योगी संशुद्धकिल्बिषः । अनेकजन्मसंसिद्धः , ततो याति परां गतिम् ॥ ६.४५

prayatnaadyatamaanastu, yogii sa.m"suddhakilbi.sa.h |

anekajanmasa.msiddha.h, tato yaati paraa.m gatim || 6.45

6.45 With sincerity and dependability the seeker sheds weakness and becomes strong. He overcomes cowardice and becomes brave.

And achieves the perfection that accrues over repeated cycles of birth i.e. that comes from facing and experiencing many ups and downs in life.

तपस्विभ्योऽधिको योगी , ज्ञानिभ्योऽपि मतोऽधिकः । कर्मिभ्यश्चाधिको योगी , तस्माद्योगी भवार्जुन ॥ ६.४६

tapasvibhyo'dhiko yogii, j~naanibhyo'pi mato'dhika.h |

karmibhya"scaadhiko yogii, tasmaadyogii bhavaarjuna || 6.46

6.46 Such a sincere seeker, such an ardent devotee, such a dutiful householder, such a persevering student, such a responsible leader is to be considered the standard for others to follow. He is greater than many on this planet. Greater than most he is the epitome of manhood. Of humanity. Of a race. Of a human birth. You too be one O Arjuna, O Reader, O Listener, O Devotee!

योगिनामपि सर्वेषाम् , मद्गतेनान्तरात्मना । श्रद्धावान्भजते यो माम् , स मे युक्ततमो मतः ॥ ६.४७

yoginaamapi sarve.saam, madgatenaantaraatmanaa |

"sraddhaavaanbhajate yo maam, sa me yuktatamo mata.h || 6.47

6.47 And amongst them all, amongst the best and the brightest, amongst the greatest of the great; the one who is a Bhakta, who is filled with devotion, whose faith is irresolute, who adores Me fully, he gets my vote!

ॐ तत् सत् । इति श्रीमद्भगवद्गीतासु उपनिषत्सु ब्रह्मविद्यायां योगशास्त्रे श्रीकृष्णार्जुनसंवादे

आत्मसंयम-योगो नाम षष्ठोऽध्यायः ॥ ६॥ (ध्यान-योगो नाम)

o.m tat sat | iti "sriimadbhagavadgiitaasu upani.satsu

brahmavidyaayaa.m yoga"saastre "sriik.r.s.naarjunasa.mvaade

aatmasa.myamayogo naama .sa.s.tho'dhyaaya.h

|| 6 ||

7 Yoga of Divine Qualities

Qualities of the Truth = Divinity, so that we may aim for them and imbibe them

ॐ श्री परमात्मने नमः । अथ सप्तमोऽध्यायः

oṁ śrī paramātmane namaḥ I atha saptamo'dhyāyaḥ

श्री भगवान् उवाच

मय्यासक्तमनाः पार्थ , योगं युञ्जन् मदाश्रयः । असंशयं समग्रं माम् , यथा ज्ञास्यसि तच्छृणु ॥ ७.१

śrī bhagavān uvāca

mayyāsaktamanāḥ pārtha , yogaṁ yuñjan madāśrayaḥ I

asaṁśayaṁ samagraṁ mām , yathā jñāsyasi tacchr̥ṇu II 7.1

The gracious Lord said

7.1 With concentration and earnestness, practice the alignment of heart-head-breath, i.e. perform duty wholeheartedly. By this attitude you shall come to realize the highest truth.

ज्ञानं तेऽहं सविज्ञानम् , इदं वक्ष्याम्यशेषतः । यज्ज्ञात्वा नेह भूयोऽन्यत् , ज्ञातव्यम् अवशिष्यते ॥ ७.२

jñānaṁ te'haṁ savijñānam , idaṁ vakṣyāmyaśeṣataḥ I

yajjñātvā neha bhūyo'nyat , jñātavyam avaśiṣyate II 7.2

7.2 The Truth shall be revealed to you and it shall be assimilated by your core. Knowing That, all the natural laws shall be known in one unified principle. (upanishad - by knowing what is all known)?

मनुष्याणां सहस्रेषु , कश्चिद् यतति सिद्धये । यतताम् अपि सिद्धानाम् , कश्चिन् मां वेत्ति तत्त्वतः ॥ ७.३

manuṣyāṇāṁ sahasreṣu , kaścid yatati siddhaye I

yatatām api siddhānām , kaścin māṁ vetti tattvataḥ II 7.3

7.3 Among the vast populace very few have the spirit of enquiry for the truth. Even amongst those, few go all out to realize it fully. (After all the Olympics and Grammies and Mount Everest are commonly available, however the rare go for it, even rarer make it to the top).

भूमिरापोऽनलो वायुः , खं मनो बुद्धिरेव च । अहङ्कार इतीयं मे , भिन्ना प्रकृतिर् अष्टधा ॥ ७.४

bhūmirāpo'nalo vāyuḥ , khaṁ mano buddhireva ca I

ahaṅkāra itīyaṁ me , bhinnā prakr̥tir aṣṭadhā ॥ 7.4

7.4 The manifest creation consists of the 5 measurable elements space-air-fire-water-earth that constitute the bodies and objects. The same subtle-immeasurable elements form 6 the sensory mind that sees and hears, 7 the judging intellect and 8 the sense of I-ness. This eight-fold principle constitutes all of the visible creation with life and inanimate matter.

अपरेयमितस्त्वन्याम् , प्रकृतिं विद्धि मे पराम् । जीवभूतां महाबाहो , ययेदं धार्यते जगत् ॥ ७.५

apareyamitastvanyām , prakr̥tiṁ viddhi me parām ।

jīvabhūtāṁ mahābāho , yayedaṁ dhāryate jagat ॥ 7.5

7.5 The law stated above is cognizable and recognizable by the sharpest intellect. There is however a realm of the unknowable-by-the-intellect. It is that unknowable dark matter that upholds and regulates this manifest creation.

एतद् योनीनि भूतानि , सर्वाणीत्युपधारय । अहं कृत्स्नस्य जगतः , प्रभवᳲ प्रलयस् तथा ॥ ७.६

etad yonīni bhūtāni , sarvāṇītyupadhāraya ।

ahaṁ kr̥tsnasya jagataḥ , prabhavaᳲ pralayas tathā ॥ 7.6

7.6 Understand that the eightfold measurable principle and the unknowable dark matter go together. The underlying Truth is that which can be felt in the purest heart yet it cannot be formulated precisely in words nor stated concretely in any manner.

मत्तᳲ परतरं नान्यत् , किञ्चिद् अस्ति धनञ्जय । मयि सर्वमिदं प्रोतम् , सूत्रे मणिगणा इव ॥ ७.७

mattaᳲ parataraṁ nānyat , kiñcid asti dhanañjaya ।

mayi sarvamidaṁ protam , sūtre maṇigaṇā iva ॥ 7.7

7.7 The highest Truth supports all and is present in all and everything. You may loosely think of the Truth as a chain on which pearls are strung to form a necklace.
1) The chain is in every pearl 2) The chain is yet not the pearl
3) The chain is also there where the pearl is not.
Here pearl means an animate or inanimate object.

रसोऽहमप्सु कौन्तेय , प्रभास्मि शशिसूर्ययोः । प्रणवस् सर्ववेदेषु , शब्दᳲ खे पौरुषं नृषु ॥ ७.८

raso'hamapsu kaunteya , prabhāsmi śaśisūryayoḥ ।

praṇavas sarvavedeṣu , śabdaᳲ khe pauruṣaṁ nr̥ṣu ॥ 7.8

7.8 Visualize the Truth as the Taste in water and juice, the Light in the heavenly bodies sun and moon, the Sacred syllable Om in the scriptures, the Sound in space and the Virility in man.

पुण्यो गन्धः पृथिव्यां च , तेजश् चास्मि विभावसौ । जीवनं सर्वभूतेषु , तपश् चास्मि तपस्विषु ॥ ७.९

puṇyo gandhaḥ pṛthivyāṁ ca , tejaś cāsmi vibhāvasau ।

jīvanaṁ sarvabhūteṣu , tapaś cāsmi tapasviṣu ॥ 7.9

7.9 Also imagine it to be the heady fragrance in flowers and inanimate earthy stuff, the brilliance in fire and fiery matter, the lifeforce in animate matter and the quality of I SHALL DO IT in brave hearts.

बीजं मां सर्वभूतानाम् , विद्धि पार्थ सनातनम् । बुद्धिर् बुद्धिमताम् अस्मि , तेजस् तेजस्विनाम् अहम् ॥ ७.१०

bījaṁ māṁ sarvabhūtānām , viddhi pārtha sanātanam ।

buddhir buddhimatām asmi , tejas tejasvinām aham ॥ 7.10

7.10 Consider the Truth to be the imperishable seed in all beings, the sharp intelligence of the wise, and the attraction in any desirable maiden, gadget or phenomenon.

बलं बलवतां चाहम् , कामरागविवर्जितम् । धर्माविरुद्धो भूतेषु , कामोऽस्मि भरतर्षभ ॥ ७.११

balaṁ balavatāṁ cāham , kāmarāgavivarjitam ।

dharmāviruddho bhūteṣu , kāmo'smi bharatarṣabha ॥ 7.11

7.11 Of the Able, the Truth is the quality that is devoid of harm and injustice. Of the rest, the Truth is the will that does not align to unfair means.
The Mighty Rule, so in them the Truth is likened to the sense of protective righteousness. In the ruled, Truth is a desire not colluding with foul play.

ये चैव सात्त्विका भावाः , राजसास् तामसाश् च ये । मत्त एवेति तान् विद्धि , न त्वहं तेषु ते मयि ॥ ७.१२

ye caiva sāttvikā bhāvāḥ , rājasās tāmasāś ca ye ।

matta eveti tān viddhi , na tvahaṁ teṣu te mayi ॥ 7.12

7.12 All that is pure, all that is active and all at rest are regulated by the Truth. The Truth is fundamental to all three, yet it is something intangible, not capturable.

त्रिभिर् गुणमयैर् भावैः , एभिस् सर्वम् इदं जगत् । मोहितं नाभिजानाति , मामेभ्यः परम् अव्ययम् ॥ ७.१३

tribhir guṇamayair bhāvaiḥ , ebhis sarvam idaṁ jagat ।

mohitaṁ nābhijānāti , māmebhyaḥ param avyayam ॥ 7.13

7.13 The animate beings are so engrossed in their duty, some other activity, or resting, that the Truth eludes them. Its distinctness and all enveloping nature is not at all grasped by any.
(After all to know something one must be separate from that at a distance, to remedy a situation one must be outside that situation.)

दैवी ह्येषा गुणमयी , मम माया दुरत्यया । मामेव ये प्रपद्यन्ते , मायामेतां तरन्ति ते ॥ ७.१४

daivī hyeṣā guṇamayī , mama māyā duratyayā ।

māmeva ye prapadyante , māyāmetāṁ taranti te ॥ 7.14

7.14 Verily the nature of divinity is hard to figure out. Only to a devoted heart does it reveal itself.

न मां दुष्कृतिनो मूढाः , प्रपद्यन्ते नराधमाः । माययापहृतज्ञानाः , आसुरं भावमाश्रिताः ॥ ७.१५

na māṁ duṣkṛtino mūḍhāḥ , prapadyante narādhamāḥ ।

māyayāpahṛtajñānāḥ , āsuraṁ bhāvamāśritāḥ ॥ 7.15

7.15 Whom we see as cruel and stubborn are the farthest from realizing Divinity. Such are the terrorists to whom justice is always delayed.

चतुर्विधा भजन्ते माम् , जनास् सुकृतिनोऽर्जुन । आर्तो जिज्ञासुर् अर्थार्थी , ज्ञानी च भरतर्षभ ॥ ७.१६

caturvidhā bhajante mām , janās sukṛtino'rjuna ।

ārto jijñāsur arthārthī , jñānī ca bharatarṣabha ॥ 7.16

7.16 Rest of mankind falls in 4 categories, the distressed seeking a way out, the industrious seeking to amass wealth, the devoted seeking to realize god, and the Saints with god realization.

तेषां ज्ञानी नित्ययुक्तः , एकभक्तिर् विशिष्यते । प्रियो हि ज्ञानिनोऽत्यर्थम् , अहं स च मम प्रियः ॥ ७.१७

teṣāṁ jñānī nityayuktaḥ , ekabhaktir viśiṣyate ।

priyo hi jñānino'tyartham , ahaṁ sa ca mama priyaḥ ॥ 7.17

7.17 Of them, the Saintly are so pure and loving, their compassion encompasses all and they are one with the Divine.

उदारास् सर्व एवैते , ज्ञानी त्वात्मैव मे मतम् । आस्थितस् स हि युक्तात्मा , मामेवानुत्तमां गतिम् ॥ ७.१८

udārās sarva evaite , jñānī tvātmaiva me matam ।

āsthitas sa hi yuktātmā , māmevānuttamāṁ gatim ॥ 7.18

7.18 Of course the other three types are also evolving, yet the Saintly have already reached the goal.

बहूनां जन्मनाम् अन्ते , ज्ञानवान् मां प्रपद्यते । वासुदेवस् सर्वम् इति , स महात्मा सुदुर्लभः ॥ ७.१९

bahūnāṁ janmanām ante , jñānavān māṁ prapadyate ।

vāsudevas sarvam iti , sa mahātmā sudurlabhaḥ ॥ 7.19

7.19 It does take a lot many experiences and some rather hard knocks for a man to start seeking the Divine. Such a man who goes all out in this direction is rare and the great one who actually realizes the Truth is hard to find.

कामैस् तैस् तैर् हृतज्ञानाः , प्रपद्यन्तेऽन्यदेवताः । तं तं नियममास्थाय , प्रकृत्या नियतास् स्वया ॥ ७.२०

kāmais tais tair hr̥tajñānāḥ , prapadyante'nyadevatāḥ ।

taṁ taṁ niyamamāsthāya , prakr̥tyā niyatās svayā ॥ 7.20

7.20 Most men do not have the gold medal as their prime target. Satisfied by puny desires they lead an ordinary life.

यो यो यां यां तनुं भक्तः , श्रद्धयार्चितुम् इच्छति । तस्य तस्याचलां श्रद्धाम् , ताम् एव विदधाम्यहम् ॥ ७.२१

yo yo yāṁ yāṁ tanuṁ bhaktaḥ , śraddhayārcitum icchati ।

tasya tasyācalāṁ śraddhām , tām eva vidadhāmyaham ॥ 7.21

7.21 In any case whatever aim man fixes his heart on that he attains, that is for sure. Nature is designed to fulfill all wants.

स तया श्रद्धया युक्तः , तस्याराधनमीहते । लभते च ततः कामान् , मयैव विहितान् हि तान् ॥ ७.२२

sa tayā śraddhayā yuktaḥ , tasyārādhanamīhate ।

labhate ca tata× kāmān , mayaiva vihitān hi tān ॥ 7.22

7.22 Man's efforts whatever they may be always bear fruit. The laws of creation see to that.

अन्तवत् तु फलं तेषाम् , तद्भवत्यल्पमेधसाम् । देवान् देवयजो यान्ति , मद्भक्ता यान्ति माम् अपि ॥ ७.२३

antavat tu phalaṁ teṣām , tadbhavatyalpamedhasām I

devān devayajo yānti , madbhaktā yānti mām api II 7.23

7.23 Intelligent are those who seek the Divine. They tower head and shoulders above the seekers of other joys.

अव्यक्तं व्यक्तिमापन्नम् , मन्यन्ते माम् अबुद्धयः । परं भावम् अजानन्तः , ममाव्ययम् अनुत्तमम् ॥ ७.२४

avyaktaṁ vyaktimāpannam , manyante mām abuddhayaḥ I

paraṁ bhāvam ajānantaḥ , mamāvyayam anuttamam II 7.24

7.24 Foolish is the one caught up in the run-of-the-mill jobs since he has no passion for the highest goal, that is all-encompassing and Divine.

नाहं प्रकाशस् सर्वस्य , योगमायासमावृतः । मूढोऽयं नाभिजानाति , लोको माम् अजम् अव्ययम् ॥ ७.२५

nāhaṁ prakāśas sarvasya , yogamāyāsamāvṛtaḥ I

mūḍho'yaṁ nābhijānāti , loko mām ajam avyayam II 7.25

7.25 Men remain beguiled by trifles and small pastimes, only stuck in the measurable. Such beings do not grasp the Divinity, that is omnipotent omnipresent.

वेदाहं समतीतानि , वर्तमानानि चार्जुन । भविष्याणि च भूतानि , मां तु वेद न कश्चन ॥ ७.२६

vedāhaṁ samatītāni , vartamānāni cārjuna I

bhaviṣyāṇi ca bhūtāni , māṁ tu veda na kaścana II 7.26

7.26 The Divine is omniscient, with complete knowledge of the past present and future. Being omniscient is a rarity in mankind.

इच्छाद्वेषसमुत्थेन , द्वन्द्वमोहेन भारत । सर्वभूतानि सम्मोहम् , सर्गे यान्ति परन्तप ॥ ७.२७

icchādveṣasamutthena , dvandvamohena bhārata I

sarvabhūtāni sammoham , sarge yānti parantapa II 7.27

7.27 Being born to two parents with quite contrary qualities in terms of intellect and emotion, yet with a desire to cohabit and pull along, man is vulnerable to infatuation in the beginning.

येषां त्वन्तगतं पापम् , जनानां पुण्यकर्मणाम् । ते द्वन्द्वमोहनिर्मुक्ताः , भजन्ते मां दृढव्रताः ॥ ७.२८

yeṣāṁ tvantagataṁ pāpam , janānāṁ puṇyakarmaṇām ।

te dvandvamohanirmuktāḥ , bhajante māṁ dṛḍhavratāḥ ॥ 7.28

7.28 But by performing virtuous acts this infatuation melts away and the chain of entanglement is also broken. Such men are drawn to the Truth and become steadfast in their pursuit.

जरामरणमोक्षाय , माम् आश्रित्य यतन्ति ये । ते ब्रह्म तद् विदुः कृत्स्नम् , अध्यात्मं कर्म चाखिलम् ॥ ७.२९

jarāmaraṇamokṣāya , mām āśritya yatanti ye ।

te brahma tad viduḥ kṛtsnam , adhyātmaṁ karma cākhilam ॥ 7.29

7.29 Those who so strive for perfection, take refuge in the Truth, and thus mature to wholesome living, complete within with inner fulfilment.

साधिभूताधिदैवं माम् , साधियज्ञं च ये विदुः । प्रयाणकालेऽपि च माम् , ते विदुर् युक्तचेतसः ॥ ७.३०

sādhibhūtādhidaivaṁ mām , sādhiyajñaṁ ca ye viduḥ ।

prayāṇakāle'pi ca mām , te vidur yuktacetasaḥ ॥ 7.30

7.30 These men know the 5-fold nature pertaining to the elements and 3-fold nature pertaining to the subtle. Being steadfast in their duty and at harmony within, they meet a peaceful death.

ॐ तत् सत् । इति श्रीमद्भगवद्गीतासु उपनिषत्सु ब्रह्मविद्यायां योगशास्त्रे श्रीकृष्णार्जुनसंवादे

ज्ञान-विज्ञान-योगो नाम सप्तमोऽध्यायः ॥ ७॥

oṁ tat sat । iti śrīmadbhagavadgītāsu upaniṣatsu brahmavidyāyāṁ yogaśāstre śrīkṛṣṇārjunasaṁvāde jñāna-vijñāna-yogo nāma saptamo'dhyāyaḥ

॥ 7 ॥

8 Yoga of Demystifying Death

Death Demystified and Divine realm explained

ॐ श्री परमात्मने नमः । अथ अष्टमोऽध्यायः

oṁ śrī paramātmane namaḥ । atha aṣṭamo'dhyāyaḥ

अर्जुन उवाच

किं तद् ब्रह्म किम् अध्यात्मम् , किं कर्म पुरुषोत्तम । अधिभूतं च किं प्रोक्तम् , अधिदैवं किम् उच्यते ॥ ८.१

arjuna uvāca

kiṁ tad brahma kim adhyātmam , kiṁ karma puruṣottama ।

adhibhūtaṁ ca kiṁ proktam , adhidaivaṁ kim ucyate ॥ 8.1

Arjun asks based on 7.29 and 7.30
8.1 Please enlighten me regarding Brahman. What does the term Adhyatma mean and what is Action related to it? Please also clarify Adibhuta and Adhideva.

अधियज्ञ× कथं कोऽत्र , देहेऽस्मिन् मधुसूदन । प्रयाणकाले च कथम् , ज्ञेयोऽसि नियतात्मभिः ॥ ८.२

adhiyajña× kathaṁ ko'tra , dehe'smin madhusūdana ।

prayāṇakāle ca katham , jñeyo'si niyatātmabhiḥ ॥ 8.2

8.2 Also what doth Adhiyagna mean as applied to body? By what self-control is the peaceful death to be premeditated?

श्री भगवान् उवाच

अक्षरं ब्रह्म परमम् , स्वभावोऽध्यात्मम् उच्यते । भूतभावोद्भवकरः , विसर्ग× कर्मसञ्ज्ञितः ॥ ८.३

śrī bhagavān uvāca

akṣaraṁ brahma paramam , svabhāvo'dhyātmam ucyate ।

bhūtabhāvodbhavakaraḥ , visarga× karmasañjñitaḥ ॥ 8.3

The Lord immediately supplies
8.3 Brahman is a technical term in Vedanta philosophy. It refers to the Truth, the Divinity that is always present. The nature of Divine is to be experienced within as all that is sacred. This self-experience activity is known as Adhyatma. Action in this case is all that is noble, virtuous and righteous. Especially that is called 'Action' that keeps the fabric of society intact and civilization evolving.

अधिभूतं क्षरो भावः , पुरुषश् चाधिदैवतम् । अधियज्ञोऽहमेवात्र , देहे देहभृतां वर ॥ ८.४

adhibhūtaṁ kṣaro bhāvaḥ , puruṣaś cādhidaivatam ।

adhiyajño'hamevātra , dehe dehabhṛtāṁ vara ॥ 8.4

8.4 Adhibuta refers to the fivefold nature that is impermanent or changing, composed of the 5 gross elements. Adhideva refers to the 3 subtle energies that constitute life or animate matter. Adhiyagna in this case is applied to the primal all-pervading Divinity within all bodies and objects.

अन्तकाले च माम् एव , स्मरन् मुक्त्वा कलेवरम् । यः प्रयाति स मद्भावम् , याति नास्त्यत्र संशयः ॥ ८.५

antakāle ca mām eva , smaran muktvā kalevaram ।

yaḥ prayāti sa madbhāvam , yāti nāstyatra saṁśayaḥ ॥ 8.5

8.5 And a peaceful death or a worthy transition, akin to a bumpless transfer is most priced, sought for and desirable. That is a big boost to the new life or new job or new partner as well, ensuring a long term, stable and successful union.

यं यं वापि स्मरन् भावम् , त्यजत्यन्ते कलेवरम् । तं तमेवैति कौन्तेय , सदा तद्भावभावितः ॥ ८.६

yaṁ yaṁ vāpi smaran bhāvam , tyajatyante kalevaram ।

taṁ tamevaiti kaunteya , sadā tadbhāvabhāvitaḥ ॥ 8.6

8.6 Remember that at a transition point or a milestone in one's life, one most naturally gets what is uppermost in one's mind and thoughts. Whenever we make a U-turn, or stop and ponder, or make a fresh start, then effortlessly we go the way of our current aim.

तस्मात् सर्वेषु कालेषु , माम् अनुस्मर युध्य च । मय्यर्पितमनोबुद्धिः , मामेवैष्यस्यसंशयम् ॥ ८.७

tasmāt sarveṣu kāleṣu , mām anusmara yudhya ca ।

mayyarpitamanobuddhiḥ , māmevaiṣyasyasaṁśayam ॥ 8.7

8.7 Hence it is a moot point to identify and prioritize one's life and aims. Undoubtedly that will lead to fulfilment sooner.

अभ्यासयोगयुक्तेन , चेतसा नान्यगामिना । परमं पुरषं दिव्यम् , याति पार्थानुचिन्तयन् ॥ ८.८

abhyāsayogayuktena , cetasā nānyagāminā ।

paramaṁ puraṣaṁ divyam , yāti pārthānucintayan ॥ 8.8

8.8 With the practice of long habit to assimilate and synthesize, and enough contemplation regarding one's aim, one achieves the Divine Splendour within.

कविं पुराणम् अनुशासितारम् , अणोरणीयांसम् अनुस्मरेद् यः ।

सर्वस्य धातारम् अचिन्त्यरूपम् , आदित्यवर्णं तमसः परस्तात् ॥ ८.९

kaviṁ purāṇam anuśāsitāram , aṇoraṇīyāṁsam anusmared yaḥ I

sarvasya dhātāram acintyarūpam ,ādityavarṇaṁ tamasaḥ parastāt II 8.9

8.9 Whosoever contemplates on the Lord of the Universe, having an inconceivable form hence variable for each individual, who is at the core of all creation, who can be assumed to be shining as the bright sun, beyond all notions and limitations...

प्रयाणकाले मनसाचलेन , भक्त्या युक्तो योगबलेन चैव ।

भ्रुवोर् मध्ये प्राणम् आवेश्य सम्यक् , स तं परं पुरुषम् उपैति दिव्यम् ॥ ८.१०

prayāṇakāle manasācalena , bhaktyā yukto yogabalena caiva I

bhruvor madhye prāṇam āveśya samyak ,

sa taṁ paraṁ puruṣam upaiti divyam II 8.10

8.10 At the hour of Death, devoted and steadfast, withdrawing one's thoughts, and focussing on the third-eye or Ajna Chakra between the eyebrows, one attains to the Divine realm i.e. an infinite peace.

यद् अक्षरं वेदविदो वदन्ति , विशन्ति यद् यतयो वीतरागाः ।

यदिच्छन्तो ब्रह्मचर्यं चरन्ति , तत्ते पदं सङ्ग्रहेण प्रवक्ष्ये ॥ ८.११

yad akṣaraṁ vedavido vadanti , viśanti yad yatayo vītarāgāḥ I

yadicchanto brahmacaryaṁ caranti , tatte padaṁ saṅgraheṇa pravakṣye II 8.11

8.11 The infinitely peaceful realm talked about in the scriptures, that which is the abode of the introverted dispassionate souls, that which is the aim of those practicing celibacy, hear in brief about the same.

सर्वद्वाराणि संयम्य , मनो हृदि निरुध्य च । मूर्ध्न्याधायात्मनः प्राणम् , आस्थितो योगधारणाम् ॥ ८.१२

sarvadvārāṇi saṁyamya , mano hṛdi nirudhya ca I

mūrdhnyādhāyātmanaḥ prāṇam , āsthito yogadhāraṇām II 8.12

8.12 At the hour of death, Shutting off the senses, with a focus on the Heart Center or the A chakra, and holding the prana or life force at the top of the head or the Sahasrara Chakra, thereby engaged...

ॐ इत्येकाक्षरं ब्रह्म , व्याहरन् माम् अनुस्मरन् । यः प्रयाति त्यजन् देहम् , स याति परमां गतिम् ॥ ८.१३

oṁ ityekākṣaraṁ brahma , vyāharan mām anusmaran ।

yaḥ prayāti tyajan deham , sa yāti paramāṁ gatim ॥ 8.13

8.13 in japa of the sacred single syllable Om, with a cheerful heart fixed on the Lord, the one that passeth away attains an infinite peace.

अनन्यचेतास् सततम् , यो मां स्मरति नित्यशः । तस्याहं सुलभः पार्थ , नित्ययुक्तस्य योगिनः ॥ ८.१४

ananyacetās satatam , yo māṁ smarati nityaśaḥ ।

tasyāhaṁ sulabhaḥ pārtha , nityayuktasya yoginaḥ ॥ 8.14

8.14 Also, Union with the Divine or infinite peace at the time of parting is surely attainable by the one who engages regularly in honest and virtuous acts.

माम् उपेत्य पुनर्जन्म , दुःखालयम् अशाश्वतम् । नाप्नुवन्ति महात्मानः , संसिद्धिं परमां गताः ॥ ८.१५

mām upetya punarjanma , duḥkhālayam aśāśvatam ।

nāpnuvanti mahātmānaḥ , saṁsiddhiṁ paramāṁ gatāḥ ॥ 8.15

8.15 Being united with the Divine or infinite peace, the noble souls are never reborn to a temporary life of grief or hardship. They have attained Salvation.

आब्रह्मभुवनाल्लोकाः , पुनरावर्तिनोऽर्जुन । माम् उपेत्य तु कौन्तेय , पुनर्जन्म न विद्यते ॥ ८.१६

ābrahmabhuvanāllokāḥ , punarāvartino'rjuna ।

mām upetya tu kaunteya , punarjanma na vidyate ॥ 8.16

8.16 The many layers and levels of creation have a cyclic nature. Even a King has to go through ups and downs. However the one who unites with the Divine attains lasting peace.

सहस्रयुगपर्यन्तम् , अहर्यद्ब्रह्मणो विदुः । रात्रिं युगसहस्रान्ताम् , तेऽहोरात्रविदो जनाः ॥ ८.१७

sahasrayugaparyantam , aharyadbrahmaṇo viduḥ ।

rātriṁ yugasahasrāntām , te'horātravido janāḥ ॥ 8.17

8.17 Those men who are intuitive regarding Time's relativistic nature and who can travel across time zones, understand the Truth that Time is simply a notion. Day and

Night are notional and relative.

अव्यक्ताद् व्यक्तयस् सर्वा: , प्रभवन्त्यहरागमे । रात्र्यागमे प्रलीयन्ते , तत्रैवाव्यक्तसञ्ज्ञके ॥ ८.१८

avyaktād vyaktayas sarvā:, prabhavantyaharāgame I

rātryāgame pralīyante , tatraivāvyaktasañjñake II 8.18

8.18 Day is simply a time-frame for activity. Night is simply a time-frame for rest. The manifest (active) in one time-frame might be unmanifest (inactive) in another, this being a normal cyclical system.

भूतग्रामस् स एवायम् , भूत्वा भूत्वा प्रलीयते । रात्र्यागमेऽवश× पार्थ , प्रभवत्यहरागमे ॥ ८.१९

bhūtagrāmas sa evāyam , bhūtvā bhūtvā pralīyate I

rātryāgame'vaśa× pārtha , prabhavatyaharāgame II 8.19

8.19 As if helplessly, all animate beings undergo a period of activity followed by a period of rest.
Some might wish the day was longer than 24 hours, many of us easily run out of time, or are otherwise delayed or out-of-sync.

परस् तस्मात् तु भावोऽन्यः,अव्यक्तोऽव्यक्तात् सनातनः। यस् स सर्वेषु भूतेषु , नश्यत्सु न विनश्यति ॥ ८.२०

paras tasmāt tu bhāvo'nyaḥ , avyakto'vyaktāt sanātanaḥ I

yas sa sarveṣu bhūteṣu , naśyatsu na vinaśyati II 8.20

8.20 However there is also a plane that is steady, non-cyclic and eternal. That is the unknown plane of indestructibility i.e. without grief and also that is not a common experience for the majority of beings in creation.

अव्यक्तोऽक्षर इत्युक्तः , तमाहु× परमां गतिम् । यं प्राप्य न निवर्तन्ते , तद्धाम परमं मम ॥ ८.२१

avyakto'kṣara ityuktaḥ , tamāhu× paramāṁ gatim I

yaṁ prāpya na nivartante , taddhāma paramaṁ mama II 8.21

8.21 Such is that plane unknown to many, indestructible without grief of any kind, that plane is said to be the highest in the scriptures. That orbit or frequency or latitude is the Divine abode. Meaning that even though the Divine is present at all times in each and every being in entire expanse of space, yet the Divine is in a plane or frequency sans grief.

पुरुषस् स परः पार्थ , भक्त्या लभ्यस् त्वनन्यया । यस्यान्तःस्थानि भूतानि , येन सर्वम् इदं ततम् ॥ ८.२२

puruṣas sa paraḥ pārtha , bhaktyā labhyas tvananyayā ।

yasyāntaḥsthāni bhūtāni , yena sarvam idaṁ tatam ॥ 8.22

8.22 That plane is achievable in life through a Yogic lifestyle. After death to those who lived a Yogic lifestyle. Yogic lifestyle simply means a honest cheerful life, a virtuous or noble life.

यत्र काले त्वनावृत्तिम् , आवृत्तिं चैव योगिनः । प्रयाता यान्ति तं कालम् , वक्ष्यामि भरतर्षभ ॥ ८.२३

yatra kāle tvanāvṛttim , āvṛttiṁ caiva yoginaḥ ।

prayātā yānti taṁ kālam , vakṣyāmi bharatarṣabha ॥ 8.23

8.23 Now also hear regarding the seasons and their effect on man's temperament and attitude. That in turn determines the hour of attainment to the Divine plane.

अग्निर् ज्योतिरहः शुक्लः , षण्मासा उत्तरायणम् । तत्र प्रयाता गच्छन्ति , ब्रह्म ब्रह्मविदो जनाः ॥ ८.२४

agnir jyotirahaḥ śuklaḥ , ṣaṇmāsā uttarāyaṇam ।

tatra prayātā gacchanti , brahma brahmavido janāḥ ॥ 8.24

8.24 A light and cheerful ambience, a glowing hour when the heart is in devotion, those sunny days when one is in love, the seasons when the temperature is comfortable, such times are favourable to transcend this plane and move onto that Divine plane; for honest unblemished souls, for eternity.

धूमो रात्रिस् तथा कृष्णः , षण्मासा दक्षिणायनम् । तत्र चान्द्रमसं ज्योतिः , योगी प्राप्य निवर्तते ॥ ८.२५

dhūmo rātris tathā kṛṣṇaḥ , ṣaṇmāsā dakṣiṇāyanam ।

tatra cāndramasaṁ jyotiḥ , yogī prāpya nivartate ॥ 8.25

8.25 If a honest soul happens to get ejected from this plane to the Divine plane during moments of gloomy and oppressive nature, the moments of dullness, and the seasons of turmoil and agitation, then that soul is again thrust onto the lower planes. *The phrase goes - Timing is Everything. Also in sports - He sweet times the ball.*

शुक्लकृष्णे गती ह्येते , जगतश् शाश्वते मते । एकया यात्यनावृत्तिम् , अन्ययावर्तते पुनः ॥ ८.२६

śuklakṛṣṇe gatī hyete , jagataś śāśvate mate ।

ekayā yātyanāvṛttim , anyayāvartate punaḥ ॥.8 26

8.26 So we might say there are two paths of ejecting from this plane to the Divine plane. A one way street of eternal salvation, and a two way street of temporary relief.

नैते सृती पार्थ जानन् , योगी मुह्यति कश्चन । तस्मात् सर्वेषु कालेषु , योगयुक्तो भवार्जुन ॥ ८.२७

naite sr̥tī pārtha jānan , yogī muhyati kaścana ।

tasmāt sarveṣu kāleṣu , yogayukto bhavārjuna ॥ 8.27

8.27 A cheerful honest man develops intuitive knowledge regarding these paths to the Divine, so he verily chooses to lead a noble lifestyle.

वेदेषु यज्ञेषु तपःसु चैव , दानेषु यत् पुण्यफलं प्रदिष्टम् ।
अत्येति तत् सर्वमिदं विदित्वा , योगी परं स्थानम् उपैति चाद्यम् ॥ ८.२८

vedeṣu yajñeṣu tapaḥsu caiva , dāneṣu yat puṇyaphalaṁ pradiṣṭam ।

atyeti tat sarvamidaṁ viditvā , yogī paraṁ sthānam upaiti cādyam ॥ 8.28

8.28 Thus do the scriptures declare the noble and righteous deeds, for mankind to excel in those and attain to the Divine realm.

ॐ तत् सत् । इति श्रीमद्भगवद्गीतासु उपनिषत्सु ब्रह्मविद्यायां योगशास्त्रे श्रीकृष्णार्जुनसंवादे
अक्षर-ब्रह्म-योगो नाम अष्टमोऽध्यायः ॥ ८॥

oṁ tat sat । iti śrīmadbhagavadgītāsu upaniṣatsu brahmavidyāyāṁ yogaśāstre
śrīkr̥ṣṇārjunasaṁvāde akṣara-brahma-yogo nāma **aṣṭamo'dhyāyaḥ**
॥ 8 ॥

9 Yoga of Royal Secrets

The Secrets of where the Divine manifests

ॐ श्री परमात्मने नमः । अथ नवमोऽध्यायः

oṁ śrī paramātmane namaḥ । atha navamo'dhyāyaḥ

श्री भगवान् उवाच

इदं तु ते गुह्यतमम् , प्रवक्ष्याम्यनसूयवे । ज्ञानं विज्ञानसहितम् , यज्ज्ञात्वा मोक्ष्यसेऽशुभात् ॥ ९.१

śrī bhagavān uvāca

idaṁ tu te guhyatamam , pravakṣyāmyanasūyave ।

jñānaṁ vijñānasahitam , yajjñātvā mokṣyase'śubhāt ॥ 9.1

The gracious Lord said

9.1 The Truth shall be told to those who do not grumble or complain. The Truth is a great mystery, the Divine is surrounded by an impregnable veil, however it reveals to an attitude of cheerfulness. When the Divine so blesses, both knowledge and its assimilation happen. When that happens, one is freed from the inauspicious.

राजविद्या राजगुह्यम् , पवित्रम् इदम् उत्तमम् । प्रत्यक्षावगमं धर्म्यम् , सुसुखं कर्तुम् अव्ययम् ॥ ९.२

rājavidyā rājaguhyam , pavitram idam uttamam ।

pratyakṣāvagamaṁ dharmyam , susukhaṁ kartum avyayam ॥ 9.2

9.2 This is the Royal treasure, the secret of secrets that is like a brilliant shower of purity. Intuition is its gateway, the very nature is its body, it is simplicity personified and everlasting is its impact.

अश्रद्दधानाः पुरुषाः , धर्मस्यास्य परन्तप । अप्राप्य मां निवर्तन्ते , मृत्युसंसारवर्त्मनि ॥ ९.३

aśraddadhānāḥ puruṣāḥ , dharmasyāsya parantapa ।

aprāpya māṁ nivartante , mṛtyusaṁsāravartmani ॥ 9.3

9.3 The Doubting creatures returns empty handed, unable to bear the brilliance of justice, they literally fall down flat.

मया ततम् इदं सर्वम् , जगद् अव्यक्तमूर्तिना । मत्स्थानि सर्वभूतानि , न चाहं तेष्ववस्थितः ॥ ९.४

mayā tatam idaṁ sarvam , jagad avyaktamūrtinā ।

matsthāni sarvabhūtāni , na cāhaṁ teṣvavasthitaḥ ॥ 9.4

9.4 The Divine is threaded and woven into the very fabric of this creation and through all bodies. It is yet untouched unblemished unstained, being of a frequency or quality whose laws are unexplainable.

न च मत्स्थानि भूतानि , पश्य मे योगमैश्वरम् । भूतभृन्न च भूतस्थः , ममात्मा भूतभावनः ॥ ९.५

na ca matsthāni bhūtāni , paśya me yogamaiśvaram I

bhūtabhṛnna ca bhūtasthaḥ ,mamātmā bhūtabhāvanaḥ II 9.5

9.5 Similarly, even though united physically with all and sundry, the Divine maintains absolute union only with the pure at heart.

यथाकाशस्थितो नित्यम् , वायुस् सर्वत्रगो महान् । तथा सर्वाणि भूतानि , मत्स्थानीत्युपधारय ॥ ९.६

yathākāśasthito nityam , vāyus sarvatrago mahān I

tathā sarvāṇi bhūtāni , matsthānītyupadhāraya II 9.6

9.6 Just as the strong winds and turbulent waves arise in all corners of the globe, yet are wholly contained in space, so does all animate and inanimate matter rest on the Divine plane.

सर्वभूतानि कौन्तेय , प्रकृतिं यान्ति मामिकाम् । कल्पक्षये पुनस् तानि , कल्पादौ विसृजाम्यहम् ॥ ९.७

sarvabhūtāni kaunteya , prakṛtiṁ yānti māmikām I

kalpakṣaye punas tāni , kalpādau visṛjāmyaham II 9.7

9.7 All sentient beings go into deep sleep periodically, and also awaken in due course of time. All inanimate matter also perishes after a while, and takes on new forms afresh.

प्रकृतिं स्वाम् अवष्टभ्य , विसृजामि पुन× पुनः । भूतग्रामम् इमं कृत्स्नम् , अवशं प्रकृतेर्वशात् ॥ ९.८

prakṛtiṁ svām avaṣṭabhya , visṛjāmi puna× punaḥ I

bhūtagrāmam imaṁ kṛtsnam , avaśaṁ prakṛtervaśāt II 9.8

9.8 Such is the cyclical design of the mighty primeval laws and forces.

न च मां तानि कर्माणि , निबध्नन्ति धनञ्जय । उदासीनवदासीनम् , असक्तं तेषु कर्मसु ॥ ९.९

na ca māṁ tāni karmāṇi , nibadhnanti dhanañjaya I

udāsīnavadāsīnam , asaktaṁ teṣu karmasu II 9.9

9.9 These formidable forces do not act upon the Divine plane. It remains unknown and untouched by the currents operating in creation.

मयाध्यक्षेण प्रकृतिः , सूयते सचराचरम् । हेतुनानेन कौन्तेय , जगद् विपरिवर्तते ॥ ९.१०

mayādhyakṣeṇa prakr̥tiḥ , sūyate sacarācaram ।

hetunānena kaunteya , jagad viparivartate ॥ 9.10

9.10 The Divine is the prime mover of creation. Activity and rest for all heavenly bodies and beings on earth is regulated by the Divine Nature.

अवजानन्ति मां मूढाः , मानुषीं तनुम् आश्रितम् । परं भावम् अजानन्तः , मम भूतमहेश्वरम् ॥ ९.११

avajānanti māṁ mūḍhāḥ , mānuṣīṁ tanum āśritam ।

paraṁ bhāvam ajānantaḥ , mama bhūtamaheśvaram ॥ 9.11

9.11 Divine manifests from time to time just as it manifested as Sri Krishna. However common man cannot relate to an avatar, is oblivious to the workings of Divine, and is unable to elevate anybody as having Divine potential.

मोघाशा मोघकर्माणः , मोघज्ञाना विचेतसः । राक्षसीम् आसुरीं चैव , प्रकृतिं मोहिनीं श्रिताः ॥ ९.१२

moghāśā moghakarmāṇaḥ , moghajñānā vicetasaḥ ।

rākṣasīm āsurīṁ caiva , prakr̥tiṁ mohinīṁ śritāḥ ॥ 9.12

9.12 Vanity and pettiness rules a large section of the populace, their behaviour is accordingly rather inhuman.

महात्मानस् तु मां पार्थ , दैवीं प्रकृतिम् आश्रिताः । भजन्त्यनन्यमनसः , ज्ञात्वा भूतादिम् अव्ययम् ॥ ९.१३

mahātmānas tu māṁ pārtha , daivīṁ prakr̥tim āśritāḥ ।

bhajantyananyamanasaḥ , jñātvā bhūtādim avyayam ॥ 9.13

9.13 On the other hand devout humans being intuitive about Divinity, take it upon themselves to contemplate on the Divine qualities, with faith that these qualities are worth striving for.

सततं कीर्तयन्तो माम् , यतन्तश्च दृढव्रताः । नमस्यन्तश्च मां भक्त्या , नित्ययुक्ता उपासते ॥ ९.१४

satataṁ kīrtayanto mām , yatantaśca dr̥ḍhavratāḥ ।

namasyantaśca māṁ bhaktyā , nityayuktā upāsate ॥ 9.14

9.14 They are regular in their singing of devotional songs and doing elaborate pujas with meticulous decorations.

ज्ञानयज्ञेन चाप्यन्ये , यजन्तो माम् उपासते । एकत्वेन पृथक्त्वेन , बहुधा विश्वतोमुखम् ॥ ९.१५

jñānayajñena cāpyanye , yajanto mām upāsate ।

ekatvena pr̥thaktvena , bahudhā viśvatomukham ॥ 9.15

9.15 Other souls who have a logical temperament seek me through their hardwork, in their one-pointed attention to detail, in the manifold architectures they fashion.

अहं क्रतुरहं यज्ञः , स्वधाहमहमौषधम् । मन्त्रोऽहमहमेवाज्यम् , अहम् अग्निर् अहं हुतम् ॥ ९.१६

ahaṁ kraturahaṁ yajñaḥ , svadhāhamahamauṣadham ।

mantro'hamahamevājyam , aham agnir ahaṁ hutam ॥ 9.16

9.16 The Divine is glorified by performing Yagna, the fire ritual, agnihotra, homa, etc. It is also invoked by producing ayurvedic and natural formulations and by Vedic Chants or playing devotional music. Also by the due remembrance of ancestors during specific ceremonies e.g. by getting made their framed images.

पिताहमस्य जगतः , माता धाता पितामहः । वेद्यं पवित्रम् ॐकारः , ऋक् साम यजुर् एव च ॥ ९.१७

pitāhamasya jagataḥ , mātā dhātā pitāmahaḥ ।

vedyaṁ pavitram ॐkāraḥ, r̥k sāma yajur eva ca ॥ 9.17

9.17 Divinity manifests in fatherhood, in motherhood, in able administrators, and in the wise old grandparents. Divine is available to those who chant Om and also to those who hear, read and study the Rig, Sama and Yajur hymns.
(The Vedic texts contain these hymns, Atharva Veda and supplementary Vedic texts are all composed of hymns in these three meters.)

गतिर् भर्ता प्रभुस् साक्षी , निवासश् शरणं सुहृत् । प्रभवꭗ प्रलयस् स्थानम् , निधानं बीजम् अव्ययम् ॥ ९.१८

gatir bhartā prabhus sākṣī , nivāsaś śaraṇaṁ suhr̥t ।

prabhavaꭗ pralayas sthānam,nidhānaṁ bījam avyayam ॥ 9.18

9.18 Divine manifests in any virtuous aim, in people who support noble causes, in Just kings, in calm and composed humans, in safe and sound homes and workplaces, in friendship, and in sacred temples. The Divinity is the cause for birth and death and maintenance. It is the sought for outstanding emotion.

तपाम्यहमहं वर्षम् , *निगृह्णाम्युत्सृजामि* च । अमृतं चैव मृत्युश्च , सद् असच्चाहम् अर्जुन ॥ ९.१९

tapāmyahamahaṁ varṣam , nigr̥hṇāmyutsr̥jāmi ca ।

amṛtaṁ caiva mṛtyuśca , sad asaccāham arjuna ‖ 9.19

9.19 The Divine is in the Sun that nourishes, awakens and gives warmth, it is in the sunshine and in the rainfall. Nectar, Change, Existence and Vacuum are other names for the Divine.

त्रैविद्या मां सोमपाः पूतपापाः , यज्ञैरिष्ट्वा स्वर्गतिं प्रार्थयन्ते ।

ते पुण्यमासाद्य सुरेन्द्रलोकम् , अश्नन्ति दिव्यान् दिवि देवभोगान् ॥ ९.२०

traividyā māṁ somapāḥ pūtapāpāḥ, yajñairiṣṭvā svargatiṁ prārthayante।

te puṇyamāsādya surendralokam , aśnanti divyān divi devabhogān ‖ 9.20

9.20 The students who take up a study of the three R's - reading writing arithmetic - get a passport to Heaven. Those who partake of sermons and seminars also obtain such a visa, having overcome their shortcomings thereby. Know that by visas and passports one gains entry to comfortable, pleasurable and heavenly lands.

ते तं भुक्त्वा स्वर्गलोकं विशालम् , क्षीणे पुण्ये मर्त्यलोकं विशन्ति ।

एवं त्रयीधर्मम् अनुप्रपन्नाः , गतागतं कामकामा लभन्ते ॥ ९.२१

te taṁ bhuktvā svargalokaṁ viśālam , kṣīṇe puṇye martyalokaṁ viśanti ।

evaṁ trayīdharmam anuprapannāḥ , gatāgataṁ kāmakāmā labhante ‖21

9.21 Heavenly lands are temporary places of sensual enjoyments and pleasures. They are not the ultimate goal, yet they are yearned for by many, and that is quite normal for the novice, rookie or greenhorn.

अनन्याश् चिन्तयन्तो माम् , ये जनाः पर्युपासते । तेषां नित्याभियुक्तानाम् , योगक्षेमं वहाम्यहम् ॥ ९.२२

ananyāś cintayanto mām , ye janāḥ paryupāsate ।

teṣāṁ nityābhiyuktānām , yogakṣemaṁ vahāmyaham ‖ 9.22

9.22 However pragmatic virtuous souls who strive for the Divine - unmixed with pleasures - obtain long lasting tryst with safety, security, and a productive life.

येऽप्यन्यदेवता भक्ताः , यजन्ते श्रद्धयान्विताः । तेऽपि मामेव कौन्तेय , यजन्त्यविधिपूर्वकम् ॥ ९.२३

ye'pyanyadevatā bhaktāḥ , yajante śraddhayānvitāḥ ।

te'pi māmeva kaunteya , yajantyavidhipūrvakam ‖ 9.23

9.23 Harking for Heaven is a half-attempt, so not altogether to be decried. Sooner or later such men also turn to striving for the highest Divinity.

अहं हि सर्वयज्ञानाम् , भोक्ता च प्रभुरेव च । न तु माम् अभिजानन्ति , तत्त्वेनातश् च्यवन्ति ते ॥ ९.२४

ahaṁ hi sarvayajñānām , bhoktā ca prabhureva ca ।

na tu mām abhijānanti , tattvenātaś cyavanti te ॥ 9.24

9.24 Not knowing the merit of purity, not realizing the essence of purity, the novice seek pleasures over purity, so need to work again.

यान्ति देवव्रता देवान् , पितन्यान्ति पितृव्रताः । भूतानि यान्ति भूतेज्याः , यान्ति मद्याजिनोऽपि माम् ॥ ९.२५

yānti devavratā devān , pitṝnyānti pitṛvratāḥ ।

bhūtāni yānti bhūtejyāḥ , yānti madyājino'pi mām ॥ 9.25

9.25 Those who strive for district-level, state-level and national level achieve the same. However those who strive for international glory are the best.

पत्रं पुष्पं फलं तोयम् , यो मे भक्त्या प्रयच्छति । तद् अहं भक्त्युपहृतम् , अश्नामि प्रयतात्मनः ॥ ९.२६

patraṁ puṣpaṁ phalaṁ toyam , yo me bhaktyā prayacchati ।

tad ahaṁ bhaktyupahṛtam , aśnāmi prayatātmanaḥ ॥ 9.26

9.26 Whether thee be an illiterate villager, or a skilled artisan, or a highly accomplished and cultured personality, all qualify to attain Divine union since a pure heart is the only permit. Leaf-flower-fruit is an oft quoted simile for the buffoon-mediocre-intelligent.

यत् करोषि यद् अश्नासि , यज्जुहोषि ददासि यत् । यत् तपस्यसि कौन्तेय , तत् कुरुष्व मदर्पणम् ॥ ९.२७

yat karoṣi yad aśnāsi , yajjuhoṣi dadāsi yat ।

yat tapasyasi kaunteya , tat kuruṣva madarpaṇam ॥ 9.27

9.27 Purity of heart means humility, kindness, patience. It is an attitude of cheerfulness, calmness, simplicity and devotion.

शुभाशुभफलैरेवम् , मोक्ष्यसे कर्मबन्धनैः । सन्न्यासयोगयुक्तात्मा , विमुक्तो माम् उपैष्यसि ॥ ९.२८

śubhāśubhaphalairevam , mokṣyase karmabandhanaiḥ ।

sannyāsayogayuktātmā , vimukto mām upaiṣyasi ॥ 9.28

9.28 That attitude frees one from self-imposed bonds and limitations. It removes ones impurities. It makes one steadfast in one's Divine pursuit.

समोऽहं सर्वभूतेषु , न मे द्वेष्योऽस्ति न प्रियः । ये भजन्ति तु मां भक्त्या , मयि ते तेषु चाप्यहम् ॥ ९.२९

samo'haṁ sarvabhūteṣu , na me dveṣyo'sti na priyaḥ ।

ye bhajanti tu māṁ bhaktyā , mayi te teṣu cāpyaham ॥ 9.29

9.29 Divinity is actually impervious to righthood and wronghood. However the righteous transcend their bonds and attain escape velocity to freedom.

अपि चेत् सुदुराचारः , भजते माम् अनन्यभाक् । साधुरेव स मन्तव्यः , सम्यग्व्यवसितो हि सः ॥ ९.३०

api cet sudurācāraḥ , bhajate mām ananyabhāk ।

sādhureva sa mantavyaḥ , samyagvyavasito hi saḥ ॥ 9.30

9.30 Even after much blundering and waywardness, one may stumble to the right track and make steady progress.

क्षिप्रं भवति धर्मात्मा , शश्वच्छान्तिं निगच्छति । कौन्तेय प्रतिजानीहि , न मे भक्त× प्रणश्यति ॥ ९.३१

kṣipraṁ bhavati dharmātmā , śaśvacchāntiṁ nigacchati ।

kaunteya pratijānīhi , na me bhakta× praṇaśyati ॥ 9.31

9.31 Making steady progress on the path to cultivating Divine qualities, one attains the desired goal of safety and freedom in life.

मां हि पार्थ व्यपाश्रित्य , येऽपि स्यु× पापयोनयः । स्त्रियो वैश्यास् तथा शूद्राः , तेऽपि यान्ति परां गतिम् ॥ ९.३२

māṁ hi pārtha vyapāśritya , ye'pi syu× pāpayonayaḥ ।

striyo vaiśyās tathā śūdrāḥ , te'pi yānti parāṁ gatim ॥ 9.32

9.32 A child climbs up the ladder through kindergarten, primary school, college and ultimately a high class university education. Similarly even the destitute/orphan/handicapped and the performer singer who gives pleasure like Kishore Kumar/ sportsman like Sachin Tendulkar / heroine like Hema Malini and the stakeholder in a business or profitmaking venture, and the maid or a white collar worker in a bank or multinational or the government, any of these who direct their efforts to the Divine in a honest manner are capable of receiving Grace.

किं पुनर् ब्राह्मणा× पुण्याः ,भक्ता राजर्षयस् तथा । अनित्यम् असुखं लोकम् , इमं प्राप्य भजस्व माम् ॥ ९.३३

kiṁ punar brāhmaṇā× puṇyāḥ , bhaktā rājarṣayas tathā ।

anityam asukhaṁ lokam , imaṁ prāpya bhajasva mām ॥ 9.33

9.33 Then what to talk about the sincere seekers like Sadhus and Monks and the capable administrators striving whole heartedly for common welfare, disregarding any praise or acclaim knowing it to be temporary.

मन्मना भव मद्भक्तः , मद्याजी मां नमस्कुरु । मामेवैष्यसि युक्त्वैवम् , आत्मानं मत्परायणः ॥ ९.३४

manmanā bhava madbhaktaḥ , madyājī māṁ namaskuru I

māmevaiṣyasi yuktvaivam , ātmānaṁ matparāyaṇaḥ II 9.34

9.34 Focus on the task at hand with a clean heart, remembering the Divine in all actions. With such an attitude of supreme devotion, your life becomes worth living and a blessing to all.

ॐ तत् सत् । इति श्रीमद्भगवद्गीतासु उपनिषत्सु ब्रह्मविद्यायां योगशास्त्रे श्रीकृष्णार्जुनसंवादे

राजविद्या-राजगुह्य-योगो नाम नवमोऽध्यायः ॥ ९॥

oṁ tat sat I iti śrīmadbhagavadgītāsu upaniṣatsu brahmavidyāyāṁ yogaśāstre śrīkr̥ṣṇārjunasaṁvāde rājavidyā-rājaguhya-yogo nāma **navamo'dhyāyaḥ**

II 9 II

10 Yoga of Divine Manifestations

Occasions, attributes and dwellings of the Divine and manifestation of Divinity.

ॐ श्री परमात्मने नमः । अथ दशमोऽध्यायः

oṁ śrī paramātmane namaḥ I atha daśamo'dhyāyaḥ

श्री भगवान् उवाच

भूय एव महाबाहो , शृणु मे परमं वचः । यत्तेऽहं प्रीयमाणाय , वक्ष्यामि हितकाम्यया ॥ १०.१

śrī bhagavān uvāca

bhūya eva mahābāho , śṛṇu me paramaṁ vacaḥ I

yatte'haṁ prīyamāṇāya , vakṣyāmi hitakāmyayā II 10.1

The gracious Lord continues

10.1 Listen O Supreme Devotee to the glory of Divine manifestation. Thee are most dear and it shall be to your welfare.

न मे विदुस् सुरगणाः , प्रभवं न महर्षयः । अहम् आदिर् हि देवानाम् , महर्षीणां च सर्वशः ॥ १०.२

na me vidus suragaṇāḥ , prabhavaṁ na maharṣayaḥ I

aham ādir hi devānām , maharṣīṇāṁ ca sarvaśaḥ II 10.2

10.2 Neither the denizens of heaven, nor the skilled intellectuals have any clue to the Divine presence, since Divinity is far ahead of the greatest intellect as well as of the heavenly abode.

यो माम् अजम् अनादिं च , वेत्ति लोकमहेश्वरम् । असम्मूढस् स मर्त्येषु , सर्वपापैः प्रमुच्यते ॥ १०.३

yo mām ajam anādiṁ ca , vetti lokamaheśvaram I

asammūḍhas sa martyeṣu , sarvapāpaiḥ pramucyate II 10.3

10.3 The humble disciple who reposes faith in the eternal timeless Supreme force, his veil drops and he attains freedom from the vagaries of change.

बुद्धिर् ज्ञानम् असम्मोहः , क्षमा सत्यं दमश् शमः । सुखं दुःखं भवोऽभावः , भयं चाभयम् एव च ॥ १०.४

buddhir jñānam asammohaḥ , kṣamā satyaṁ damaś śamaḥ I

sukhaṁ duḥkhaṁ bhavo'bhāvaḥ , bhayaṁ cābhayam eva ca II 10.4

10.4 The qualities of Intelligence, Wisdom, Being not infatuated, Forgiveness, Truthfulness, Self-restraint, Peacefulness, Joy-Sorrow, Birth-Death, Fear-Fearlessness, and...

अहिंसा समता तुष्टिः , तपो दानं यशोऽयशः । भवन्ति भावा भूतानाम् , मत्त एव पृथग्विधाः ॥ १०.५

ahiṁsā samatā tuṣṭiḥ , tapo dānaṁ yaśo'yaśaḥ ।

bhavanti bhāvā bhūtānām , matta eva pr̥thagvidhāḥ ॥ 10.5

10.5 Non-violence, Equanimity, Contentment, Discipline, Charity and Fame-Ignominy arise from Divinity alone and in different degrees.

महर्षयस् सप्त पूर्वे , चत्वारो मनवस् तथा । मद्भावा मानसा जाताः , येषां लोक इमा× प्रजाः ॥ १०.६

maharṣayas sapta pūrve , catvāro manavas tathā ।

madbhāvā mānasā jātāḥ , yeṣāṁ loka imā× prajāḥ ॥ 10.6

10.6 The seven greatest sages, the four earliest born ascetics, and also the first law-givers were possessed of Divine powers. They were willed by the Divine and thus began the production of animate and inanimate matter.

एतां विभूतिं योगं च , मम यो वेत्ति तत्त्वतः । सोऽविकम्पेन योगेन , युज्यते नात्र संशयः ॥ १०.७

etāṁ vibhūtiṁ yogaṁ ca , mama yo vetti tattvataḥ ।

so'vikampena yogena , yujyate nātra saṁśayaḥ ॥ 10.7

10.7 He who reposes firm faith in the Divine presence and in the wonderful ways of the Divine, gets a life away from vicissitudes without any doubt.

अहं सर्वस्य प्रभवः , मत्तस् सर्वं प्रवर्तते । इति मत्वा भजन्ते माम् , बुधा भावसमन्विताः ॥ १०.८

ahaṁ sarvasya prabhavaḥ , mattas sarvaṁ pravartate ।

iti matvā bhajante mām , budhā bhāvasamanvitāḥ ॥ 10.8

10.8 The wise devotee reposes faith in the Divine presence, understanding through contemplation that all is willed by the Divine alone.

मच्चित्ता मद्गतप्राणाः , बोधयन्त× परस्परम् । कथयन्तश्च मां नित्यम् , तुष्यन्ति च रमन्ति च ॥ १०.९

maccittā madgataprāṇāḥ , bodhayanta× parasparam ।

kathayantaśca māṁ nityam , tuṣyanti ca ramanti ca ॥ 10.9

10.9 Such devotees frequently partake of Divine stories and glories, delighting themselves and deriving contentment from such pastimes.

तेषां सततयुक्तानाम् , भजतां प्रीतिपूर्वकम् । ददामि बुद्धियोगं तम् , येन माम् उपयान्ति ते ॥ १०.१०

teṣāṁ satatayuktānām , bhajatāṁ prītipūrvakam I

dadāmi buddhiyogaṁ tam , yena mām upayānti te II 10.10

10.10 In the earnest devotees who spends time in taking the Divine name with regularity, Discrimination springs forth paving the path for their emancipation.

तेषाम् एवानुकम्पार्थम् , अहम् अज्ञानजं तमः । नाशयाम्यात्मभावस्थः , ज्ञानदीपेन भास्वता ॥ १०.११

teṣām evānukampārtham , aham ajñānajaṁ tamaḥ I

nāśayāmyātmabhāvasthaḥ , jñānadīpena bhāsvatā II 10.11

10.11 Sharing extreme compassion with them, the Divine surges forth in their activities, and their limitations are overcome by the lamp of knowledge.

अर्जुन उवाच

परं ब्रह्म परं धाम , पवित्रं परमं भवान् । पुरुषं शाश्वतं दिव्यम् , आदिदेवम् अजं विभुम् ॥ १०.१२

arjuna uvāca

paraṁ brahma paraṁ dhāma , pavitraṁ paramaṁ bhavān I

puruṣaṁ śāśvataṁ divyam , ādidevam ajaṁ vibhum II 10.12

The spotless seeker glorifies

10.12 O Lord thou art the supreme brahman consciousness, the best abode, the genuine purifier. Thou art eternal, thou art excellent, thou art the first adorable. Thou art beginningless and all-pervading.

आहुस् त्वाम् ऋषयस् सर्वे , देवर्षिर् नारदस् तथा । असितो देवलो व्यासः , स्वयं चैव ब्रवीषि मे ॥ १०.१३

āhus tvām ṛṣayas sarve , devarṣir nāradas tathā I

asito devalo vyāsaḥ , svayaṁ caiva bravīṣi me II 10.13

10.13 All the sages have thus declared. So has the heavenly sage Narada eulogized. So also have Buddha's contemporary the sage Asita, sage Devala and composer of Mahabharata epic sage Vyasa stated. And now thee yourself O Lord so speak to me.

सर्वम् एतद् ऋतं मन्ये , यन्मां वदसि केशव । न हि ते भगवन् व्यक्तिम् , विदुर् देवा न दानवाः ॥ १०.१४

sarvam etad ṛtaṁ manye , yanmāṁ vadasi keśava I

na hi te bhagavan vyaktim , vidur devā na dānavāḥ II 10.14

10.14 I fully believe in your words O Lord, O Supreme Delight. It is correct that the neither the heavenly beings nor the demons can sense thy presence.

स्वयम् एवात्मनात्मानम् , वेत्थ त्वं पुरुषोत्तम । भूतभावन भूतेश , देवदेव जगत्पते ॥ १०.१५

svayam evātmanātmānam , vettha tvaṁ puruṣottama I

bhūtabhāvana bhūteśa , devadeva jagatpate II 10.15

10.15 Surely the devotee senses it in the heart of his heart. O Supremo! O Boss! O Source of all! O Ruler of all! O God of gods! O Emperor!

वक्तुम् अर्हस्यशेषेण , दिव्या ह्यात्मविभूतयः । याभिर् विभूतिभिर् लोकान् , इमांस्त्वं व्याप्य तिष्ठसि ॥ १०.१६

vaktum arhasyaśeṣeṇa , divyā hyātmavibhūtayaḥ I

yābhir vibhūtibhir lokān , imāṁstvaṁ vyāpya tiṣṭhasi II 10.16

10.16 Please describe without reserve of thy Divine manifestations and the occasions by which thee make thy presence felt across time and space.

कथं विद्यामहं योगिन् , त्वां सदा परिचिन्तयन् । केषु केषु च भावेषु , चिन्त्योऽसि भगवन् मया ॥ १०.१७

kathaṁ vidyāmahaṁ yogin , tvāṁ sadā paricintayan I

keṣu keṣu ca bhāveṣu , cintyo'si bhagavan mayā II 10.17

10.17 How shall i as a devotee in contemplation seek thee? In what aspect, object, thought or attribute should i remember, recognize and know about you O Lord?

विस्तरेणात्मनो योगम् , विभूतिं च जनार्दन । भूयꣳ कथय तृप्तिर् हि , शृण्वतो नास्ति मेऽमृतम् ॥ १०.१८

vistareṇātmano yogam , vibhūtiṁ ca janārdana I

bhūyaꣳ kathaya tr̥ptir hi , śr̥ṇvato nāsti me'mr̥tam II 10.18

10.18 O Janardana! Describe again in flowing detail thy Yogic prowess and Siddhis. My ears are still not satiated with what i have heard by your nectarine words. (Listening to the Lord's glory and glorious feats is a supreme pastime of the earnest devotee, and it is this Shravanam that is regarded so highly in the Upanishads and sacred scriptures everywhere.)

श्री भगवान् उवाच

हन्त ते कथयिष्यामि , दिव्या ह्यात्मविभूतयः । प्राधान्यतꣳ कुरुश्रेष्ठ , नास्त्यन्तो विस्तरस्य मे ॥ १०.१९

śrī bhagavān uvāca

hanta te kathayiṣyāmi , divyā hyātmavibhūtayaḥ I

prādhānyata× kuruśreṣṭha , nāstyanto vistarasya me II 10.19

The gracious Lord complies

10.19 Very well O Best among the Kuru clan! I shall talk about some prominent Divine qualities. Verily there is no end to the stories and details that recount them.

अहम् आत्मा गुडाकेश , सर्वभूताशयस्थितः । अहम् आदिश्च मध्यं च , भूतानामन्त एव च ॥ १०.२०

aham ātmā guḍākeśa , sarvabhūtāśayasthitaḥ I

aham ādiśca madhyaṁ ca , bhūtānāmanta eva ca II 10.20

10.20 O Gudakesha! I am the Soul present within the hearts of all beings. From me is the Birth, the Life and the Death for all.

आदित्यानाम् अहं विष्णुः,ज्योतिषां रविर् अंशुमान् । मरीचिर् मरुताम् अस्मि ,नक्षत्राणाम् अहं शशी॥ १०.२१

ādityānām ahaṁ viṣṇuḥ , jyotiṣāṁ ravir aṁśumān I

marīcir marutām asmi , nakṣatrāṇām ahaṁ śaśī II 10.21

10.21 Of the 12 Suns I am the one named Vishnu, the largest and longest lived. Among the radiant fiery bodies I am the Sun, the closest to Earth. Of the 48 directional winds I am the wind named Marichi, the coolest and stormiest. I am the lustrous Moon that visits each of the 27 lunar mansion for the duration of a tithi.

वेदानां सामवेदोऽस्मि , देवानाम् अस्मि वासवः। इन्द्रियाणां मनश् चास्मि ,भूतानाम् अस्मि चेतना ॥ १०.२२

vedānāṁ sāmavedo'smi , devānām asmi vāsavaḥ I

indriyāṇāṁ manaś cāsmi , bhūtānām asmi cetanā II 10.22

10.22 Among the Vedas I am the Sama Veda that gives hymns composed in the highly structured and most potent Sama meter. Among the various heavenly deities or office bearers I am their king named Vasava, another name for Indra. Of the senses I am their controller, the thought provoking faculty known as Mind. In the living beings I am the Awareness, the quality that shows that the being is alive and functioning.

रुद्राणां शङ्करश् चास्मि ,वित्तेशो यक्षरक्षसाम् । वसूनां पावकश् चास्मि , मेरुश् शिखरिणाम् अहम् ॥ १०.२३

rudrāṇāṁ śaṅkaraś cāsmi , vitteśo yakṣarakṣasām I

vasūnāṁ pāvakaś cāsmi , meruś śikhariṇām aham II 23

10.23 Among the 11 Rudras(5 Pranas, 5 Subpranas and the thinking faculty Mind) I am the one named Shankar. Of the Yakshas and Rakshasas I am the Chief Financial Officer named Kuber. Among the 8 Vasus(5 Elements, Sun, Moon and Stars) I am the Fire element named Pavaka, the purifier.

पुरोधसां च मुख्यं माम् , विद्धि पार्थ बृहस्पतिम् । सेनानीनाम् अहं स्कन्दः ,सरसाम् अस्मि सागरः ॥ १०.२४

purodhasāṁ ca mukhyaṁ mām , viddhi pārtha bṛhaspatim I

senānīnām ahaṁ skandaḥ , sarasām asmi sāgaraḥ II 10.24

10.24 Of all family priests I am Brihaspati (the chief counsel for the heavenly ruler Indra), Of all army generals I am Skanda (another name for Lord Shiva's son Kartikeya), Of all water bodies I am the ocean (in Indian mythology the Pacific, Atlantic and Indian are a combined ocean named Sagar.)

महर्षीणां भृगुर् अहम् , गिराम् अस्म्येकम् अक्षरम् । यज्ञानां जपयज्ञोऽस्मि ,स्थावराणां हिमालयः ॥ १०.२५

maharṣīṇāṁ bhṛgur aham , girām asmyekam akṣaram I

yajñānāṁ japayajño'smi , sthāvarāṇāṁ himālayaḥ II 10.25

10.25 Among the 7 great sages (saptarishis) I am the sage named Bhrigu, Of all words I am the monosyllable Om, Of all prayer forms I am the Japa (silent mental prayer of repeating a Lord's name), among the stationary mountain ranges I am the Himalayas.

अश्वत्थस् सर्ववृक्षाणाम् , देवर्षीणां च नारदः । गन्धर्वाणां चित्ररथः , सिद्धानां कपिलो मुनिः ॥ १०.२६

aśvatthas sarvavṛkṣāṇām , devarṣīṇāṁ ca nāradaḥ I

gandharvāṇāṁ citrarathaḥ , siddhānāṁ kapilo muniḥ II 10.26

10.26 Of all trees I am the sacred Peepul tree (a large shady tree that gives maximum oxygen - also the tree under which Lord Buddha attained enlightenment at Bodh Gaya), Of all the heavenly sages I am Narada - depicted with a musical instrument sitar - who connects the Devas and the Asuras, or any opposing beings, since his spontaneous frank hearted style is welcomed by all), Of all celebrities I am Chitraratha - who can mesmerize any onlooker by his picture perfect looks and moving style, Of all talented ones I am Kapila muni - the one who gave salvation to his mother.

उच्चैःश्रवसम् अश्वानाम् , विद्धि माम् अमृतोद्भवम् । ऐरावतं गजेन्द्राणाम् , नराणां च नराधिपम् ॥ १०.२७

uccaiḥśravasam aśvānām , viddhi mām amṛtodbhavam I

airāvataṁ gajendrāṇām , narāṇāṁ ca narādhipam II 10.27

10.27 Of all fleet footed horses I am Ucchaishravas - born of churning the ocean for nectar, Of all the majestic elephants - I am Airavata born of churning the ocean - the elephant who knew to fly (and who had a memorable duel with the crocodile - the king of waters who is an amphibian), Of all humans I am the resident Emperor - i.e. Prime Minister or President.

आयुधानाम् अहं वज्रम् , धेनूनाम् अस्मि कामधुक् । प्रजनश् चास्मि कन्दर्पः , सर्पाणाम् अस्मि वासुकिः ॥ १०.२८

āyudhānām ahaṁ vajram , dhenūnām asmi kāmadhuk ।

prajanaś cāsmi kandarpaḥ , sarpāṇām asmi vāsukiḥ ॥ 10.28

10.28 Of all weapons I am the Vraja Thunderbolt - that is like a reusable guided missile with firepower soundpower and lightening velocity, Of all cattle I am the Divine cow Kamadhenu - born of ocean churning for nectar - that means wish fulfilling, Of romance I am the love arouser Kamadeva known as Kandarpa, Of all the deadly serpents I am Vasuki - a hoodless reptile that is equally at ease on land, under water, and in the subterranean depths of earth - hoodless here simply means that cannot be eliminated in a duel - no head i.e. no fatal injury prone part of the body.

अनन्तश् चास्मि नागानाम् , वरुणो यादसाम् अहम् । पितृणाम् अर्यमा चास्मि , यमस् संयमताम् अहम् ॥ १०.२९

anantaś cāsmi nāgānām , varuṇo yādasām aham ।

pitṝṇām aryamā cāsmi , yamas saṁyamatām aham ॥ 10.29

10.29 Of all the king cobras I am Ananta - meaning unkillable - cobras are large headed snakes that never die or rather are reborn immediately at death, I rule over all water molecules H_2O by the name Varuna, I am the first and ideal ancestor Aryaman to all beings, Of all the Officers I am called Yama - the inbuilt energy that keeps a Sanyam or natural control over the lifespan (technically working span) of all beings - who causes anyone to resign in appropriate and due course of time.

प्रह्लादश् चास्मि दैत्यानाम् , कालः कलयतामहम् । मृगाणां च मृगेन्द्रोऽहम् , वैनतेयश्च पक्षिणाम् ॥ १०.३०

prahlādaś cāsmi daityānām , kāla× kalayatāmaham ।

mṛgāṇāṁ ca mṛgendro'ham , vainateyaśca pakṣiṇām ॥ 10.30

10.30 Of all the sons of Diti I am Prahlada - Diti is the mother that has unrighteousness as offspring - but as an exception Prahlada happened to be uncommonly righteous and an exceptional devotee, Of all dimensions I am Time that ticks away marking the milestones, Of all forest beasts I am their king large-hearted courageous Lion, Of all winged arial creatures I am Vainateya - the Garuda or Vulture - that scavenges and clears all rotten carcasses.

पवन× पवताम् अस्मि , रामश् शस्त्रभृतामहम् । झषाणां मकरश् चास्मि , स्रोतसाम् अस्मि *जाह्नवी* ॥ १०.३१

pavana× pavatām asmi , rāmaś śastrabhr̥tāmaham I

jhaṣāṇāṁ makaraś cāsmi , srotasām asmi jāhnavī II 10.31

10.31 Of the fleetest I am the Wind - the fastest among the fast, Of all expert in warfare I am Lord Ram, Of the swimming beasts I am the crocodile, Among the flowing waters
I am the Ganges - the dearest - hence called Jahnvi.

सर्गाणाम् आदिरन्तश्च , मध्यं चैवाहम् अर्जुन । अध्यात्मविद्या विद्यानाम् , वाद× प्रवदताम् अहम् ॥ १०.३२

sargāṇām ādirantaśca , madhyaṁ caivāham arjuna I

adhyātmavidyā vidyānām , vāda× pravadatām aham II 10.32

10.32 O beloved seeker Arjuna! Of all created objects and beings I am the producer/birthgiver-the sustainer-the dissolver/end. Of all studies and disciplines I am the Study of the Soul- i.e. Mind and Consciousness, Of people involved in debates and discussions I am the Orator with best reasoning.

अक्षराणाम् अकारोऽस्मि , द्वन्द्वस् सामासिकस्य च । अहम् एवाक्षय× कालः ,धाताहं विश्वतोमुखः ॥ १०.३३

akṣarāṇām akāro'smi , dvandvas sāmāsikasya ca I

aham evākṣaya× kālaḥ , dhātāhaṁ viśvatomukhaḥ II 10.33

10.33 Among the 56 letters of the Vedic Sanskrit Alphabet I am the starting vowel sound "A as in Among", Of all compounds and unions and marriages and partnerships I am the Equal Partner, Of Time I am the Present Moment, Among the EastWestNorthSouth cardinal directions - corner intermediate directions - Up-middle-below locations I am them all.

मृत्युस् सर्वहरश् चाहम् , उद्भवश्च भविष्यताम् । कीर्तिः श्रीर्वाक् च नारीणाम् , स्मृतिर् मेधा धृतिः क्षमा ॥ १०.३४

mr̥tyus sarvaharaś cāham , udbhavaśca bhaviṣyatām I

kīrtiḥ śrīrvāk ca nārīṇām , smr̥tir medhā dhr̥tiḥ kṣamā II 10.34

10.34 And I am devouring Death and Ending of all, I am the business instinct of the Wealthy. I am dazzling beauty-gold and diamonds-honeyed tongue-strong emotion-intuition-passion and fickleness of the feminine.

बृहत्साम तथा साम्नाम् , गायत्री छन्दसाम् अहम् । मासानां मार्गशीर्षोऽहम् , ऋतूनां कुसुमाकरः ॥ १०.३५

bṛhatsāma tathā sāmnām , gāyatrī chandasām aham I

māsānāṁ mārgaśīrṣo'ham , ṛtūnāṁ kusumākaraḥ II 10.35

10.35 Among the Rik-Sama-Yajur hymns I am the great Sama verse, Of all metrical verses I am the 24 syllabled Gayatri meter, Among the 12 months I am the Margashirsha - the crown of months that is ideal to attain fitness, Among the 6 seasons I am the spring - ideal for romance and love.

द्यूतं छलयताम् अस्मि , तेजस् तेजस्विनाम् अहम् । जयोऽस्मि व्यवसायोऽस्मि , सत्त्वं सत्त्ववताम् अहम् ॥ १०.३६

dyūtaṁ chalayatām asmi , tejas tejasvinām aham I

jayo'smi vyavasāyo'smi , sattvaṁ sattvavatām aham II 10.36

10.36 Of all deceiving tricks I am the Deception, I am the Talent of the geniuses, Victory of the victorious, Determination of the bold, Goodness of the good.

वृष्णीनां वासुदेवोऽस्मि , पाण्डवानां धनञ्जयः । मुनीनाम् अप्यहं व्यासः , कवीनाम् उशना कविः ॥ १०.३७

vṛṣṇīnāṁ vāsudevo'smi , pāṇḍavānāṁ dhanañjayaḥ I

munīnām apyahaṁ vyāsaḥ , kavīnām uśanā kaviḥ II 10.37

10.37 Among the Vrishni clan of Yadavas I am Vasudeva, Among the 5 pandavas I am Dhananjaya i.e. Arjuna. Of all enlightened masters I am Ved Vyasa - composer of the Mahabharata - that contains the Bhagavad Gita, Of all poets I am Ushana.

दण्डो दमयताम् अस्मि , नीतिर् अस्मि जिगीषताम् । मौनं चैवास्मि गुह्यानाम् , ज्ञानं ज्ञानवताम् अहम् ॥ १०.३८

daṇḍo damayatām asmi , nītir asmi jigīṣatām I

maunaṁ caivāsmi guhyānām , jñānaṁ jñānavatām aham II 10.38

10.38 Of all punishments I am the Striking Rod, Of all plans and ambitions I am the Strategy, I am the Mystery in the unexplainable, I am the wisdom in the wise.

यच्चापि सर्वभूतानाम् , बीजं तद् अहम् अर्जुन । न तदस्ति विना यत् स्यात् , मया भूतं चराचरम् ॥ १०.३९

yaccāpi sarvabhūtānām , bījaṁ tad aham arjuna I

na tadasti vinā yat syāt , mayā bhūtaṁ carācaram II 10.39

10.39 O Arjuna! I am the source-cause-seed for all beings and objects. Naught is there that exists without me.

नान्तोऽस्ति मम दिव्यानाम् , विभूतीनां परन्तप । एष तूद्देशतः प्रोक्तः , विभूतेर् विस्तरो मया ॥ १०.४०

nānto'sti mama divyānām , vibhūtīnāṁ parantapa I

eṣa tūddeśataḥ proktaḥ , vibhūter vistaro mayā II 10.40

10.40 O Arjuna! Endless are my manifestations and numerous are the occasions and ways of my Expression. This is but a brief description of my Divine presence and glories.

यद् यद् विभूतिमत् सत्त्वम् , श्रीमद् ऊर्जितम् एव वा ।

तत् तद् एवावगच्छत्वम् , मम तेजोऽंशसम्भवम् ॥ १०.४१ (तेजः अंश-सम्भवम् , तेजोंऽशसम्भवम्)

yad yad vibhūtimat sattvam , śrīmad ūrjitam eva vā I

tat tad evāvagacchatvam,mama tejo'ṁśasambhavam II 10.41

(tejaḥ aṁśa-sambhavam , tejoṁ'śasambhavam)

10.41 Simply keep in mind that wherever and whenever there is something extraordinary, brilliant, intelligent or superlative, know that to be My manifestation. A flash of My presence. My handiwork. (Remember it to be in the time dependent moment - not the physical being or object or event).

अथवा बहुनैतेन , किं ज्ञातेन तवार्जुन । विष्टभ्याहम् इदं कृत्स्नम् , एकांशेन स्थितो जगत् ॥ १०.४२

athavā bahunaitena , kiṁ jñātena tavārjuna I

viṣṭabhyāham idaṁ kṛtsnam , ekāṁśena sthito jagat II 10.42

10.42 This is an infinite and unending detail, and not particularly of much erudition O Arjuna! Just know all of it to be an insignificant part of My Divinity.

ॐ तत् सत् । इति श्रीमद्भगवद्गीतासु उपनिषत्सु ब्रह्मविद्यायां योगशास्त्रे श्रीकृष्णार्जुनसंवादे

विभूति-योगो नाम दशमोऽध्यायः ॥ १० ॥

oṁ tat sat I iti śrīmadbhagavadgītāsu upaniṣatsu brahmavidyāyāṁ yogaśāstre śrīkṛṣṇārjunasaṁvāde vibhūti-yogo nāma daśamo'dhyāyaḥ

II 10 II

11 Yoga of Cosmic Personality

The Gigantic Cosmic Personality and how to Praise the Lord

ॐ श्री परमात्मने नमः । अथ एकादशोऽध्यायः

oṁ śrī paramātmane namaḥ । atha ekādaśo'dhyāyaḥ

अर्जुन उवाच

मदनुग्रहाय परमम् , गुह्यम् अध्यात्मसञ्ज्ञितम् । यत् त्वयोक्तं वचस्तेन , मोहोऽयं विगतो मम ॥ ११.१

arjuna uvāca

madanugrahāya paramam , guhyam adhyātmasañjñitam ।

yat tvayoktaṁ vacastena , moho'yaṁ vigato mama ॥ 11.1

Arjuna states

11.1 By your wondrous description of the secret of secrets concerning thy Self outlined by thee for my emancipation, my infatuation has dropped.

भवाप्ययौ हि भूतानाम् , श्रुतौ विस्तरशो मया । त्वत्तः कमलपत्राक्ष , माहात्म्यम् अपि चाव्ययम् ॥ ११.२

bhavāpyayau hi bhūtānām , śrutau vistaraśo mayā ।

tvattaḥ kamalapatrākṣa , māhātmyam api cāvyayam ॥ 11.2

11.2 From thee is the cause of Coming and Going of beings, and also thy infinite greatness and qualities have been heard in much detail by me O Lotus eyed One!

एवम् एतद् यथात्थ त्वम् , आत्मानं परमेश्वर । द्रष्टुम् इच्छामि ते रूपम् , ऐश्वरं पुरुषोत्तम ॥ ११.३

evam etad yathāttha tvam , ātmānaṁ parameśvara ।

draṣṭum icchāmi te rūpam , aiśvaraṁ puruṣottama ॥ 11.3

11.3 Now O Lord! As thou has described yourself, please grant me the vision of that Magnificent form.

मन्यसे यदि तच्छक्यम् , मया द्रष्टुम् इति प्रभो । योगेश्वर ततो मे त्वम् , दर्शयात्मानम् अव्ययम् ॥ ११.४

manyase yadi tacchakyam , mayā draṣṭum iti prabho ।

yogeśvara tato me tvam , darśayātmānam avyayam ॥ 11.4

11.4 O dear Lord! If thou think fit that i can behold thy Mighty figure, please dear accomplished one! Give me the glimpse.

श्री भगवान् उवाच

पश्य मे पार्थ रूपाणि , शतशोऽथ सहस्रशः । नानाविधानि दिव्यानि , नानावर्णाकृतीनि च ॥ ११.५

śrī bhagavān uvāca

paśya me pārtha rūpāṇi , śataśo'tha sahasraśaḥ ।

nānāvidhāni divyāni , nānāvarṇākṛtīni ca ॥ 11.5

Happily the Lord acquiesced
11.5 O dear Partha! Behold my multitudinous forms in hundreds and thousands, of exquisite contours, colours, lustres and hues.

पश्यादित्यान् वसून् रुद्रान् , अश्विनौ मरुतस् तथा । बहून्यदृष्टपूर्वाणि , पश्याश्चर्याणि भारत ॥ ११.६

paśyādityān vasūn rudrān , aśvinau marutas tathā ।

bahūnyadṛṣṭapūrvāṇi , paśyāścaryāṇi bhārata ॥ 11.6

11.6 Behold the 12 Adityas (suns), 8 Vasus (five elements, sun, moon and stars), 11 Rudras (vital airs), twin ashwini kumars (gifted celestial physicians), 48 Maruts (geographical breezes and winds and storms). O Bharata! Also behold most wondrous, exceptional, incredible never seen before figures.

इहैकस्थं जगत् कृत्स्नम् , पश्याद्य सचराचरम् । मम देहे गुडाकेश , यच्चान्यद् द्रष्टुम् इच्छसि ॥ ११.७

ihaikasthaṁ jagat kṛtsnam , paśyādya sacarācaram ।

mama dehe guḍākeśa , yaccānyad draṣṭum icchasi ॥ 11.7

11.7 O Gudakesha! Now behold in my body the entire universe, with all its mobile and stationary bodies-beings-objects-flora-fauna and whatever else you might desire to see or know.

न तु मां शक्यसे द्रष्टुम् , अनेनैव स्वचक्षुषा । दिव्यं ददामि ते चक्षुः , पश्य मे योगम् ऐश्वरम् ॥ ११.८

na tu māṁ śakyase draṣṭum , anenaiva svacakṣuṣā ।

divyaṁ dadāmi te cakṣuḥ , paśya me yogam aiśvaram ॥ 11.8

11.8 For this you have been granted special senses and extra sensory perception, so that you may see (and hear) what our limited faculties cannot comprehend or absorb or divine or process.

सञ्जय उवाच

एवम् उक्त्वा ततो राजन् , महायोगेश्वरो हरिः । दर्शयामास पार्थाय , परमं रूपम् ऐश्वरम् ॥ ११.९

sañjaya uvāca

evam uktvā tato rājan , mahāyogeśvaro hariḥ ।

darśayāmāsa pārthāya , paramaṁ rūpam aiśvaram ॥ 11.9

Sanjaya - the charioteer and butler of King Dhritarashtra - speaks, just like a TV commentator. So far we have been hearing the live dialogue between the protagonists in the playfield. Now we hear the TV commentary.

11.9 O King! Having thus spoken in the preceding 8 verses, the great accomplished Lord Hari showed his extraordinary divine form to Partha.

अनेकवक्त्रनयनम् , अनेकाद्भुतदर्शनम् । अनेकदिव्याभरणम् , दिव्यानेकोद्यतायुधम् ॥ ११.१०

anekavaktranayanam , anekādbhutadarśanam ।

anekadivyābharaṇam , divyānekodyatāyudham ॥ 11.10

11.10 Consisting of countless faces of wonderful qualities and adorned with their individual clothing-hairstyle-glittering ornaments and flashing respective toolkits-weaponry-insignia...

दिव्यमाल्याम्बरधरम् , दिव्यगन्धानुलेपनम् । सर्वाश्चर्यमयं देवम् , अनन्तं विश्वतोमुखम् ॥ ११.११

divyamālyāmbaradharam , divyagandhānulepanam ।

sarvāścaryamayaṁ devam , anantaṁ viśvatomukham ॥ 11.11

11.11 Wearing sparkling necklaces and apparel, and emitting heady fragrances, the wonderful, resplendent, multitudinous figures.

दिवि सूर्यसहस्रस्य , भवेद् युगपद् उत्थिता । यदि भास् सदृशी सा स्यात् , भासस् तस्य महात्मनः ॥ ११.१२

divi sūryasahasrasya , bhaved yugapad utthitā ।

yadi bhās sadṛśī sā syāt , bhāsas tasya mahātmanaḥ ॥ 11.12

11.12 Immense blazing lights of a thousand highpower lamps in various spectrums were as it were simultaneously put on. Such was the spectacle of that Extraordinary Mighty Form.

तत्रैकस्थं जगत् कृत्स्नम् , प्रविभक्तम् अनेकधा । अपश्यद् देवदेवस्य , शरीरे पाण्डवस् तदा ॥ ११.१३

tatraikasthaṁ jagat kṛtsnam , pravibhaktam anekadhā ।

apaśyad devadevasya , śarīre pāṇḍavas tadā ॥ 11.13

11.13 There held in a single body, the whole universe with its sights and sounds, hustle and bustle, and intricate mosaic was thus seen by the Pandava.

ततस् स विस्मयाविष्टः , हृष्टरोमा धनञ्जयः । प्रणम्य शिरसा देवम् , कृताञ्जलिर् अभाषत ॥ ११.१४

tatas sa vismayāviṣṭaḥ , hṛṣṭaromā dhanañjayaḥ ।

praṇamya śirasā devam , kṛtāñjalir abhāṣata ॥ 11.14

11.14 Then with wonderstruck eyes, frozen countenance, goosebumps and hair standing on end, Dhananjaya bowed low to Divinity and spoke with joined palms...

अर्जुन उवाच

पश्यामि देवांस्तव देव देहे , सर्वांस्तथा भूतविशेषसङ्घान् ।

ब्रह्माणम् ईशं कमलासनस्थम् , ऋषींश्च सर्वान् उरगांश्च दिव्यान् ॥ ११.१५

arjuna uvāca

paśyāmi devāṁstava deva dehe , sarvāṁstathā bhūtaviśeṣasaṅghān ।

brahmāṇam īśaṁ kamalāsanastham , ṛṣīṁśca sarvān uragāṁśca divyān ॥ 11.15

Arjuna speaks - live dialog from the sports arena resumed
Gurudev Kutir, Ganges bank - strong smell of kumkum tilak - it is empty there is not a soul, no signs of any puja either - possibly a Yaksha - Who rules God? What is God's purpose?
11.15 I see Heavenly beings, celestial comets, a lustrous aura emanating. Also a multitude of figures and figurines - various shapes and forms. I see the 4 headed creator ensconced on a lotus shape, and men in flowing beards.

The truth is that the Seeker sees (will see) what is uppermost in his mind. The devotee sees the Lord just as he envisions. The mind - projects on the Lord's white screen - paints on the blank canvas - just what it wills. Whatever it has been desiring, experiencing and fantasizing.

The following verses are a concrete indication that our fancies, dreams, memories and plans all come true. Here the verses depict them coming true all at once - that is rather rare, bewildering and upsetting. However they certainly come true in due course of time and well-spaced out too, so one can enjoy and savour and be suitably quenched.

अनेकबाहूदरवक्त्रनेत्रम् , पश्यामि त्वां सर्वतोऽनन्तरूपम् ।

नान्तं न मध्यं न पुनस् तवादिम् , पश्यामि विश्वेश्वर विश्वरूप ॥ ११.१६

anekabāhūdaravaktranetram , paśyāmi tvāṁ sarvato'nantarūpam ।

nāntaṁ na madhyaṁ na punas tavādim , paśyāmi viśveśvara viśvarūpa ॥ 11.16

11.16 I see the Divine form stretching out for miles in all directions. Wherever I look there is some expression, some emotion, some attraction and some colour.

किरीटिनं गदिनं चक्रिणं च , तेजोराशिं सर्वतो दीप्तिमन्तम् ।

पश्यामि त्वां दुर्निरीक्ष्यं समन्तात् , दीप्तानलार्कद्युतिम् अप्रमेयम् ॥ ११.१७

kirīṭinaṁ gadinaṁ cakriṇaṁ ca , tejorāśiṁ sarvato dīptimantam I

paśyāmi tvāṁ durnirīkṣyaṁ samantāt, dīptānalārkadyutim aprameyam II 11.17

11.17 I see the Divine Sri Krishna just as I have read and heard about him with - a Kiriti - the radiant gemstone that turns all heads, a mace that vanquishes hardened egos, a discus - the sudarshan chakra that purifies one's intellect and corrects one's attitude, and a resplendent aura like the harsh noon sun.

त्वम् अक्षरं परमं वेदितव्यम् , त्वम् अस्य विश्वस्य परं निधानम् ।

त्वम् अव्ययश् शाश्वतधर्मगोप्ता , सनातनस्त्वं पुरुषो मतो मे ॥ ११.१८

tvam akṣaraṁ paramaṁ veditavyam , tvam asya viśvasya paraṁ nidhānam I

tvam avyayaś śāśvatadharmagoptā,sanātanastvaṁ puruṣo mato me II18

11.18 Thou art the undecaying one that is supremely coveted, the precious treasure that draws all, that remains full though richly partaken of by many. Thou art the sustainer and protector of nature. Thou art very ancient and traditional since times immemorial i feel.

अनादिमध्यान्तम् अनन्तवीर्यम् , अनन्तबाहुं शशिसूर्यनेत्रम् ।

पश्यामि त्वां दीप्तहुताशवक्त्रम् , स्वतेजसा विश्वम् इदं तपन्तम् ॥ ११.१९

anādimadhyāntam anantavīryam , anantabāhuṁ śaśisūryanetram I

paśyāmi tvāṁ dīptahutāśavaktram , svatejasā viśvam idaṁ tapantam II19

11.19 I see on all sides a brilliance, a radiance, a resplendence that is lighting up the entire cosmos.

द्यावापृथिव्योर् इदम् अन्तरं हि , व्याप्तं त्वयैकेन दिशश्च सर्वाः ।

दृष्ट्वाद्भुतं रूपम् उग्रं तवेदम् , लोकत्रयं प्रव्यथितं महात्मन् ॥ ११.२०

dyāvāpṛthivyor idam antaraṁ hi , vyāptaṁ tvayaikena diśaśca sarvāḥ I

dṛṣṭvādbhutaṁ rūpam ugraṁ tavedam ,

lokatrayaṁ pravyathitaṁ mahātman ll 11.20

11.20 The entire space and visible spectrum and all directions are filled by a gigantic incredible wonder. All around is a pulsation and changing sensation.

अमी हि त्वां सुरसङ्घा विशन्ति , केचिद्भीताः प्राञ्जलयो गृणन्ति ।

स्वस्तीत्युक्त्वा महर्षिसिद्धसङ्घाः , स्तुवन्ति त्वां स्तुतिभिः पुष्कलाभिः ॥ ११.२१

amī hi tvāṁ surasaṅghā viśanti , kecidbhītāḥ prāñjalayo gr̥ṇanti l

svastītyuktvā maharṣisiddhasaṅghāḥ ,

stuvanti tvāṁ stutibhiḥ puṣkalābhiḥ ll 11.21

11.21 There is a hustle and bustle and a stream of moving energies. Some regular, some with harmonics, some resounding and intermingling. There are sounds of singing and chanting of sacred verses by hosts of great souls and talented be ings.

रुद्रादित्या वसवो ये च साध्याः , विश्वेऽश्विनौ मरुतश्चोष्मपाश्च ।

गन्धर्वयक्षासुरसिद्धसङ्घाः , वीक्षन्ते त्वां विस्मिताश्चैव सर्वे ॥ ११.२२

rudrādityā vasavo ye ca sādyāḥ , viśve'śvinau marutaścoṣmapāśca l

gandharvayakṣāsurasiddhasaṅghāḥ , vīkṣante tvāṁ vismitāścaiva sarve ll 11.22

11.22 What thee described earlier and what virtues and qualities thou extolled - The Rudras, Adityas, Vasus, Sadhyas, Vishvadevas, twin Ashwini Kumars, Maruts, Ushmapas, Gandharvas, Yakshas, Asuras, Siddhas - all have manifested and come alive.

रूपं महत्ते बहुवक्त्रनेत्रम् , महाबाहो बहुबाहूरुपादम् ।

बहूदरं बहुदंष्ट्राकरालम् , दृष्ट्वा लोकाः प्रव्यथितास् तथाहम् ॥ ११.२३

rūpaṁ mahatte bahuvaktranetram , mahābāho bahubāhūrupādam l

bahūdaraṁ bahudaṁṣṭrākarālam , dr̥ṣṭvā lokāḥ pravyathitās tathāham ll 11.23

11.23 Having experienced such intense emotions and sensations and having stared at the numerous bright lights, i am shaky, stunned and my whole being is now exhausted.

नभःस्पृशं दीप्तम् अनेकवर्णम् , व्यात्ताननं दीप्तविशालनेत्रम् ।

दृष्ट्वा हि त्वां प्रव्यथितान्तरात्मा , धृतिं न विन्दामि शमं च विष्णो ॥ ११.२४

nabhaḥspr̥śaṁ dīptam anekavarṇam , vyāttānanaṁ dīptaviśālanetram I

dr̥ṣṭvā hi tvāṁ pravyathitāntarātmā , dhr̥tiṁ na vindāmi śamaṁ ca viṣṇo II 11.24

11.24 The core of my heart has been touched and has become tender. Am losing my patience and equanimity. Enough of such a grand spectacle O Lord!

(isn't that so - all good things come to an end - verily need to come to an end. the best of the best stands ground for some time then melts away. Change is so desirable - our senses and faculties get satiated and need a break after a while).

दंष्ट्राकरालानि च ते मुखानि , दृष्ट्वैव कालानलसन्निभानि ।

दिशो न जाने न लभे च शर्म , प्रसीद देवेश जगन्निवास ॥ ११.२५

daṁṣṭrākarālāni ca te mukhāni , dr̥ṣṭvaiva kālānalasannibhāni I

diśo na jāne na labhe ca śarma , prasīda deveśa jagannivāsa II 11.25

11.25 The great movie has thrilled me and rocked me no end, the superlative performance has left me gaping, and now i wish a bit of rest. Kindly end the show, please turn off the lights.

अमि च त्वां धृतराष्ट्रस्य पुत्राः , सर्वे सहैवावनिपालसङ्घैः ।

भीष्मो द्रोणस् सूतपुत्रस् तथासौ , सहास्मदीयैर् अपि योधमुख्यैः ॥ ११.२६

ami ca tvāṁ dhr̥tarāṣṭrasya putrāḥ , sarve sahaivāvanipālasaṅghaiḥ I

bhīṣmo droṇas sūtaputras tathāsau , sahāsmadīyair api yodhamukhyaiḥ II 11.26

11.26 Credits and names appear across the screen - all famous personalities - knaves and kings - the patriarch, the teacher, the driver - the protagonists...

वक्त्राणि ते त्वरमाणा विशन्ति , दंष्ट्राकरालानि भयानकानि ।

केचिद् विलग्ना दशनान्तरेषु , सन्दृश्यन्ते चूर्णितैर् उत्तमाङ्गैः ॥ ११.२७

vaktrāṇi te tvaramaṇā viśanti , daṁṣṭrākarālāni bhayānakāni I

kecid vilagnā daśanāntareṣu , sandr̥śyante cūrṇitair uttamāṅgaiḥ II 11.27

11.27 Dropping and cavorting in myriad circles, Fading away quickly towards the end, Eaten and chewed so to say.

यथा नदीनां बहवोऽम्बुवेगाः , समुद्रम् एवाभिमुखा द्रवन्ति ।

तथा तवामी नरलोकवीराः , विशन्ति वक्त्राण्यभिविज्वलन्ति ॥ ११.२८

yathā nadīnāṁ bahavo'mbuvegāḥ , samudram evābhimukhā dravanti ।

tathā tavāmī naralokavīrāḥ , viśanti vaktrāṇyabhivijvalanti ॥ 11.28

11.28 Just as river currents gush past torrentially towards the ocean, so does the all-star cast vanish off the sides of the screen.

यथा प्रदीप्तं ज्वलनं पतङ्गाः , विशन्ति नाशाय समृद्धवेगाः ।

तथैव नाशाय विशन्ति लोकाः , तवापि वक्त्राणि समृद्धवेगाः ॥ ११.२९

yathā pradīptaṁ jvalanaṁ pataṅgāḥ , viśanti nāśāya samṛddhavegāḥ ।

tathaiva nāśāya viśanti lokāḥ , tavāpi vaktrāṇi samṛddhavegāḥ ॥ 11.29

11.29 Just as moths making a bee-line towards the glowing lamps and falling to an end in the torching flames, so are all creatures longing for the good Lord entering his great bosom and attaining final rest.

लेलिह्यसे ग्रसमानस् समन्तात् , लोकान् समग्रान् वदनैर् ज्वलद्भिः ।

तेजोभिर् आपूर्य जगत् समग्रम् , भासस् तवोग्रा× प्रतपन्ति विष्णो ॥ ११.३०

lelihyase grasamānas samantāt , lokān samagrān vadanair jvaladbhiḥ ।

tejobhir āpūrya jagat samagram , bhāsas tavogrā× pratapanti viṣṇo ॥ 30

11.30 Time devours creations and beings on all sides, none escape its grasp. Fierce and Fiery are the rays that illumine all.

आख्याहि मे को भवान् उग्ररूपः , नमोऽस्तु ते देववर प्रसीद ।

विज्ञातुम् इच्छामि भवन्तम् आद्यम् , न हि प्रजानामि तव प्रवृत्तिम् ॥ ११.३१

ākhyāhi me ko bhavān ugrarūpaḥ , namo'stu te devavara prasīda ।

vijñātum icchāmi bhavantam ādyam , na hi prajānāmi tava pravṛttim ॥ 31

11.31 Difficult to comprehend is the Lord, unfathomable are his ways. One can only wonder and offer praise.

श्री भगवान् उवाच

कालोऽस्मि लोकक्षयकृत्प्रवृतद्धः , लोकान् समाहर्तुम् इह प्रवृत्तः ।

ऋतेऽपि त्वां न भविष्यन्ति सर्वे , येऽवस्थिता× प्रत्यनीकेषु योधाः ॥ ११.३२

śrī bhagavān uvāca

kālo'smi lokakṣayakr̥tpravr̥taddhaḥ , lokān samāhartum iha pravr̥ttaḥ ।

r̥te'pi tvāṁ na bhaviṣyanti sarve , ye'vasthitā× pratyanīkeṣu yodhāḥ ॥ 32

The maginficient Presence responds

11.32 The Divine is the cause of all endings. Presiding over peoples and situations, he alone wills. All dualities get absorbed in him.

तस्मात् त्वम् उत्तिष्ठ यशो लभस्व , जित्वा शत्रून् भुङ्क्ष्व राज्यं समृद्धम् ।

मयैवैते निहता× पूर्वम् एव , निमित्तमात्रं भव सव्यसाचिन् ॥ ११.३३

tasmāt tvam uttiṣṭha yaśo labhasva , jitvā śatrūn bhuṅkṣva rājyaṁ samr̥ddham ।

mayaivaite nihatā× pūrvam eva , nimittamātraṁ bhava savyasācin ॥11.33

11.33 Hence play your part to the full, participate in every endeavour that comes your way, face up to challenges willingly and enjoy remarkable fame. Perform to the hilt like an actor, play your role whether heroic or villainous.

द्रोणं च भीष्मं च जयद्रथं च , कर्णं तथान्यान् अपि योधवीरान् ।

मया हतांस्त्वं जहि मा व्यथिष्ठाः , युध्यस्व जेतासि रणे सपत्नान् ॥ ११.३४

droṇaṁ ca bhīṣmaṁ ca jayadrathaṁ ca ,karṇaṁ tathānyān api yodhavīrān ।

mayā hatāṁstvaṁ jahi mā vyathiṣṭhāḥ , yudhyasva jetāsi raṇe sapatnān ॥ 11.34

11.34 All the great roles of Bhishma, Dronacharya, Jayadratha, Karna and the brave performers have been planned by the Divine. Your role also is the Divine will, enact it unerringly with gusto and you shall overcome guilt and remorse.

सञ्जय उवाच

एतच्छ्रुत्वा वचनं केशवस्य , कृताञ्जलिर् वेपमान× किरीटी ।

नमस्कृत्वा भूय एवाह कृष्णम् , सगद्गदं भीतभीत× प्रणम्य ॥ ११.३५

sañjaya uvāca

etacchrutvā vacanaṁ keśavasya , kr̥tāñjalir vepamāna× kirīṭī ।

namaskr̥tvā bhūya evāha kr̥ṣṇam,sagadgadaṁ bhītabhīta× praṇamya ॥ 11.35

Sanjaya interjects here (the voice of the TV commentator is heard)

11.35 Becoming mesmerized by the Divine dictum, our man Kiriti with folded palms and choking voice and head bowed low spoke with a tremble.

अर्जुन उवाच

स्थाने हृषीकेश तव प्रकीर्त्या , जगत् प्रहृष्यत्यनुरज्यते च ।

रक्षांसि भीतानि दिशो द्रवन्ति , सर्वे नमस्यन्ति च सिद्धसङ्घाः ॥ ११.३६

arjuna uvāca

sthāne hṛṣīkeśa tava prakīrtyā , jagat prahṛṣyatyanurajyate ca ।

rakṣāṁsi bhītāni diśo dravanti , sarve namasyanti ca siddhasaṅghāḥ ॥ 11.36

Arjuna speaks

11.36 It is the world's way to delight and rejoice in the heroic act that causes the villain to flee in fear. It is the way of the world that the host of righteous, talented and pure hearted worship and extol the Divine.

कस्माच्च ते न नमेरन् महात्मन् , गरीयसे ब्रह्मणोऽप्यादिकर्त्रे ।

अनन्त देवेश जगन्निवास , त्वम् अक्षरं सद् असत् तत् परं यत् ॥ ११.३७

kasmācca te na nameran mahātman , garīyase brahmaṇo'pyādikartre ।

ananta deveśa jagannivāsa , tvam akṣaraṁ sad asat tat paraṁ yat ॥ 11.37

11.37 And why wouldn't they praise the Divine, they who see their own virtues magnified in nature and creation everywhere.

(Arjuna also begins to shower praise)

त्वम् आदिदेवः पुरुषः पुराणः , त्वम् अस्य विश्वस्य परं निधानम् ।

वेत्तासि वेद्यं च परं च धाम , त्वया ततं विश्वम् अनन्तरूप ॥ ११.३८

tvam ādidevaḥ puruṣaḥ purāṇaḥ , tvam asya viśvasya paraṁ nidhānam ।

vettāsi vedyaṁ ca paraṁ ca dhāma , tvayā tataṁ viśvam anantarūpa ॥38

11.38 Thou art the first luminary, the traditional master, the supreme refuge of us all. Thou art the Subject, the Object and the foundation of it all. By thee is everyone pervaded, thee are in each form.

वायुर् यमोऽग्निर् वरुणश् शशाङ्कः , प्रजापतिस् त्वं प्रपितामहश्च ।

नमो नमस्तेऽस्तु सहस्रकृत्वः , पुनश्च भूयोऽपि नमो नमस्ते ॥ ११.३९

vāyur yamo'gnir varuṇaś śaśāṅkaḥ , prajāpatis tvaṁ prapitāmahaśca ।

namo namaste'stu sahasrakṛtvaḥ , punaśca bhūyo'pi namo namaste ॥ 39

11.39 Thou art the soothing breeze, the restraining of evil, the protective fire, the nourishing water, the beautiful moon. Thou art my ancestor, a thousand salutations to thee. Again and again i glorify, salute and bow down to thee.

नमः पुरस्ताद् अथ पृष्ठतस् ते , नमोऽस्तु ते सर्वत एव सर्व ।

अनन्तवीर्यामितविक्रमस् त्वम् , सर्वं समाप्नोषि ततोऽसि सर्वः ॥ ११.४०

nama× purastād atha pṛṣṭhatas te , namo'stu te sarvata eva sarva I

anantavīryāmitavikramas tvam , sarvaṁ samāpnoṣi tato'si sarvaḥ ॥11.40

11.40 Accept my humble prostrations to thee. Accept my little words of glee. O all Powerful! O all-Pervading! O the one who hath become Me!

सखेति मत्वा प्रसभं यद् उक्तम् , हे कृष्ण हे यादव हे सखेति ।

अजानता महिमानं तवेदम् , मया प्रमादात् प्रणयेन वापि ॥ ११.४१

sakheti matvā prasabhaṁ yad uktam , he kṛṣṇa he yādava he sakheti I

ajānatā mahimānaṁ tavedam , mayā pramādāt praṇayena vāpi ॥ 11.41

11.41 So many times have i given you fond names, so many are the words i have addressed you by. All my praises fall short of thee yet all my love is showered on thee.

यच्चावहासार्थम् असत्कृतोऽसि , विहारशय्यासनभोजनेषु ।

एकोऽथवाप्यच्युत तत् समक्षम् , तत् क्षामये त्वाम् अहम् अप्रमेयम् ॥ ११.४२

yaccāvahāsārtham asatkṛto'si , vihāraśayyāsanabhojaneṣu I

eko'thavāpyacyuta tat samakṣam , tat kṣāmaye tvām aham aprameyam ॥ 11.42

11.42 So many are the friendly pastimes spent with the Divine, so often are we engrossed in the Divine. In the company of the beloved many are the moments of carefree unawareness.

पितासि लोकस्य चराचरस्य , त्वम् अस्य पूज्यश्च गुरुर् गरीयान् ।

न त्वत्समोऽस्त्यभ्यधिकः कुतोऽन्यः, लोकत्रयेऽप्यप्रतिमप्रभाव ॥ ११.४३

pitāsi lokasya carācarasya , tvam asya pūjyaśca gurur garīyān I

na tvatsamo'styabhyadhika× kuto'nyaḥ ,lokatraye'pyapratimaprabhāva ॥ 11.43

11.43 Thou art the benefactor of this world. Thou enliven all that moves and grace all that is still. Thou art adored by all. Thou art the greatest guide. There is none that matches thee, there is none that is not reverential to thee. Thee are all talented.

तस्मात् प्रणम्य प्रणिधाय कायम् , प्रसादये त्वाम् अहम् ईशम् ईड्यम् ।

पितेव पुत्रस्य सखेव सख्युः , प्रियः प्रियायार्हसि देव सोढुम् ॥ ११.४४

tasmāt praṇamya praṇidhāya kāyam , prasādaye tvām aham īśam īḍyam I

piteva putrasya sakheva sakhyuḥ , priyaḥ priyāyārhasi deva soḍhum II 44

11.44 Hence bless me who salutes thee. Bless the one who acknowledges thee. Shower your grace as father on son, as friend on friend, as lover on mate.

अदृष्टपूर्वं हृषितोऽस्मि दृष्ट्वा , भयेन च प्रव्यथितं मनो मे ।

तदेव मे दर्शय देवरूपम् , प्रसीद देवेश जगन्निवास ॥ ११.४५

adr̥ṣṭapūrvaṁ hr̥ṣito'smi dr̥ṣṭvā , bhayena ca pravyathitaṁ mano me I

tadeva me darśaya devarūpam , prasīda deveśa jagannivāsa II 11.45

11.45 I am all agog with delightfulness, i shake as a flower dances in the breeze. Please now return to thy friendly divine form so that i feel again one with thee.

किरीटिनं गदिनं चक्रहस्तम् , इच्छामि त्वां द्रष्टुम् अहं तथैव ।

तेनैव रूपेण चतुर्भुजेन , सहस्रबाहो भव विश्वमूर्ते ॥ ११.४६

kirīṭinaṁ gadinaṁ cakrahastam , icchāmi tvāṁ draṣṭum ahaṁ tathaiva I

tenaiva rūpeṇa caturbhujena , sahasrabāho bhava viśvamūrte II 11.46

11.46 Please show me your most favourite form in radiant blue wearing a crown of diamonds and holding a mace in one hand, and sporting the sudarshan chakra in a finger of the other hand. Also two more hands, one raised to Protect, the other lowered to grant all wishes.

श्री भगवान् उवाच

मया प्रसन्नेन तवार्जुनेदम् , रूपं परं दर्शितम् आत्मयोगात् ।

तेजोमयं विश्वम् अनन्तम् आद्यम् , यन्मे त्वद् अन्येन न दृष्टपूर्वम् ॥ ११.४७

śrī bhagavān uvāca

mayā prasannena tavārjunedam , rūpaṁ paraṁ darśitam ātmayogāt I

tejomayaṁ viśvam anantam ādyam , yanme tvad anyena na dr̥ṣṭapūrvam II 11.47

The magnificent Lord assented

11.47 O Arjuna! With pleasure I revealed this sacrosanct cosmic form of mine that could not be seen with ordinary eyes.

न वेदयज्ञाध्ययनैर् न दानैः , न च क्रियाभिर् न तपोभिर् उग्रैः ।

एवंरूपश् शक्य अहं नृलोके , द्रष्टुं त्वद् अन्येन कुरुप्रवीर ॥ ११.४८

na vedayajñādhyayanair na dānaiḥ , na ca kriyābhir na tapobhir ugraiḥ ।

evaṁrūpaś śakya ahaṁ nr̥loke , draṣṭuṁ tvad anyena kurupravīra ॥11.48

11.48 O Kurupravir! The gigantic form is so rare that not even the best and brightest have had its vision. Neither have those engaged in brutal living.

मा ते व्यथा मा च विमूढभावः , दृष्ट्वा रूपं घोरम् ईदृङ् ममेदम् ।

व्यपेतभीः प्रीतमनाः पुनस् त्वम् , तद् एव मे रूपम् इदं प्रपश्य ॥ ११.४९

mā te vyathā mā ca vimūḍhabhāvaḥ , dr̥ṣṭvā rūpaṁ ghoram īdr̥ṅ mamedam ।

vyapetabhīḥ prītamanāḥ punas tvam , tad eva me rūpam idaṁ prapaśya ॥ 11.49

11.49 Be not subdued nor excited by having seen the Gigantic form. With your senses calmed and with a loving heart now behold the Divinity in its most pleasing and pacifying appearance with a discus and mace.

सञ्जय उवाच

इत्यर्जुनं वासुदेवस् तथोक्त्वा , स्वकं रूपं दर्शयामास भूयः ।

आश्वासयामास च भीतम् एनम् , भूत्वा पुनस् सौम्यवपुर् महात्मा ॥ ११.५०

sañjaya uvāca

ityarjunaṁ vāsudevas tathoktvā , svakaṁ rūpaṁ darśayāmāsa bhūyaḥ ।

āśvāsayāmāsa ca bhītam enam , bhūtvā punas saumyavapur mahātmā ॥ 11.50

Sanjaya spoke

11.50 Then the great Lord transformed from the Gigantic to the Pacifying Divinity, and then again assumed his friendly human figure, and his devotee experienced the soothing bliss.

अर्जुन उवाच

दृष्ट्वेदं मानुषं रूपम् , तव सौम्यं जनार्दन । इदानीम् अस्मि संवृत्तः , सचेताः प्रकृतिं गतः ॥ ११.५१

arjuna uvāca

dr̥ṣṭvedaṁ mānuṣaṁ rūpam , tava saumyaṁ janārdana ।

idānīm asmi saṁvr̥ttaḥ , sacetā× prakr̥tiṁ gataḥ ॥ 11.51

Arjuna recovers
11.51 Having you back as my bosom buddy is such a relief, my senses have cooled and my intellect has cleared.

श्री भगवान् उवाच

सुदुर्दर्शम् इदं रूपम् , दृष्टवानसि यन्मम । देवा अप्यस्य रूपस्य , नित्यं दर्शनकाङ्क्षिणः ॥ ११.५२

śrī bhagavān uvāca

sudurdarśam idaṁ rūpam , dr̥ṣṭavānasi yanmama ।

devā apyasya rūpasya , nityaṁ darśanakāṅkṣiṇaḥ ॥ 11.52

The good Lord adds
11.52 Really uncommon it is to experience the all-encompassing Gigantic nature of the Lord. Even the heavenly deities and noble beings are ever longing to get such a direct vision up close.

नाहं वेदैर्न तपसा , न दानेन न चेज्यया । शक्य एवंविधो द्रष्टुम् , दृष्टवानसि मां यथा ॥ ११.५३

nāhaṁ vedairna tapasā , na dānena na cejyayā ।

śakya evaṁvidho draṣṭum , dr̥ṣṭavānasi māṁ yathā ॥ 11.53

11.53 Not by efforts of any sort nor by vain works alone can anyone experience Divinity. Your experience is caused by something else altogether.

भक्त्या त्वनन्यया शक्यः , अहम् एवंविधोऽर्जुन । ज्ञातुं द्रष्टुं च तत्त्वेन , प्रवेष्टुं च परन्तप ॥ ११.५४

bhaktyā tvananyayā śakyaḥ , aham evaṁvidho'rjuna ।

jñātuṁ draṣṭuṁ ca tattvena , praveṣṭuṁ ca parantapa ॥ 11.54

11.54 By the fruit of undying devotion full of humility is my presence granted, and the Divine accessed O Parantapa!

मत्कर्मकृन्मत्परमः , मद्भक्तस् सङ्गवर्जितः । निर्वैरस् सर्वभूतेषु , यस् स माम् एति पाण्डव ॥ ११.५५

matkarmakr̥nmatparamaḥ , madbhaktas saṅgavarjitaḥ ।

nirvairas sarvabhūteṣu , yas sa mām eti pāṇḍava ॥ 11.55

11.55 He who offers all actions and day to day mundane tasks to the Divine, he who is worshipful and reverential in his attitude, he who is not blown away by his senses, and he who harbours no ill will, he qualifies for Divine grace, he gets united with Divinity.

ॐ तत् सत् । इति श्रीमद्भगवद्गीतासु उपनिषत्सु ब्रह्मविद्यायां योगशास्त्रे श्रीकृष्णार्जुनसंवादे

विश्व-रूप-दर्शन-योगो नाम एकादशोऽध्यायः ॥ ११ ॥

oṁ tat sat । iti śrīmadbhagavadgītāsu upaniṣatsu brahmavidyāyāṁ yogaśāstre śrīkṛṣṇārjunasaṁvāde viśva-rūpa-darśana-yogo nāma ekādaśo'dhyāyaḥ ॥ 11 ॥

12 Yoga of Devotion

Faith Bhakti and Distinct Temperaments of Devotees

ॐ श्री परमात्मने नमः । अथ द्वादशोऽध्यायः

oṁ śrī paramātmane namaḥ । atha dvādaśo'dhyāyaḥ

अर्जुन उवाच

एवं सततयुक्ता ये , भक्तास् त्वां पर्युपासते । ये चाप्यक्षरम् अव्यक्तम् , तेषां के योगवित्तमाः ॥ १२.१

arjuna uvāca

evaṁ satatayuktā ye , bhaktās tvāṁ paryupāsate ।

ye cāpyakṣaram avyaktam , teṣāṁ ke yogavittamāḥ ॥ 12.1

Arjuna asks (based on 11.55)
12.1 Those who consider it an offering to thee their daily work and action compared to those who contemplate on the unknown and unknowable, who is a better Yogi of the two?

श्री भगवान् उवाच

मय्यावेश्य मनो ये माम् , नित्ययुक्ता उपासते । श्रद्धया परयोपेताः , ते मे युक्ततमा मताः ॥ १२.२

śrī bhagavān uvāca

mayyāveśya mano ye mām , nityayuktā upāsate ।

śraddhayā parayopetāḥ , te me yuktatamā matāḥ ॥ 12.2

The gracious Lord replies
12.2 Those who endowed by faith consider the Divine the object of their life in their day to day thought, speech and deed are indeed laudable.

ये त्वक्षरम् अनिर्देश्यम् , अव्यक्तं पर्युपासते । सर्वत्रगम् अचिन्त्यं च , कूटस्थम् अचलं ध्रुवम् ॥ १२.३

ye tvakṣaram anirdeśyam , avyaktaṁ paryupāsate ।

sarvatragam acintyaṁ ca , kūṭastham acalaṁ dhruvam ॥ 12.3

12.3 Those who meditate on the unknown indefinable uncognizable all-pervading timeless fixed constant...

सन्नियम्येन्द्रियग्रामम् , सर्वत्र समबुद्धयः । ते प्राप्नुवन्ति माम् एव , सर्वभूतहिते रताः ॥ १२.४

sanniyamyendriyagrāmam , sarvatra samabuddhayaḥ ।

te prāpnuvanti mām eva , sarvabhūtahite ratāḥ ॥ 12.4

12.4 With balanced restraint on senses and thoughts, intent on general welfare of all, they certainly make the top grade.

क्लेशोऽधिकतरस् तेषाम् , अव्यक्तासक्तचेतसाम् । अव्यक्ता हि गतिर् दुःखम् , देहवद्भिर् अवाप्यते ॥ १२.५

kleśo'dhikataras teṣām , avyaktāsaktacetasām ।

avyaktā hi gatir duḥkham , dehavadbhir avāpyate ॥ 12.5

12.5 Their Challenges and Aims are much tougher, since correctly negating the body-mind complex is possible only for the very brave.

ये तु सर्वाणि कर्माणि , मयि सन्न्यस्य मत्पराः । अनन्येनैव योगेन , मां ध्यायन्त उपासते ॥ १२.६

ye tu sarvāṇi karmāṇi , mayi sannyasya matparāḥ ।

ananyenaiva yogena , māṁ dhyāyanta upāsate ॥ 12.6

12.6 And those who glorify the Divine, being grateful for what the day brings, having their final aim as Divine beatitude, and spend enough time contemplating on the Lord and singing his praises...

तेषाम् अहं समुद्धर्ता , मृत्युसंसारसागरात् । भवामि नचिरात् पार्थ , मय्यावेशितचेतसाम् ॥ १२.७

teṣām ahaṁ samuddhartā , mṛtyusaṁsārasāgarāt ।

bhavāmi nacirāt pārtha , mayyāveśitacetasām ॥ 12.7

12.7 Verily very soon they attain their aim and are transported to the Divine dimension sans misery.

As seen earlier, Lord taught the Yoga of Action in the 3rd Chapter and the Yoga of Reflection in the 4th. Also in the 7th Chapter he had classified his devotees into 4 types -
a) those seeking a way out of sorrow
b) those seeking wealth or success
c) those seeking the truth
d) the enlightened souls
Here the Lord reclassifies his devotees into
a) those with supreme devotion
b) those with supreme discipline

c) those seeking wealth and success
d) general populace
or
the Lord outlines the faculties of the अन्तःकरण, and puts them all on a level playing ground so that each category of men can apply wholeheartedly, without feeling inferior or left out.
a) 12.8 Chitta based
b) 12.9 Intellect based
c) 12.10 Sensory based
d) 12.11 Ego based

मय्येव मन आधत्स्व , मयि बुद्धिं निवेशय ।

निवसिष्यसि मय्येव , अत ऊर्ध्वं न संशयः ॥ १२.८

mayyeva mana ādhatsva , mayi buddhiṁ niveśaya ।

nivasiṣyasi mayyeva , ata ūrdhvaṁ na saṁśayaḥ ॥ 12.8

12.8 Remember the Lord while doing any task, let there be a place for the Lord in your decision making intellect, surely without doubt you shall transcend to the Divine plane.
(This fits those having the temperament of a Bhakta - supreme devotee - who is generally immersed in the Lord.)

अथ चित्तं समाधातुम् , न शक्नोषि मयि स्थिरम् । अभ्यासयोगेन ततः , माम् इच्छाप्तुं धनञ्जय ॥ १२.९

atha cittaṁ samādhātum , na śaknoṣi mayi sthiram ।

abhyāsayogena tataḥ , mām icchāptuṁ dhanañjaya ॥ 12.9

12.9 In case your mind wavers and is unable to remember the Lord at all times, then keep up your practice of desiring for the Lord at some regular intervals.
(This fits those having the temperament of supreme discipline - Abhyaasa)

अभ्यासेऽप्यसमर्थोऽसि , मत्कर्मपरमो भव । मदर्थम् अपि कर्माणि , कुर्वन् सिद्धिम् अवाप्स्यसि ॥ १२.१०

abhyāse'pyasamartho'si , matkarmaparamo bhava ।

madartham api karmāṇi , kurvan siddhim avāpsyasi ॥ 12.10

12.10 In case your mind slips and your practice of remembering is also too few and far between, then while working put up a sticky note of giving thanks to the Lord. At your work place keep the Lord's name or his image so that for each job done you can be grateful. (Fits those seeking wealth and success.)

अथैतदप्यशक्तोऽसि , कर्तुं मद्योगम् आश्रितः । सर्वकर्मफलत्यागम् , ततः कुरु यतात्मवान् ॥ १२.११

athaitadapyaśakto'si , kartuṁ madyogam āśritaḥ I

sarvakarmaphalatyāgam , tataḥ kuru yatātmavān II 12.11

12.11 If even such a task is not to your liking, then for each job done just do not have the sense of doership. Do not take credit for your success, think that it is simply due to Nature and Natural forces, thereby relinquishing any residue of doership.
(Fits the maximum populace. For any profile or economic status - whether student, housewife, shopkeeper, artist, musician, sportsman, officegoer, politician or lay worker.)

This verse grades the distinct temperaments, for the sole purpose of encouraging and inspiring people on the borderline or those rather unsure, to aim for the higher virtues. The gradation is done with the fine motive of inspiring, rather than simply showing the contrast.

Remember the number 4 Types is used as a pointer to specify the 4 paths at a crossing. Each reaches the center. From 4 cardinal directions one may arrive. Any 4 varnas can pursue. Any 4 ashramas can attain.

श्रेयो हि ज्ञानम् अभ्यासात् , ज्ञानाद् ध्यानं विशिष्यते ।

ध्यानात् कर्मफलत्यागः , त्यागाच्छान्तिर् अनन्तरम् ॥ १२.१२

śreyo hi jñānam abhyāsāt , jñānād dhyānaṁ viśiṣyate I

dhyānāt karmaphalatyāgaḥ ,tyāgācchāntir anantaram II 12.12

12.12 Verily Understanding the great Lord - a cosmic principle - Nature and its ways - and doing is better than mere mechanical practice of remembering the Lord by engaging in rituals listlessly and without honour.
i.e. use of Intellect and Reason is better than just applying Mind and Senses.
Being Meditative and calm in working is better than mere Understanding.
i.e. Balancing Head and Heart is better than Intellect alone.

However Dropping the Doership in Action excels all since it results in peace instantly. i.e. Relinquishing the ego takes the cake as it delivers what is most cherished - p e a c e.

The following 8 verses have been declared to be the Amritashtakam - nectar that banishes fear, grief.

अद्वेष्टा सर्वभूतानाम् , मैत्रः करुण एव च । निर्ममो निरहङ्कारः , समदुःखसुखः क्षमी ॥ १२.१३

adveṣṭā sarvabhūtānām , maitraḥ karuṇa eva ca ।

nirmamo nirahaṅkāraḥ , samaduḥkhasukhaḥ kṣamī ॥ 12.13

12.13 Free from judging any being, they have acceptance and kindliness towards all. Not attaching to things, emotions or thoughts and without a sense of vanity are they. They maintain their composure and wits during thick and thin. They are ready to forgive and forget...

सन्तुष्टस् सततं योगी , यतात्मा दृढनिश्चयः । मय्यर्पितमनोबुद्धिः , यो मद्भक्तस् स मे प्रियः ॥ १२.१४

santuṣṭas satataṁ yogī , yatātmā dṛḍhaniścayaḥ ।

mayyarpitamanobuddhiḥ , yo madbhaktas sa me priyaḥ ॥ 12.14

12.14 Cheerfulness and Peace radiates from such Yogis. A strong dedication to realize the highest is evident in their lifestyle. Such are the beloved of the Lord.

यस्मान्नोद्विजते लोकः , लोकान्नोद्विजते च यः । हर्षामर्षभयोद्वेगैः , मुक्तो यस् स च मे प्रियः ॥ १२.१५

yasmānnodvijate lokaḥ , lokānnodvijate ca yaḥ ।

harṣāmarṣabhayodvegaiḥ , mukto yas sa ca me priyaḥ ॥ 12.15

12.15 Neither do they fear the vagaries of life, nor is society alarmed in their presence. They who are beyond excitement-depression-anxiety-frustration are the beloved of the Lord.

अनपेक्षः शुचिर्दक्षः , उदासीनो गतव्यथः । सर्वारम्भपरित्यागी , यो मद्भक्तस् स मे प्रियः ॥ १२.१६

anapekṣaḥ śucirdakṣaḥ , udāsīno gatavyathaḥ ।

sarvārambhaparityāgī , yo madbhaktas sa me priyaḥ ॥ 12.16

12.16 Without feverishness in head, pure in heart, skillful in action, non-interfering non-nagging Ones. They have overcome loss in their emotions, they merge into the landscape well. Their capacity to be unruffled and cause no flutter is remarkable, they are the beloved of the Lord.

यो न हृष्यति न द्वेष्टि , न शोचति न काङ्क्षति । शुभाशुभपरित्यागी , भक्तिमान्यस् स मे प्रियः ॥ १२.१७

yo na hṛṣyati na dveṣṭi , na śocati na kāṅkṣati ।

śubhāśubhaparityāgī , bhaktimānyas sa me priyaḥ ॥ 12.17

12.17 They are neither delirious nor deluded, they are neither blameful nor anxious. The brave ones who neither offend nor are offended are the beloved of the Lord.

समश् शत्रौ च मित्रे च , तथा मानापमानयोः । शीतोष्णसुखदुःखेषु , समस् सङ्गविवर्जितः ॥ १२.१८

samaś śatrau ca mitre ca , tathā mānāpamānayoḥ ।

śītoṣṇasukhaduḥkheṣu , samas saṅgavivarjitaḥ ॥ 12.18

12.18 Pleasing to friends and not aggravating to foes, gallant in handling praise and disgrace. Productive in all seasons and conditions with that endurance, and mastering their body and senses...

तुल्यनिन्दास्तुतिर् मौनी , सन्तुष्टो येन केनचित् । अनिकेतस् स्थिरमतिः , भक्तिमान् मे प्रियो नरः ॥ १२.१९

tulyanindāstutir maunī , santuṣṭo yena kenacit ।

aniketas sthiramatiḥ , bhaktimān me priyo naraḥ ॥ 12.19

12.19 Affable in failure and success, Contented come what may, without Ownership of land or property, and having a reliable intellect, is the beloved of the Lord.

ये तु धर्म्यामृतम् इदम् , यथोक्तं पर्युपासते । श्रद्दधाना मत्परमाः , भक्तास् तेऽतीव मे प्रियाः ॥ १२.२०

ye tu dharmyāmṛtam idam , yathoktaṁ paryupāsate ।

śraddadhānā matparamāḥ , bhaktās te'tīva me priyāḥ ॥ 12.20

12.20 And those who sing the glories of the Lord, those who listen to the glories of the Lord, those who eulogize the devotees of the Lord, and those who devoutedly contemplate on these aforesaid verses, are all the Lord's beloved.

Refer Guru Granth Sahib

ਸੁਣਤੇ ਪੁਨੀਤ ਕਹਤੇ ਪਵਿਤੁ ਸਤਿਗੁਰੁ ਰਹਿਆ ਭਰਪੂਰੇ ॥

ਬਿਨਵੰਤਿ ਨਾਨਕੁ ਗੁਰ ਚਰਣ ਲਾਗੇ ਵਾਜੇ ਅਨਹਦ ਤੂਰੇ ॥

सुणते पुनीत कहते पवितु सतिगुरु रहिआ भरपूरे ॥ बिनवंति नानकु गुर चरण लागे वाजे अनहद तूरे ॥

ॐ तत् सत् । इति श्रीमद्भगवद्गीतासु उपनिषत्सु ब्रह्मविद्यायां योगशास्त्रे श्रीकृष्णार्जुनसंवादे

भक्ति-योगो नाम द्वादशोऽध्यायः ॥ १२॥

oṁ tat sat । iti śrīmadbhagavadgītāsu upaniṣatsu brahmavidyāyāṁ yogaśāstre

śrīkṛṣṇārjunasaṁvāde bhakti-yogo nāma dvādaśo'dhyāyaḥ ॥ 12 ॥

13 Yoga of Matter & Consciousness

Alive_yet_Listless vs Alive_with_Spark
The mystery of Duality
all is one yet it is two too
Isn't it Three? Nope TWO...
But living, non-living and god?
Living = Matter+Mind+God
Non-Living = Matter+God

Mind = a special type of Matter+God
What do you mean Special?
Umm let us take an analogy.
Mobile Phone = Matter+ Battery+ User

Based on the level of one's vision,
1. One may view all as one in the heart and act as one with each - only possible for the so called heavenly bodies or for the five great elements or even for that which is "classified" as inert or lifeless, and also for the Brahman.
2. One may view all as one in the heart and act with intelligent discrimination with each - like a Saint, or the King or an Administrator.
3. One may view it all different in the heart and act mixedly - like human beings in different stages of evolution
4. One may view it all different in the heart and yet act according to a mechanical program - like flora and fauna.

The Kshetra and the Kshetrajna
The Field and the Player
The Arena and the Sportsman
The Stage and the Actor
The Car and the Driver
Chariot and Charioteer

A most educative and enlightening discussion on - Is there any difference between Matter and Energy and their Controller or User? What is the nature of Matter and Energy and what exactly is the Being that seems to be Alive? How does one define LIFE?

Nothing happens without Bhaiya = nothing happens without Bhaiya's laws = The good act is his laws' will. the bad act is his laws' will.

Then what is the laws' will?
If i proceed on this path i make this karma or else otherwise. Does that mean a bit of free will component is there??? YES. For the common man lots and lots of free will is there to neutralize bad karma and transcend into the divine realm (or vice versa). For the saint, devotee or yogi however, each thought is the Lord's will. Be very sure of THIS.

ॐ श्री परमात्मने नमः । अथ त्रयोदशोऽध्यायः

oṁ śrī paramātmane namaḥ । atha trayodaśo'dhyāyaḥ

Some editions of the Gita have this extra verse.

अर्जुन उवाच -

प्रकृतिं पुरुषं चैव, क्षेत्रं क्षेत्रज्ञम् एव च । एतद् वेदितुम् इच्छामि, ज्ञानं ज्ञेयं च केशव ॥

(This changes the count of verses in the Gita from 700 to 701).

arjuna uvāca

prakṛtiṁ puruṣaṁ caiva , kṣetraṁ kṣetrajñam eva ca ।

etad veditum icchāmi , jñānaṁ jñeyaṁ ca keśava ॥

श्री भगवान् उवाच

इदं शरीरं कौन्तेय , क्षेत्रम् इत्यभिधीयते । एतद् यो वेत्ति तं प्राहुः , क्षेत्रज्ञ इति तद्विदः ॥ १३.१

śrī bhagavān uvāca

idaṁ śarīraṁ kaunteya , kṣetram ityabhidhīyate ।

etad yo vetti taṁ prāhuḥ , kṣetrajña iti tadvidaḥ ॥ 13.1

The good Lord throws light

13.1 Know O Seeker - this Body of yours is named as the Field. And That principle which knows, cognizes and perceives this body - that the wise define as the FieldKnower.
The Lord thus introduces two principles - the Matter principle and the Conscious principle. The teaching begins with a duality. The duality is introduced to highlight our day to day lifestyle.
There are temporary changing things like flowers blooming, desire for an ice cream, going to Bangalore Ashram.
Then there are "unchanging" or at least seemingly permanent things like Kindness, the vast sky, the sunrise.

There are seemingly inert things like rocks and sand and water and beaches. There are seemingly alive things like men and flora and fauna. There is the employee and there is the employer. There is the student and there is the teacher. There is the wallet and there is the cash. There is a bottle and there is the milk.

Simply put this chapter highlights the Duality Principle And in the onset introduces a "notion" that the Purusha and Prakriti = Kshetra and Kshetrajna = Knower and Known are distinct/independent/governed by entirely different laws.
i.e. both these Principles have to be respected and allotted their due.

क्षेत्रज्ञं चापि मां विद्धि , सर्वक्षेत्रेषु भारत । क्षेत्रक्षेत्रज्ञयोर् ज्ञानम् , यत् तज्ज्ञानं मतं मम ॥ १३.२

kṣetrajñaṁ cāpi māṁ viddhi , sarvakṣetreṣu bhārata I

kṣetrakṣetrajñayor jñānam , yat tajjñānaṁ mataṁ mama II 13.2

13.2 And understand the sublime fact that it is the great Lord himself who is the Kshetrajna in all the Fields everywhere. Just bring it to your notice that it is the Divinity in all Bodies across the world. Such understanding is very precious, very crucial, most helpful in daily life.

तत् क्षेत्रं यच्च यादृक् च , यद्विकारि यतश्च यत् । स च यो यत्प्रभावश् च , तत् समासेन मे शृणु ॥ १३.३

tat kṣetraṁ yacca yādṛk ca , yadvikāri yataśca yat I

sa ca yo yatprabhāvaś ca , tat samāsena me śṛṇu II 13.3

13.3 We shall now delve deeper into the nature of this Field and its properties. We shall also hear about the splendorous virtues of the Divine.

ऋषिभिर् बहुधा गीतम् , छन्दोभिर् विविधैः पृथक् । ब्रह्मसूत्रपदैश् चैव , हेतुमद्भिर् विनिश्चितैः ॥ १३.४

ṛṣibhir bahudhā gītam , chandobhir vividhaiḥ pṛthak I

brahmasūtrapadaiś caiva , hetumadbhir viniścitaiḥ II 13.4

13.4 The same teaching has been taught by the Sages and seers in their own words. It has been revealed in the Scriptures to suit various personalities. The great statements, the phrases in every language and culture, and the inviolable rulings of administrators and statesmen also illumine the same knowledge regarding Matter and Spirit.

महाभूतान्यहङ्कारः , बुद्धिर् अव्यक्तम् एव च । इन्द्रियाणि दशैकं च , पञ्च चेन्द्रियगोचराः ॥ १३.५

mahābhūtānyahaṅkāraḥ , buddhir avyaktam eva ca I

indriyāṇi daśaikaṁ ca , pañca cendriyagocarāḥ II 13.5

13.5 The great Elements, the Ego, the Intellect and That which cannot be put in words; The ten Senses and organs, and their controller the Mind, and the Objects that move the senses.

Since there are five great elements - space, air, fire, water and earth; and there are five objects sabda, sparsha, rupa, rasa and gandha that move the senses, hence,
In all we can count 5+1+1+1+10+1+5 = 24 attributes have been listed in this verse.

इच्छा द्वेषस् सुखं दुःखम् , सङ्घातश् चेतना धृतिः । एतत् क्षेत्रं समासेन , सविकारम् उदाहृतम् ॥ १३.६

icchā dveṣas sukhaṁ duḥkham , saṅghātaś cetanā dhṛtiḥ I

etat kṣetraṁ samāsena , savikāram udāhṛtam II 13.6

13.6 A bundle of Desires and Dislikes resulting in Joys and Sorrows, and decision making or avoiding Will, this whole consortium has a Reflective capability. To reflect Divinity. To mirror the Luminosity. To exhibit sentience.

(This body has a faculty called अन्तःकरणः I We have body, mind, soul. The body and mind are inert matter, the soul is consciousness. However the mind reflects the light of the soul and shines like the moon, and gets mistaken for consciousness.)
Secondly, no being or object or principle has any capacity of its own to influence. However the moment Desire and Dislike arise, any inert matter gets endowed with the capacity to cause pleasure and pain. This is how with strangers one is fine, but soon new colleagues at work or new roommates in college become a headache or entangle-ache.

The Lord thus gives the 24 attributes of matter i.e. the Field. He also says that the inert matter called Field expresses in cycles of DesireDislike causing PleasurePain and exhibiting Will.

Now the Lord defines the attributes of a wise soul, of a saint, or of what is desirable and to be cultivated by human beings.

अमानित्वम् अदम्भित्वम् , अहिंसा क्षान्तिर् आर्जवम् । आचार्योपासनं शौचम् , स्थैर्यम् आत्मविनिग्रहः॥ १३.७

amānitvam adambhitvam , ahiṁsā kṣāntir ārjavam I

ācāryopāsanaṁ śaucam , sthairyam ātmavinigrahaḥ II 13.7

13.7 Humility, Frankness, Non-injury, Patience, Sincerity, Looking after the Master's needs, Purity in thought, Being Steady, Introspection.

इन्द्रियार्थेषु वैराग्यम् , अनहङ्कार एव च । जन्ममृत्युजराव्याधिदुःखदोषानुदर्शनम् ॥ १३.८

indriyārtheṣu vairāgyam , anahaṅkāra eva ca ।

janma-mṛtyu-jarā-vyādhi-duḥkha-doṣānudarśanam ॥ 13.8

13.8 Restraint of senses, Free from Mineness or Doership, Observing the frailty in the process of life, illness, old-age, and death.

असक्तिर् अनभिष्वङ्गः , पुत्रदारगृहादिषु । नित्यं च समचित्तत्वम् , इष्टानिष्टोपपत्तिषु ॥ १३.९

asaktir anabhiṣvaṅgaḥ , putradāragṛhādiṣu ।

nityaṁ ca samacittatvam , iṣṭāniṣṭopapattiṣu ॥ 13.9

13.9 Dispassion, Not overly stuck in children, spouse, material possessions, Usually having a peaceful disposition in favourable and unfavourable circumstances.

मयि चानन्ययोगेन , भक्तिर् अव्यभिचारिणी । विविक्तदेशसेवित्वम् , अरतिर् जनसंसदि ॥ १३.१०

mayi cānanyayogena , bhaktir avyabhicāriṇī ।

viviktadeśasevitvam , aratir janasaṁsadi ॥ 13.10

13.10 Having undivided attention and unswerving devotion in the Lord, Maintaining a recluse temperament and not enjoying company.

अध्यात्मज्ञाननित्यत्वम् , तत्त्वज्ञानार्थदर्शनम् । एतज्ज्ञानम् इति प्रोक्तम् , अज्ञानं यदतोऽन्यथा ॥ १३.११

adhyātmajñānanityatvam , tattvajñānārthadarśanam ।

etajjñānam iti proktam , ajñānaṁ yadato'nyathā ॥ 13.11

13.11 Being engaged in Who Am I deliberation, Keeping focus on the core principles of Life, all of this is said to be worth nourishing and upholding as the highest knowledge. Whatever is retrograde and contrary to the same is said to be Ignorance or small mindedness and to be shunned at all costs.

ज्ञेयं यत् तत् प्रवक्ष्यामि , यज्ज्ञात्वामृतम् अश्नुते । अनादिमत् परं ब्रह्म , न सत् तन्नासद् उच्यते ॥ १३.१२

jñeyaṁ yat tat pravakṣyāmi , yajjñātvāmṛtam aśnute ।

anādimat paraṁ brahma , na sat tannāsad ucyate ॥ 13.12

13.12 I shall teach you that which is absolutely essential to be known; that which grants immortality i.e. a buffer from the vicissitudes. It is the knowledge of supreme Brahman, the ultimate reality that is said to be beyond truth and untruth i.e. beyond logic and ungraspable.

(In earlier verses the attributes of Matter have been detailed, and also the virtues to be practiced by a human being for attaining success. Now verses that qualify Consciousness).

सर्वतः पाणिपादं तत् , सर्वतोऽक्षिशिरोमुखम् । सर्वतः श्रुतिमल्लोके , सर्वम् आवृत्य तिष्ठति ॥ १३.१३

sarvataḥ pāṇipādaṁ tat , sarvato'kṣiśiromukham ।

sarvataḥ śrutimalloke , sarvam āvṛtya tiṣṭhati ॥ 13.13

13.13 That can act and reach everywhere. That can sense anything that goes on in the entire world. That enjoys each and every pleasure experienced by everyone. That pervades the whole world.

सर्वेन्द्रियगुणाभासम् , सर्वेन्द्रियविवर्जितम् । असक्तं सर्वभृच्चैव , निर्गुणं गुणभोक्तृ च ॥ १३.१४

sarvendriyaguṇābhāsam , sarvendriyavivarjitam ।

asaktaṁ sarvabhṛccaiva , nirguṇaṁ guṇabhoktṛ ca ॥ 13.14

13.14 That senses each sense organ impression, yet remains free of all impressions. Without attachment That supports one and all. That experiences all pleasures, pains, emotions and seasons, yet remains unaffected and untarnished. (Like the movie Screen on which a movie is projected, like the Space in which all events and phenomena occur).

बहिर् अन्तश्च भूतानाम् , अचरं चरम् एव च । सूक्ष्मत्वात् तद् अविज्ञेयम् , दूरस्थं चान्तिके च तत् ॥ १३.१५

bahir antaśca bhūtānām , acaraṁ caram eva ca ।

sūkṣmatvāt tad avijñeyam , dūrasthaṁ cāntike ca tat ॥ 13.15

13.15 That is enveloping and also indwelling in all beings and objects. That is still, yet That reaches everywhere. Being extremely subtle That escapes all faculties and intelligence and probing. That is out of reach for the one who does not seek, and near at hand for the seeker.

अविभक्तं च भूतेषु , विभक्तम् इव च स्थितम् । भूतभर्तृ च तज्ज्ञेयम् , ग्रसिष्णु प्रभविष्णु च ॥ १३.१६

avibhaktaṁ ca bhūteṣu , vibhaktam iva ca sthitam ।

bhūtabhartṛ ca tajjñeyam , grasiṣṇu prabhaviṣṇu ca ॥ 13.16

13.16 Seamless in and through all bodies and objects, yet apparently separated from body to body. Know That to be the sustainer of all beings and things. Understand That is the destroyer and That is the creator of all beings and things.

ज्योतिषाम् अपि तज्ज्योतिः , तमसः परम् उच्यते । ज्ञानं ज्ञेयं ज्ञानगम्यम् , हृदि सर्वस्य विष्ठितम् ॥ १३.१७

jyotiṣām api tajjyotiḥ , tamasaḥ param ucyate ।

jñānaṁ jñeyaṁ jñānagamyam , hr̥di sarvasya viṣṭhitam ॥ 13.17

13.17 Also, That is the glow in every light and the spark in every intelligence; That is beyond dullness and beyond ignorance of any sort and That makes one aware of stupidity and error. That is Knowledge, That is Known, and That is the aim of every Seeking and Searching. That especially sits in every heart and in everything's core.

Refer Mundaka Upanishad 2.10

न तत्र सूर्यो भाति न चन्द्रतारकं नेमा विद्युतो भान्ति कुतोऽयमग्निः ।

तमेव भान्तमनुभाति सर्वं तस्य भासा सर्वमिदं विभाति ॥

इति क्षेत्रं तथा ज्ञानम् , ज्ञेयं चोक्तं समासतः । मद्भक्त एतद् विज्ञाय , मद्भावायोपपद्यते ॥ १३.१८

iti kṣetraṁ tathā jñānam , jñeyaṁ coktaṁ samāsataḥ ।

madbhakta etad vijñāya , madbhāvāyopapadyate ॥ 13.18

13.18 Thus the Matter and the Knowledge and the Known have been taught in brief. The sincere devotee having understood this, qualifies to attain the Highest goal - the realization of Parabrahman, the realization of supreme Godliness.

प्रकृतिं पुरुषं चैव , विद्ध्यनादी उभावपि । विकारांश्च गुणांश् चैव , विद्धि प्रकृतिसम्भवान् ॥ १३.१९

prakr̥tiṁ puruṣaṁ caiva , viddhyanādī ubhāvapi ।

vikārāṁśca guṇāṁś caiva , viddhi prakr̥tisambhavān ॥ 13.19

13.19 This process of duality in creation can also be explained by using the words Purusha - Prime, and Prakriti - Derived or Secondary. Know that the entire process of differentiation and segregation and modification and infusing things and beings with qualities, is the Derived or Secondary portion of duality, i.e. a manifestation of Prakriti alone.

(the seed-plant-tree-flower-fruit; the baby-child-youth-adult; the clay-pottery-pot; the land-city-state-laws; the Space-Time-phenomena; all of this is a function and cause and effect of Prakriti alone, understand this well. And the Purusha is something else entirely).

कार्यकरणकर्तृत्वे , हेतुः प्रकृतिर् उच्यते । (कार्यकारणकर्तृत्वे)

पुरुषस् सुखदुःखानाम् , भोक्तृत्वे हेतुर् उच्यते ॥ १३.२०

kāryakaraṇakartr̥tve , hetu× prakr̥tir ucyate । (kāryakāraṇakartr̥tve)

puruṣas sukhaduḥkhānām , bhoktr̥tve hetur ucyate ॥ 13.20

13.20 The cause and doership of objects and things and bodies and beings and sensations and emotions and thoughts and wills is said to be Prakriti. The silent witness of all phenomena; the stillness that is the contrast to the changing scenario, it is said to be Purusha.

पुरुष× प्रकृतिस्थो हि , भुङ्क्ते प्रकृतिजान् गुणान् । कारणं गुणसङ्गोऽस्य , सद्असद्योनिजन्मसु ॥ १३.२१

puruṣa× prakr̥tistho hi , bhuṅkte prakr̥tijān guṇān ।

kāraṇaṁ guṇasaṅgo'sya , sadasadyonijanmasu ॥ 13.21

13.21 Residing in all of Prakriti - innate in the entire SpaceTimePhenomenaLifeDeath continuum is the distinct entity Purusha that is aware of it all.

The Cause Effect principle rules the SpaceTime creation - As the seed so is the fruit - As the reaction so is the result - As the performance so is the reward - As the attitude so is the bonding. This is the classical law of physics and chemistry, and it is governed by Prakriti.

उपद्रष्टानुमन्ता च , भर्ता भोक्ता महेश्वरः । परमात्मेति चाप्युक्तः , देहेऽस्मिन् पुरुष× परः ॥ १३.२२

upadraṣṭānumantā ca , bhartā bhoktā maheśvaraḥ ।

paramātmeti cāpyuktaḥ , dehe'smin puruṣa× paraḥ ॥ 13.22

13.22 The intimate Witness, the non-interfering Permitter, the unattached sustainer and support, the casual Awareness is the Great Lord.

The same is also called the Supreme Soul, That is present in all bodies; and That is also referred as the Supreme Personality.

(just as Guruji famously says - choice is yours blessing is mine).

य एवं वेत्ति पुरुषम् , प्रकृतिं च गुणैः सह । सर्वथा वर्तमानोऽपि , न स भूयोऽभिजायते ॥ १३.२३

ya evaṁ vetti puruṣam , prakr̥tiṁ ca guṇaiḥ saha ।

sarvathā vartamāno'pi , na sa bhūyo'bhijāyate ॥ 13.23

13.23 The one who understands the Purusha, the Prakriti and the Play in this manner, he is shielded from sorrow, no matter what his vocation or station in life.

(it means that this understanding is fundamental to bliss. such realization once it settles in the intellect takes one beyond the ups and downs, releases one from the burdens, and is the state of saints).

ध्यानेनात्मनि पश्यन्ति , केचिद् आत्मानमात्मना । अन्ये साङ्ख्येन योगेन , कर्मयोगेन चापरे ॥ १३.२४

dhyānenātmani paśyanti , kecid ātmānamātmanā I

anye sāṅkhyena yogena , karmayogena cāpare II 13.24

13.24 Some people achieve this state through Dhyana-Meditation. Others through Gyana-Knowledge through Upanishad. Yet others through Karma-Devoted work. It is called God Realization. It is called having the vision of the Great Lord.

अन्ये त्वेवम् अजानन्तः , श्रुत्वान्येभ्य उपासते । तेऽपि चातितरन्त्येव , मृत्युं श्रुतिपरायणाः ॥ १३.२५

anye tvevam ajānantaḥ , śrutvānyebhya upāsate I

te'pi cātitarantyeva , mṛtyuṁ śrutiparāyaṇāḥ II 13.25

13.25 The remaining who are not introduced to Dhyana-Gyana-Karma Yoga, can also achieve it through listening to the Guru, listening to the Vani, listening to the Bhagvatam, i.e. through committed Sravanam of the Sacred.

यावत् सञ्जायते किञ्चित् , सत्त्वं स्थावरजङ्गमम् । क्षेत्रक्षेत्रज्ञसंयोगात् , तद् विद्धि भरतर्षभ ॥ १३.२६

yāvat sañjāyate kiñcit , sattvaṁ sthāvarajaṅgamam I

kṣetrakṣetrajñasaṁyogāt , tad viddhi bharatarṣabha II 13.26

13.26 Whatever is happening, what all events and situations arise, all that starts and stops, this whole play is the union of Matter and Consciousness, realize it O noble Seeker.

(Understand that all sacred acts and all acts of error and commission also are just a happening; this knowledge will relieve you of your stress, and will allow you to boldly align your vision to the path of righteousness and dharma).

समं सर्वेषु भूतेषु , तिष्ठन्तं परमेश्वरम् । विनश्यत्स्वविनश्यन्तम् , यः पश्यति स पश्यति ॥ १३.२७

samaṁ sarveṣu bhūteṣu , tiṣṭhantaṁ parameśvaram I

vinaśyatsvavinaśyantam , yaḥ paśyati sa paśyati II 13.27

13.27 The one who realizes that the Supreme Lord dwells alike in all beings, and realizes that factor is permanent in everyone - and all appearances are illusory, he is said to be a realized soul. He is the one who is enlightened.

This is the दिव्य दृष्टि or divine vision.

समं पश्यन् हि सर्वत्र , समवस्थितम् ईश्वरम् । न हिनस्त्यात्मनात्मानम् , ततो याति परां गतिम् ॥ १३.२८

samaṁ paśyan hi sarvatra , samavasthitam īśvaram ।

na hinastyātmanātmānam , tato yāti parāṁ gatim ॥ 13.28

13.28 Indeed having an unbiased view of all events and persons, knowing that the great lord is present alike in all, by this realization he is prevented from harm and erroneous action.
He thereby sets his course on the Highest and thus attains liberation.

प्रकृत्यैव च कर्माणि , क्रियमाणानि सर्वशः । यः पश्यति तथाऽऽत्मानम् , अकर्तारं स पश्यति ॥ १३.२९

prakr̥tyaiva ca karmāṇi , kriyamāṇāni sarvaśaḥ ।

yaḥ paśyati tathā''tmānam , akartāraṁ sa paśyati ॥ 13.29

13.29 He who thus understands that the onus of doership is on Nature, and that all beings have the actionless Witness within, he alone has the correct vision. He alone perceives the Truth.

यदा भूतपृथग्भावम् , एकस्थम् अनुपश्यति । तत एव च विस्तारम् , ब्रह्म सम्पद्यते तदा ॥ १३.३०

yadā bhūtapr̥thagbhāvam , ekastham anupaśyati ।

tata eva ca vistāram , brahma sampadyate tadā ॥ 13.30

13.30 When one realizes the infinite diversity in creation to have the presence of the One Lord, and realizes that the Prime entity in creation is the Brahman or the Great Lord, then one's vision is said to be purified and one's nature is said to be Divine.

अनादित्वान्निर्गुणत्वात् , परमात्मा अयम् अव्ययः । शरीरस्थोऽपि कौन्तेय , न करोति न लिप्यते ॥ १३.३१

anāditvānnirguṇatvāt , paramātmā ayam avyayaḥ ।

śarīrastho'pi kaunteya , na karoti na lipyate ॥ 13.31

13.31 That has no beginning and no attributes. This Supreme Soul is unchanging without parts i.e. it is undecaying and seamless. Even though it is identified with body, yet it does not govern the body nor is it affected by the body-mind complex O Kaunteya.

यथा सर्वगतं सौक्ष्म्यात् , आकाशं नोपलिप्यते । सर्वत्रावस्थितो देहे , तथाऽऽत्मा नोपलिप्यते ॥ १३.३२

yathā sarvagataṁ saukṣmyāt , ākāśaṁ nopalipyate I

sarvatrāvasthito dehe , tathā''tmā nopalipyate II 13.32

13.32 Just as all expansive Space due to its infinitesimal subtlety remains unaffected, similarly even though present in each body, the Soul remains pure, untouched.

यथा प्रकाशयत्येकः , कृत्स्नं लोकम् इमं रविः । क्षेत्रं क्षेत्री तथा कृत्स्नम् , प्रकाशयति भारत ॥ १३.३३

yathā prakāśayatyekaḥ , kr̥tsnaṁ lokam imaṁ raviḥ I

kṣetraṁ kṣetrī tathā kr̥tsnam , prakāśayati bhārata II 13.33

13.33 Just as one Sun shines on the entire Planet, similarly the one Divinity infuses consciousness in the whole of matter.

क्षेत्रक्षेत्रज्ञयोर् एवम् , अन्तरं ज्ञानचक्षुषा । भूतप्रकृतिमोक्षं च , ये विदुर् यान्ति ते परम् ॥ १३.३४

kṣetrakṣetrajñayor evam , antaraṁ jñānacakṣuṣā I

bhūtaprakr̥timokṣaṁ ca , ye vidur yānti te param II 13.34

13.34 With the intellect of discrimination those who are thus firmly convinced of the one Divinity in all Matter, and have realized the playfulness of the Energies, those knowledgeable ones attain perfect rhythm i.e. perfect peace.

ॐ तत् सत् । इति श्रीमद्भगवद्गीतासु उपनिषत्सु ब्रह्मविद्यायां योगशास्त्रे श्रीकृष्णार्जुनसंवादे

क्षेत्र-क्षेत्रज्ञ-विभाग-योगो नाम त्रयोदशोऽध्यायः ॥ १३ ॥

oṁ tat sat I iti śrīmadbhagavadgītāsu upaniṣatsu brahmavidyāyāṁ yogaśāstre śrīkr̥ṣṇārjunasaṁvāde kṣetra-kṣetrajña-vibhāga-yogo nāma trayodaśo'dhyāyaḥ

II 13 II

14 Yoga of triCreative Energies

Yoga of 3 Temperaments w.r.t Temperament Free
Yoga of 3 Attitudes w.r.t Beyond Attitude
Yoga of 3 Gunas w.r.t Guna Atitah, Red Green Blue RGB fields

ॐ श्री परमात्मने नमः । अथ चतुर्दशोऽध्यायः

oṁ śrī paramātmane namaḥ I atha caturdaśo'dhyāyaḥ

श्री भगवान् उवाच

परं भूयः प्रवक्ष्यामि , ज्ञानानां ज्ञानम् उत्तमम् । यज्ज्ञात्वा मुनयस् सर्वे , परां सिद्धिम् इतो गताः ॥ १४.१

śrī bhagavān uvāca

paraṁ bhūyaḥ pravakṣyāmi , jñānānāṁ jñānam uttamam I

yajjñātvā munayas sarve , parāṁ siddhim ito gatāḥ II 14.1

The Great Teacher said

14.1 Once again I shall impart that supreme science that is the highest truth, the best amongst all sciences. Understanding which the scientists of yore attained Final beatitude starting from here.

इदं ज्ञानम् उपाश्रित्य , मम साधर्म्यम् आगताः । सर्गेऽपि नोपजायन्ते , प्रलये न व्यथन्ति च ॥ १४.२

idaṁ jñānam upāśritya , mama sādharmyam āgatāḥ I

sarge'pi nopajāyante , pralaye na vyathanti ca II 14.2

14.2 Delving and applying this science, they attained the same qualities as of the Divine. i.e. they maintained equanimity and carried on working pleasantly through each stormy upheaval. They also maintained their wits in times of wars and peril. i.e. their state is one of no regrets over past mistakes and no forebodings for future uncertainties.

मम योनिर् महद् ब्रह्म , तस्मिन् गर्भं दधाम्यहम् । सम्भवस् सर्वभूतानाम् , ततो भवति भारत ॥ १४.२

mama yonir mahad brahma , tasmin garbhaṁ dadhāmyaham I

sambhavas sarvabhūtānām , tato bhavati bhārata II 14.3

14.3 My energies in the form of the secondary reality of the great natural forces, swirl forth as if pregnant with happenings and doings. My shakti carries the potential of each thing and being, that manifests appropriately in Space Time. (Like we say Maha Shivaratri is the occasion when the Infinity touches the finite, when Consciousness touches Matter, when the Lord's energy bubbles forth and comes alive).

सर्वयोनिषु कौन्तेय , मूर्तयस् सम्भवन्ति याः । तासां ब्रह्म महद् योनिः , अहं बीजप्रदः पिता ॥ १४.४

sarvayoniṣu kaunteya , mūrtayas sambhavanti yāḥ I

tāsāṁ brahma mahad yoniḥ , ahaṁ bījapradaḥ pitā II 14.4

14.4 O Kaunteya! In all names and forms and particles, the powerful Nature becomes the bodily container. The Divine infuses soul in each, sentiency or consciousness is impregnated within each independent unit.

(The Lord clearly says this essential commonality in each one of us is the Soul. Hence each being and body is worthy of respect, honour in its due context).

सत्त्वं रजस् तम इति , गुणाः प्रकृतिसम्भवाः । निबध्नन्ति महाबाहो , देहे देहिनम् अव्ययम् ॥ १४.५

sattvaṁ rajas tama iti , guṇāḥ prakṛtisambhavāḥ I

nibadhnanti mahābāho , dehe dehinam avyayam II 14.5

14.5 Three energies named Sattva, Rajas and Tamas are born of the mighty Nature. Each body and being is a mix of these energies covering the full spectrum of probability and possibility while the changeless Soul is contained within in varying degrees of intensity.

Consider electrical energy as the 3phase output. Consider primary colours as red, green and blue. Consider light as day, dawn-dusk and night. Consider male, female and transgender hormones. Ayurvedic constitution as vata, pitta and kapha; a stable stool with 3 legs, spatial mathematical coordinates x, y and z, this creation rests on 3-dimensions.

(the Divine spark is present unmodified in each body, however in different amplitude and vitality, like a small flame and a big fire).

Sanskrit guna = quality or attribute, also guna = rope or glue, thus the 3 gunas glue the mind to the body. Mind is the reflection of the Soul.

तत्र सत्त्वं निर्मलत्वात् , प्रकाशकम् अनामयम् । सुखसङ्गेन बध्नाति , ज्ञानसङ्गेन चानघ ॥ १४.६

tatra sattvaṁ nirmalatvāt , prakāśakam anāmayam I

sukhasaṅgena badhnāti , jñānasaṅgena cānagha II 14.6

14.6 Among these energies, Sattva is gentle, glowing and non-poisonous. Its glue on the Mind is based on decency, non-invasiveness and thirst for knowledge O Innocent One!

रजो रागात्मकं विद्धि , तृष्णासङ्गसमुद्भवम् । तन्निबध्नाति कौन्तेय , कर्मसङ्गेन देहिनम् ॥ १४.७

rajo rāgātmakaṁ viddhi , tr̥ṣṇāsaṅgasamudbhavam I

tannibadhnāti kaunteya , karmasaṅgena dehinam II 14.7

14.7 Understand Rajas as strong passion, feverishness and ambition. It glues the Mind by the force of extrovert activity, hustle and bustle O Kaunteya!

तमस् त्वज्ञानजं विद्धि , मोहनं सर्वदेहिनाम् । प्रमादालस्यनिद्राभिः , तन्निबध्नाति भारत ॥ १४.८

tamas tvajñānajaṁ viddhi , mohanaṁ sarvadehinām I

pramādālasyanidrābhiḥ , tannibadhnāti bhārata II 14.8

14.8 Understand Tamas as ignorance, and the shield of strong packaging. Its glue consists of stubbornness, idleness and day-dreaming O Bharata!

सत्त्वं सुखे सञ्जयति , रजः कर्मणि भारत । ज्ञानम् आवृत्य तु तमः , प्रमादे सञ्जयत्युत ॥ १४.९

sattvaṁ sukhe sañjayati , rajaḥ karmaṇi bhārata I

jñānam āvr̥tya tu tamaḥ , pramāde sañjayatyuta II 14.9

14.9 Sattva glues the Mind to decent comforts and Rajas to workaholism. Tamas with its shielding nature makes the Mind adamant.

रजस् तमश् चाभिभूय , सत्त्वं भवति भारत । रजस् सत्त्वं तमश् चैव , तमस् सत्त्वं रजस् तथा ॥ १४.१०

rajas tamaś cābhibhūya , sattvaṁ bhavati bhārata I

rajas sattvaṁ tamaś caiva , tamas sattvaṁ rajas tathā II 14.10

14.10 A being assumes Sattvic status when his Rajas and Tamas become feeble, and similarly Rajasic status when that energy predominates, or Tamasic state as the case may be. (based on which energy is dominant in the present, the outlook, virtues and habits will assume that flavour for anybody).

सर्वद्वारेषु देहेऽस्मिन् , प्रकाश उपजायते । ज्ञानं यदा तदा विद्यात् , विवृद्धं सत्त्वम् इत्युत ॥ १४.११

sarvadvāreṣu dehe'smin , prakāśa upajāyate I

jñānaṁ yadā tadā vidyāt , vivr̥ddhaṁ sattvam ityuta II 14.11

14.11 When each opening of one's mind yearns for the light, when thoughts are thirsting for wisdom, know that Sattva is influencing.

लोभ॰ प्रवृत्तिरारम्भः , कर्मणाम् अशमस् स्पृहा । रजस्येतानि जायन्ते , विवृद्धे भरतर्षभ ॥ १४.१२

lobha॰ pravṛttirārambhaḥ , karmaṇām aśamas spṛhā ।

rajasyetāni jāyante , vivṛddhe bharatarṣabha ॥ 14.12

14.12 Ambition, Planning, Movement, Engaging and Spurt of Energy; these are the influence of Rajas O Foremost Citizen!

अप्रकाशोऽप्रवृत्तिश्च , प्रमादो मोह एव च । तमस्येतानि जायन्ते , विवृद्धे कुरुनन्दन ॥ १४.१३

aprakāśo'pravṛttiśca , pramādo moha eva ca ।

tamasyetāni jāyante , vivṛddhe kurunandana ॥ 14.13

14.13 Rigidity, Inaction, Idling and Day dreaming arise under the influence of Tamas O Kurunandana!

यदा सत्त्वे प्रवृद्धे तु , प्रलयं याति देहभृत् । तदोत्तमविदां लोकान् , अमलान् प्रतिपद्यते ॥ १४.१४

yadā sattve pravṛddhe tu , pralayaṁ yāti dehabhṛt ।

tadottamavidāṁ lokān , amalān pratipadyate ॥ 14.14

14.14 If a person goes to sleep or meditates under the influence of Sattva, then he rises up in august company, then he is naturally drawn upon waking to the community of the wise and the well settled.

रजसि प्रलयं गत्वा , कर्मसङ्गिषु जायते । तथा प्रलीनस् तमसि , मूढयोनिषु जायते ॥ १४.१५

rajasi pralayaṁ gatvā , karmasaṅgiṣu jāyate ।

tathā pralīnas tamasi , mūḍhayoniṣu jāyate ॥ 14.15

14.15 Likewise arising from a Rajasic sleep one seeks the company of the ambitious and those engaged in mechanical materialist aims. And waking up from a Tamasic state one seeks such men who are steeped in vice.

कर्मणस् सुकृतस्याहुः , सात्त्विकं निर्मलं फलम् । रजसस् तु फलं दुःखम् , अज्ञानं तमस॰ फलम् ॥ १४.१६

karmaṇas sukṛtasyāhuḥ , sāttavikaṁ nirmalaṁ phalam ।

rajasas tu phalaṁ duḥkham , ajñānaṁ tamasa॰ phalam ॥ 14.16

14.16 The wise say that the result of Sattvic action is highly rewarding, the result of Rajasic activity is Stress and Strain, and the consequence of Tamasic lifestyle is a thwarted vegetable existence.

सत्त्वात् सञ्जायते ज्ञानम् , रजसो लोभ एव च । प्रमादमोहौ तमसः , भवतोऽज्ञानम् एव च ॥ १४.१७

sattvāt sañjāyate jñānam , rajaso lobha eva ca I

pramādamohau tamasaḥ , bhavato'jñānam eva ca II 14.17

14.17 Thirst for the finer aspects is born of Sattva, High ambition is born of Rajas, and stubbornness, cloudiness and dullness are the outcome of Tamas.

ऊर्ध्वं गच्छन्ति सत्त्वस्थाः ,मध्ये तिष्ठन्ति राजसाः । जघन्यगुणवृत्तिस्थाः ,अधो गच्छन्ति तामसाः ॥ १४.१८

ūrdhvaṁ gacchanti sattvasthāḥ , madhye tiṣṭhanti rājasāḥ I

jaghanyaguṇavr̥ttisthāḥ , adho gacchanti tāmasāḥ II 14.18

14.18 Sattvic people ascend the ladder of evolution, Rajasic ones remain stuck more or less, while the Tamasic drop down into further mundane roles.

नान्यं गुणेभ्यः कर्तारम् , यदा द्रष्टा अनुपश्यति । गुणेभ्यश्च परं वेत्ति , मद्भावं सोऽधिगच्छति ॥ १४.१९

nānyaṁ guṇebhyaḥ kartāram , yadā draṣṭā anupaśyati I

guṇebhyaśca paraṁ vetti , madbhāvaṁ so'dhigacchati II 14.19

14.19 Perchance a moment comes when a person realizes the doer to be the gunas alone -the play of the energies, and sees the soul as a distinct entity; in that moment his mind gets free and merges in divinity.

गुणान् एतान् अतीत्य त्रीन् , देही देहसमुद्भवान् । जन्ममृत्युजरादुःखैः , विमुक्तोऽमृतम् अश्नुते ॥ १४.२०

guṇān etān atītya trīn , dehī dehasamudbhavān I

janmamr̥tyujarāduḥkhaiḥ , vimukto'mr̥tam aśnute II 14.20

14.20 Having overcome the might of the tri Guna energies; the mind dissociates from the natural attributes of birth i.e. excitement, death i.e. frustration, spurious limitations of old age, and assorted sorrows of body-emotion-memory. Thus it becomes perfectly pure and enjoys the simple serene state.

अर्जुन उवाच

कैर् लिङ्गैस् त्रीन् गुणान् एतान् , अतीतो भवति प्रभो । किमाचारः कथं चैतान् , त्रीन् गुणान् अतिवर्तते ॥ १४.२१

arjuna uvāca

kair liṅgais trīn guṇān etān , atīto bhavati prabho I

kimācāraḥ kathaṁ caitān , trīn guṇān ativartate II 14.21

Arjuna has a question...

14.21 O dear Lord! What differentiates such a person who has attained mastery over the tri Gunas? How does he conduct himself in the world? How does he manage to overcome and keep at bay the mighty Energies?

श्री भगवान् उवाच

प्रकाशं च प्रवृत्तिं च , मोहम् एव च पाण्डव । न द्वेष्टि सम्प्रवृत्तानि , न निवृत्तानि काङ्क्षति ॥ १४.२२

śrī bhagavān uvāca

prakāśaṁ ca pravr̥ttiṁ ca , moham eva ca pāṇḍava I

na dveṣṭi sampravr̥ttāni , na nivr̥ttāni kāṅkṣati II 14.22

The gracious Lord replies...

14.22 Such a man rejects neither delightful occasions, nor shies from hard labour when needed. Even times of stormy perils are weathered well by him O Pandava! He neither escapes from the task at hand nor does he actively solicit any particular business or ceremony.

उदासीनवदासीनः , गुणैर् यो न विचाल्यते । गुणा वर्तन्त इत्येव , योऽवतिष्ठति नेङ्गते ॥ १४.२३

udāsīnavadāsīnaḥ , guṇair yo na vicālyate I

guṇā vartanta ityeva , yo'vatiṣṭhati neṅgate II 14.23

14.23 He behaves as if unconcerned by the Guna forces, and remains unmoved by the stress and strain. Knowing fully well that it is a high drama movie only, his emotions remain flutter free and calm.

समदुःखसुखस् स्वस्थः , समलोष्टाश्मकाञ्चनः । तुल्यप्रियाप्रियो धीरः , तुल्यनिन्दात्मसंस्तुतिः ॥ १४.२४

samaduḥkhasukhas svasthaḥ , samaloṣṭāśmakāñcanaḥ I

tulyapriyāpriyo dhīraḥ , tulyanindātmasaṁstutiḥ II 14.24

14.24 He can handle sorrows as well as joys as his wits are with him. He makes good use of clay, rock, and precious metals. He can rationalize and use advantageously both favourable and unfavourable situations. He bravely weathers sharp criticism and also graciously acknowledges heaps of praise.

मानापमानयोस् तुल्यः , तुल्यो मित्रारिपक्षयोः । सर्वारम्भपरित्यागी , गुणातीतस् स उच्यते ॥ १४.२५

mānāpamānayos tulyaḥ , tulyo mitrāripakṣayoḥ I

sarvārambhaparityāgī , guṇātītas sa ucyate II 14.25

14.25 He is not shattered by defeats to friends and family, nor does he exult when enemies and antagonists come to ruin. He keeps the horses of ambition in check, shies away from lotteries, giveaways and the like. Such a one is said to have mastered the tri Guna forces.

मां च योऽव्यभिचारेण , भक्तियोगेन सेवते । स गुणान् समतीत्यैतान् , ब्रह्मभूयाय कल्पते ॥ १४.२६

mām̐ ca yo'vyabhicāreṇa , bhaktiyogena sevate I

sa guṇān samatītyaitān , brahmabhūyāya kalpate II 14.26

14.26 He who lives with the welfare of all at heart, such a one having harmonized his impulses-bursts-moods, qualifies to attain Brahman, i.e. the lasting peaceful protective nourishing existence.

ब्रह्मणो हि प्रतिष्ठाहम् , अमृतस्याव्ययस्य च । शाश्वतस्य च धर्मस्य , सुखस्यैकान्तिकस्य च ॥ १४.२७

brahmaṇo hi pratiṣṭhāham , amr̥tasyāvyayasya ca I

śāśvatasya ca dharmasya , sukhasyaikāntikasya ca II 14.27

14.27 Indeed the Divine is the provider of sweet nectar and guilt-free reward. The Divine entertains all seekers and showers abundant bounties.

ॐ तत् सत् । इति श्रीमद्भगवद्गीतासु उपनिषत्सु ब्रह्मविद्यायां योगशास्त्रे श्रीकृष्णार्जुनसंवादे

गुण-त्रय-विभाग-योगो नाम चतुर्दशोऽध्यायः ॥ १४ ॥

om̐ tat sat I iti śrīmadbhagavadgītāsu upaniṣatsu brahmavidyāyām̐ yogaśāstre

śrīkr̥ṣṇārjunasam̐vāde guṇa-traya-vibhāga-yogo nāma caturdaśo'dhyāyaḥ

|| 14 ||

15 Yoga of the Ideal Man

Lordly Traits and Parameters

ॐ श्री परमात्मने नमः । अथ पञ्चदशोऽध्यायः

oṁ śrī paramātmane namaḥ । atha pañcadaśo'dhyāyaḥ

श्री भगवान् उवाच

ऊर्ध्वमूलम् अधःशाखम् , अश्वत्थं प्राहुर् अव्ययम् । छन्दांसि यस्य पर्णानि , यस्तं वेद स वेदवित् ॥ १५.१

śrī bhagavān uvāca

ūrdhvamūlam adhaḥśākham , aśvatthaṁ prāhur avyayam ।

chandāṁsi yasya parṇāni , yastaṁ veda sa vedavit ॥ 15.1

The great Lord continues

15.1 With cause earlier and effect later, a seed grows into the mighty Peepul tree. Its leaves are nourishing chlorophyll generating and rustling sound producing. One who understands the life-cycle and purpose of a tree gets realization.

अधश् चोर्ध्वं प्रसृतास् तस्य शाखाः , गुणप्रवृद्धा विषयप्रवालाः ।

अधश्च मूलान्यनुसन्ततानि , कर्मानुबन्धीनि मनुष्यलोके ॥ १५.२

adhaś cordhvaṁ prasr̥tās tasya śākhāḥ , guṇapravr̥ddhā viṣayapravālāḥ ।

adhaśca mūlānyanusantatāni , karmānubandhīni manuṣyaloke ॥ 15.2

15.2 Majestic branches spread all around are like the virtues and vices strengthened by alert senses. Firm roots anchor the tree just as great deeds make a man well entrenched in life.

न रूपमस्येह तथोपलभ्यते , नान्तो न चादिर् न च सम्प्रतिष्ठा ।

अश्वत्थमेनं सुविरूढमूलम् ,असङ्गशस्त्रेण दृढेन छित्त्वा ॥ १५.३

na rūpamasyeha tathopalabhyate , nānto na cādir na ca sampratiṣṭhā ।

aśvatthamenaṁ suvirūḍhamūlam , asaṅgaśastreṇa dr̥ḍhena chittvā ॥ 15.3

15.3 Just as the mind of a tree is stoic and incomprehensible, so is life's journey confusing. In a flash of bravery challenge the purpose and direction of life.

ततः पदं तत् परिमार्गितव्यम् ,यस्मिन् गता न निवर्तन्ति भूयः ।

तमेव चाद्यं पुरुषं प्रपद्ये , यतः प्रवृत्तिः प्रसृता पुराणी ॥ १५.४

tata× padaṁ tat parimārgitavyam , yasmin gatā na nivartanti bhūyaḥ I

tameva cādyaṁ puruṣaṁ prapadye , yata× pravr̥tti× prasr̥tā purāṇī II 15.4

15.4 And then make a course correction so that the proper final destination is reached. Make a commitment to attain what the ancient great one accomplished.

(Seek what your noble and famous predecessors realized. They have left a clear cut path, let that be your rudder and navigation).

निर्मानमोहा जितसङ्गदोषाः , अध्यात्मनित्या विनिवृत्तकामाः ।

द्वन्द्वैर् विमुक्तास् सुखदुःखसञ्ज्ञैः , गच्छन्त्यमूढा× पदम् अव्ययं तत् ॥ १५.५

nirmānamohā jitasaṅgadoṣāḥ , adhyātmanityā vinivr̥ttakāmāḥ I

dvandvair vimuktās sukhaduḥkhasañjñaiḥ ,

gacchantyamūḍhā× padam avyayaṁ tat II 15.5

15.5 Rise above false pride and infatuation. Vanquish your entanglements and messy affairs. Be engrossed in earnest duty, free from distractions. Rescue yourself from cross purposes that leads to fits and starts. Thus being clear headed cross the finishing line with elan.

न तद्भासयते सूर्यः , न शशाङ्को न पावकः । यद्गत्वा न निवर्तन्ते , तद्धाम परमं मम ॥ १५.६

na tadbhāsayate sūryaḥ , na śaśāṅko na pāvakaḥ I

yadgatvā na nivartante , taddhāma paramaṁ mama II 15.6

15.6 That which even the light of the sun or moon nor the discerning can illumine, such is the farthest ideal you have to aim for and attempt.

ममैवांशो जीवलोके , जीवभूतस् सनातनः । मनःषष्ठानि इन्द्रियाणि , प्रकृतिस्थानि कर्षति ॥ १५.७

mamaivāṁśo jīvaloke , jīvabhūtas sanātanaḥ I

manaḥṣaṣṭhāni indriyāṇi , prakr̥tisthāni karṣati II 15.7

15.7 A part of the Supreme Soul manifests in the living creation. That part of the Supreme Consciousness present in material creation is called Jiva, since it gets identified with the senses and mind as the sixth parameter.

"a part" here means the "understandable part" or "comprehensible part". Since the Supreme Soul is otherwise beyond all comprehension. The Soul present in each individual "living" being is called Jiva. Whereas the consciousness present in "non-

living" objects is simply called unidentified soul. Technically the difference between living and non-living is thus
LIVING = Soul+Mind+Senses+Body = Jiva+Body.
NON-LIVING = Soul+Body.
where Mind+Senses is that part of the body which travels along with the Soul even after the body perishes, and attains a new body. Mind+Senses is a kind of veil or shade that gets identified with the Soul and preserves its "independent separate status", until a particular Soul gets free and obtains nirvana.

शरीरं यदवाप्नोति , यच्चाप्युत्क्रामतीश्वरः । गृहीत्वैतानि संयाति , वायुर् गन्धानिवाशयात् ॥ १५.८

śarīraṁ yadavāpnoti , yaccāpyutkrāmatīśvaraḥ ।

gṛhītvaitāni saṁyāti , vāyur gandhānivāśayāt ॥ 15.8

15.8 Thus the Supreme Consciousness acquires a body and when it leaves the body, it takes them - mind and senses - just as a gust of wind carries the scent away from an object.

श्रोत्रं चक्षुस् स्पर्शनं च , रसनं घ्राणम् एव च । अधिष्ठाय मनश् चायम् , विषयान् उपसेवते ॥ १५.९

śrotraṁ cakṣus sparśanaṁ ca , rasanaṁ ghrāṇam eva ca ।

adhiṣṭhāya manaś cāyam , viṣayān upasevate ॥ 15.9

15.9 Controlling the ear, eye, skin, tongue and nose, the mind in the presence of this - the soul - enjoys the objects of senses.

(This verse emphasises that the body and senses and mind function only due to the soul's presence. One may wonder, and what exactly is the bodySensesMind stuff and how is it different from the Soul? Vedanta answers this with the analogy of the spider and its web. Another metaphor is that the bodySensesMind stuff is simply the leela, the shadow, the shakti of Brahman. The simile is the Lord and his Sport, or Man and his reflection in the mirror.).

उत्क्रामन्तं स्थितं वापि , भुञ्जानं वा गुणान्वितम् । विमूढा नानुपश्यन्ति , पश्यन्ति ज्ञानचक्षुषः ॥ १५.१०

utkrāmantaṁ sthitaṁ vāpi , bhuñjānaṁ vā guṇānvitam ।

vimūḍhā nānupaśyanti , paśyanti jñānacakṣuṣaḥ ॥ 15.10

15.10 The unevolved cannot discriminate these components within themselves, of the Travels and the Stops from one body to next of the Soul shaded by the Mind and Senses. Only the wise are aware of these things.

(the foolish think the bodySensesMindSoul is one Thing, they cannot distinguish the fourfold stature, i.e. they think it all perishes when the body perishes. So they do not attempt to learn and form habits that will extricate their soul. And what are these habits? A combination - multivitamin - multigrain - of Sadhana Yoga Pranayama Meditation, Seva social works and protecting the ecosystem, Satsang company of the Guru and wise people and scriptures).

यतन्तो योगिनश् चैनम् ,पश्यन्त्यात्मन्यवस्थितम् । यतन्तोऽप्यकृतात्मानः, नैनं पश्यन्त्यचेतसः ॥ १५.११

yatanto yoginaś cainam , paśyantyātmanyavasthitam ।

yatanto'pyakr̥tātmānaḥ , nainaṁ paśyantyacetasaḥ ॥ 15.11

15.11 With self-effort the seeker of truth gets this discrimination. The others who are not after the ultimate reality can toil and strive all to no avail, lacking intelligence for the highest.

यदादित्यगतं तेजः , जगद्भासयतेऽखिलम् । यच्चन्द्रमसि यच्चाग्नौ , तत् तेजो विद्धि मामकम् ॥ १५.१२

yadādityagataṁ tejaḥ , jagadbhāsayate'khilam ।

yaccandramasi yaccāgnau , tat tejo viddhi māmakam ॥ 15.12

15.12 The luminous rays of the sun that shine all over the globe, and the moonlight that nourishes all herbs, and the Will that propels all beings, know these to be due to the Supreme Soul.

गामाविश्य च भूतानि , धारयाम्यहमोजसा । पुष्णामि चौषधीस् सर्वाः , सोमो भूत्वा रसात्मकः ॥ १५.१३

gāmāviśya ca bhūtāni , dhārayāmyahamojasā ।

puṣṇāmi cauṣadhīs sarvāḥ , somo bhūtvā rasātmakaḥ ॥ 15.13

15.13 Permeating the planet the Supreme Soul supports all life, and nourishes the fruit producing plants, infusing nectar in them.

अहं वैश्वानरो भूत्वा , प्राणिनां देहम् आश्रितः । प्राणापानसमायुक्तः , पचाम्यन्नं चतुर्विधम् ॥ १५.१४

ahaṁ vaiśvānaro bhūtvā , prāṇināṁ deham āśritaḥ ।

prāṇāpānasamāyuktaḥ , pacāmyannaṁ caturvidham ॥ 15.14

15.14 Having become the circulatory, respiratory, digestive and nervous systems the Soul runs them all autonomously unaided. Fourfold is the four actions - sitting, standing, moving and lying. Fourfold is also the four states - awake, dreaming, deep sleep and turiya. Fourfold is again the four stages - brahmacharya childhood, grihasta householder, vanaprasta retired and sannyasa renounced. Again we see fourfold in a

match there are two teams and the umpire and the spectators. The soul makes all these four happen automatically for each being.

सर्वस्य चाहं हृदि सन्निविष्टः , मत्तस् स्मृतिर् ज्ञानम् अपोहनं च ।

वेदैश्च सर्वैर् अहमेव वेद्यः , वेदान्तकृद् वेदविदेव चाहम् ॥ १५.१५

sarvasya cāhaṁ hṛdi sanniviṣṭaḥ , mattas smṛtir jñānam apohanaṁ ca ।

vedaiśca sarvair ahameva vedyaḥ , vedāntakṛd vedavideva cāham ॥ 15.15

15.15 The soul resides in the heart of all beings. The soul directs acquisition of right knowledge, storing of experiences for helping in decision making, and erasing of unwanted and irrelevant stuff. By a study of the scriptures the soul can be sought, the soul alone is worth seeking. Indeed the soul is the director, producer and actor, the all knower and experiencer.

द्वाविमौ पुरुषौ लोके , क्षरश् चाक्षर एव च । क्षरस् सर्वाणि भूतानि , कूटस्थोऽक्षर उच्यते ॥ १५.१६

dvāvimau puruṣau loke , kṣaraś cākṣara eva ca ।

kṣaras sarvāṇi bhūtāni , kūṭastho'kṣara ucyate ॥ 15.16

15.16 The world is composed of duality, viz. the perishable and the imperishable. The bodies are called perishable while the imperishable is called rock-like invincible nature.

उत्तमᳵ पुरुषस् त्वन्यः , परमात्मेत्युदाहृतः । यो लोकत्रयमाविश्य , बिभर्त्यव्यय ईश्वरः ॥ १५.१७

uttamaᳵ puruṣas tvanyaḥ , paramātmetyudāhṛtaḥ ।

yo lokatrayamāviśya , bibhartyavyaya īśvaraḥ ॥ 15.17

15.17 However the highest being is yet another entity. This third entity is called the Supreme Soul, and he pervades the trinity - visible, invisible and nether worlds. This Lord is all sustaining, unchanging and inconceivable

यस्मात् क्षरम् अतीतोऽहम् ,अक्षराद् अपि चोत्तमः । अतोऽस्मि लोके वेदे च ,प्रथितᳵ पुरुषोत्तमः ॥ १५.१८

yasmāt kṣaram atīto'ham , akṣarād api cottamaḥ ।

ato'smi loke vede ca , prathitaᳵ puruṣottamaḥ ॥ 15.18

15.18 Since the Lord excels the perishable bodies, and since he even surpasses the imperishable nature and heavenly bodies, hence the Lord is known in the world and in the sacred scriptures as the Ideal Man. The highest being. The ultimate.

यो माम् एवम् असम्मूढः , जानाति पुरुषोत्तमम् । स सर्वविद्भजति माम् , सर्वभावेन भारत ॥ १५.१९

yo mām evam asammūḍhaḥ , jānāti puruṣottamam ।

sa sarvavidbhajati mām , sarvabhāvena bhārata ॥ 15.19

15.19 The one whose veil has dropped knows the Lord to be the highest being. And with firm conviction worships the supreme reality O Bharata!

इति गुह्यतमं शास्त्रम् , इदम् उक्तं मयानघ । एतद्बुद्ध्वा बुद्धिमान् स्यात् , कृतकृत्यश् च भारत ॥ १५.२०

iti guhyatamaṁ śāstram , idam uktaṁ mayānagha ।

etadbuddhvā buddhimān syāt , kr̥takr̥tyaś ca bhārata ॥ 15.20

15.20 Thus is this top secret science been decoded by Me, O Irreproachable One! Understanding this science, one becomes wise, perfected and fulfilled O Bharata!

ॐ तत् सत् । इति श्रीमद्भगवद्गीतासु उपनिषत्सु ब्रह्मविद्यायां योगशास्त्रे श्रीकृष्णार्जुनसंवादे

पुरुषोत्तम-योगो नाम पञ्चदशोऽध्यायः ॥ १५ ॥

oṁ tat sat । iti śrīmadbhagavadgītāsu upaniṣatsu brahmavidyāyāṁ yogaśāstre śrīkr̥ṣṇārjunasaṁvāde puruṣottama-yogo nāma pañcadaśo'dhyāyaḥ

॥ 15 ॥

16 Yoga of Good and Bad Habits

Devi Asuri Sampatti Vibhaga Yogah
Yoga of Divine and Demonic Traits
Yoga of Freeing and Binding Natures
Yoga of Caring and Heartless Inclinations

Guruji initiated reading of the Bhagavad Gita in 2004 in Bangalore Ashram. At that time he asked each ashramite to by heart 10 verses and told that he would hear us recite the same. To my ĺot came the first ten verses of the 16th chapter. I still remember i could by heart only three verses and was struggling to memorize few more...

ॐ श्री परमात्मने नमः । अथ षोडशोऽध्यायः

oṁ śrī paramātmane namaḥ I atha ṣoḍaśo'dhyāyaḥ

श्री भगवान् उवाच

अभयं सत्त्वसंशुद्धिः , ज्ञानयोगव्यवस्थितिः । दानं दमश्च यज्ञश्च , स्वाध्यायस् तप आर्जवम् ॥ १६.१

śrī bhagavān uvāca

abhayaṁ sattvasaṁśuddhiḥ , jñānayogavyavasthitiḥ I

dānaṁ damaśca yajñaśca , svādhyāyas tapa ārjavam II 16.1

The blessed Lord continues

16.1 Fearlessness in general, Sattva solidified, Steadfastness in Thought and Deed, Social Service, Self Restraint in times of difficulty, Giving oblations to fire, practice of Self Study, Enduring discipline willingly and Sincerity...

अहिंसा सत्यम् अक्रोधः , त्यागश् शान्तिर् अपैशुनम् । दया भूतेष्वलोलुप्त्वम् , मार्दवं ह्रीर् अचापलम् ॥ १६.२

ahiṁsā satyam akrodhaḥ , tyāgaś śāntir apaiśunam I

dayā bhūteṣvaloluptvam , mārdavaṁ hrīr acāpalam II 16.2

16.2 Harmlessness, Truthfulness, Lacking venomous tongue, conscious Renunciation of wrong notions and habits, Peacefulness, Avoiding cutting Slander, Kindness towards all beings, Resisting Temptation, Gentleness, Modesty, Absence of fickleness...

तेजः क्षमा धृतिश् शौचम् , अद्रोहो नातिमानिता । भवन्ति सम्पदं दैवीम् , अभिजातस्य भारत ॥ १६.३

tejaḥ kṣamā dhṛtiś śaucam , adroho nātimānitā I

bhavanti sampadaṁ daivīm , abhijātasya bhārata II 16.3

16.3 Glowing Cheerfulness, Forgiving oneself and others, Endurance and Stamina, Cleanliness, Absence of Malice, Lacking vain pride; these are the traits and habits of a good person - assets of a divine birth O Bharata!

दम्भो दर्पोऽभिमानश्च , क्रोधः पारुष्यम् एव च । अज्ञानं चाभिजातस्य , पार्थ सम्पदम् आसुरीम् ॥ १६.४

dambho darpo'bhimānaśca , krodha× pāruṣyam eva ca I

ajñānaṁ cābhijātasya , pārtha sampadam āsurīm II 16.4

16.4 False Pretense, Arrogance, Vanity and Venomous Anger; also Brutality and Rigid Stubbornness are the attributes of a bad person - liabilities of a demonic birth O Partha!

दैवी सम्पद् विमोक्षाय , निबन्धायासुरी मता । मा शुचस् सम्पदं दैवीम् , अभिजातोऽसि पाण्डव ॥ १६.५

daivī sampad vimokṣāya , nibandhāyāsurī matā I

mā śucas sampadaṁ daivīm , abhijāto'si pāṇḍava II 16.5

16.5 It is well known that the good assets lead to Success - Evolution - Liberation - Nirvana, whereas the bad liabilities lead to Failure - Stagnation - Bondage - Misery. Do not be anxious or frustrated since you are endowed with divine qualities O Pandava O Aspirant O Student!

द्वौ भूतसर्गौ लोकेऽस्मिन् , दैव आसुर एव च । दैवो विस्तरशः प्रोक्तः , आसुरं पार्थ मे श्रृणु ॥ १६.६

dvau bhūtasargau loke'smin , daiva āsura eva ca I

daivo vistaraśa× proktaḥ , āsuraṁ pārtha me śṛṇu II 16.6

16.6 In this world the creative energies balance out equally in Two proportions, namely the divine and the demonic. The humane, divine and godly instincts and traits have been described elaborately in many verses of the Gita so far in all its chapters, now is the chance to be acquainted with the inhuman parameters O Partha!

प्रवृत्तिं च निवृत्तिं च , जना न विदुर् आसुराः । न शौचं नापि चाचारः , न सत्यं तेषु विद्यते ॥ १६.७

pravṛttiṁ ca nivṛttiṁ ca , janā na vidur āsurāḥ I

na śaucaṁ nāpi cācāraḥ , na satyaṁ teṣu vidyate II 16.7

16.7 The demoniac people do not know what is to be done and what is to be avoided. They neither maintain cleanliness nor observe societal norms. They do not have any sense of Truthfulness either.

असत्यम् अप्रतिष्ठं ते , जगदाहुर् अनीश्वरम् । अपरस्परसम्भूतम् , किम् अन्यत् कामहैतुकम् ॥ १६.८

asatyam apratiṣṭhaṁ te , jagadāhur anīśvaram ।

aparasparasambhūtam , kim anyat kāmahaitukam ॥ 16.8

16.8 They have a dim and narrow viewpoint of this world. They experience the absence of divinity and thus figure that this creation is put together by lust.

एतां दृष्टिम् अवष्टभ्य , नष्टात्मानोऽल्पबुद्धयः । प्रभवन्त्युग्रकर्माणः , क्षयाय जगतोऽहिताः ॥ १६.९

etāṁ dr̥ṣṭim avaṣṭabhya , naṣṭātmāno'lpabuddhayaḥ ।

prabhavantyugrakarmāṇaḥ , kṣayāya jagato'hitāḥ ॥ 16.9

16.9 Trapped in such thinking, those scattered souls with a blocked intellect are agents of troublesome deeds wreaking havoc on the planet.

कामम् आश्रित्य दुष्पूरम् ,दम्भमानमदान्विताः । मोहाद्गृहीत्वासद्ग्राहान् ,प्रवर्तन्तेऽशुचिव्रताः ॥ १६.१०

kāmam āśritya duṣpūram , dambhamānamadānvitāḥ ।

mohādgr̥hītvāsadgrāhān , pravartante'śucivratāḥ ॥ 16.10

16.10 In the grip of blinding desire; overpowered by hypocrisy, vanity and arrogance; they blunder forth with debased maddened motives.

चिन्ताम् अपरिमेयां च , प्रलयान्ताम् उपाश्रिताः । कामोपभोगपरमाः , एतावद् इति निश्चिताः ॥ १६.११

cintām aparimeyāṁ ca , pralayāntām upāśritāḥ ।

kāmopabhogaparamāḥ , etāvad iti niścitāḥ ॥ 16.11

16.11 Clutched by lifelong abysmal fears, mired in sensual gratification, they are indoctrinated into believing this is the only pursuit.

आशापाशशतैर् बद्धाः , कामक्रोधपरायणाः । ईहन्ते कामभोगार्थम् , अन्यायेनार्थसञ्चयान् ॥ १६.१२

āśāpāśaśatair baddhāḥ , kāmakrodhaparāyaṇāḥ ।

īhante kāmabhogārtham , anyāyenārthasañcayān ॥ 16.12

16.12 Numerous excitements plague them, lust and wrath rule them, they struggle indiscriminately to amass riches for aimless indulgence.

इदम् अद्य मया लब्धम् , इमं प्राप्स्ये मनोरथम् । इदम् अस्तीदम् अपि मे , भविष्यति पुनर् धनम् ॥ १६.१३

idam adya mayā labdham , imaṁ prāpsye manoratham ।

idam astīdam api me , bhaviṣyati punar dhanam ॥ 16.13

16.13 Embroiled in reckoning their bank accounts for spending on senseless pleasures, they are stuck in nameless imaginary possessions.

असौ मया हतश् शत्रुः , हनिष्ये चापरान् अपि । ईश्वरोऽहम् अहं भोगी , सिद्धोऽहं बलवान् सुखी ॥ १६.१४

asau mayā hataś śatruḥ , haniṣye cāparān api ।

īśvaro'ham ahaṁ bhogī , siddho'haṁ balavān sukhī ॥ 16.14

16.14 They fancy crude and cruel gains by wreaking unknown antagonists. They believe they are invincible, untouchable and inviolable indulgers.

आढ्योऽभिजनवान् अस्मि , कोऽन्योऽस्ति सदृशो मया । यक्ष्ये दास्यामि मोदिष्ये , इत्यज्ञानविमोहिताः ॥ १६.१५

āḍhyo'bhijanavān asmi , ko'nyo'sti sadṛśo mayā ।

yakṣye dāsyāmi modiṣye , ityajñānavimohitāḥ ॥ 16.15

16.15 Boastful and vain they brag incessantly of repugnant possessions, while being embroiled in huge debts, non-performing assets, lurking maladies and family n friends who shall soon prove treacherous.

अनेकचित्तविभ्रान्ताः , मोहजालसमावृताः । प्रसक्ताः कामभोगेषु , पतन्ति नरकेऽशुचौ ॥ १६.१६

anekacittavibhrāntāḥ , mohajālasamāvṛtāḥ ।

prasaktāḥ kāmabhogeṣu , patanti narake'śucau ॥ 16.16

16.16 Bewildered by umpteen illusions, ensnared in the web of delusions, addicted to ruinous weaknesses, they reach a calamitous end.

आत्मसम्भावितास् स्तब्धाः, धनमानमदान्विताः । यजन्ते नामयज्ञैस् ते , दम्भेनाविधिपूर्वकम् ॥ १६.१७

ātmasambhāvitās stabdhāḥ , dhanamānamadanvitaḥ ।

yajante nāmayajñais te , dambhenāvidhipūrvakam ॥ 16.17

16.17 Conceited, Stubborn and Overpowered by haughtiness and arrogance due to money, they make their own criteria of conducting ceremonies contrary to scriptural ordinance, being muddled by pomposity.

अहङ्कारं बलं दर्पम् , कामं क्रोधं च संश्रिताः । माम् आत्मपरदेहेषु , प्रद्विषन्तोऽभ्यसूयकाः ॥ १६.१८

ahaṅkāraṁ balaṁ darpam , kāmaṁ krodhaṁ ca saṁśritāḥ ।

mām ātmaparadeheṣu , pradviṣanto'bhyasūyakāḥ ॥ 16.18

16.18 Corrupted by egotism, power, vanity, lust and wrath, these malicious men detest sanity around them and the prick of consciousness within their own self.

तान् अहं द्विषतः क्रूरान् , संसारेषु नराधमान् । क्षिपाम्यजस्रम् अशुभान् , आसुरीष्वेव योनिषु ॥ १६.१९

tān ahaṁ dviṣata× krūrān , saṁsāreṣu narādhamān I

kṣipāmyajasram aśubhān , āsurīṣveva yoniṣu II 16.19

16.19 These cruel brutes, the worst among men, get confronted again and again by barbarous endings.

आसुरीं योनिमापन्नाः , मूढा जन्मनि जन्मनि । माम् अप्राप्यैव कौन्तेय , ततो यान्त्यधमां गतिम् ॥ १६.२०

āsurīṁ yonimāpannāḥ , mūḍhā janmani janmani I

mām aprāpyaiva kaunteya , tato yāntyadhamāṁ gatim II 16.20

16.20 Ending up repeatedly in vicious traps the deluded beings passing through many journeys and births, not having obtained any succour whatsoever, become even more depraved O Kaunteya!

(that is the reason to rehabilitate the wicked, a harsh prison is not the solution).

त्रिविधं नरकस्येदम् , द्वारं नाशनम् आत्मनः । कामः क्रोधस् तथा लोभः , तस्माद् एतत् त्रयं त्यजेत् ॥ १६.२१

trividhaṁ narakasyedam , dvāraṁ nāśanam ātmanaḥ I

kāma× krodhas tathā lobhaḥ , tasmād etat trayaṁ tyajet II 16. 21

16.21 Lust, Anger and Greed constitute the three gates leading to grief and one's own destruction. Hence root out these three hellish tendencies.

एतैर् विमुक्तः कौन्तेय , तमोद्वारैस् त्रिभिर् नरः । आचरत्यात्मनः श्रेयः , ततो याति परां गतिम् ॥ १६.२२

etair vimukta× kaunteya , tamodvārais tribhir naraḥ I

ācaratyātmanaḥ śreyaḥ , tato yāti parāṁ gatim II 16.22

16.22 When he Abandons these three doorways to hell, O Kaunteya, man makes a U-turn towards his deliverance. Then his path leads to transcendent heaven.

यश् शास्त्रविधिम् उत्सृज्य , वर्तते कामकारतः। न स सिद्धिम् अवाप्नोति , न सुखं न परां गतिम् ॥ १६.२३

yaś śāstravidhim utsṛjya , vartate kāmakārataḥ I

na sa siddhim avāpnoti , na sukhaṁ na parāṁ gatim II 16.23

16.23 He who disobeys the Gurus' advice and the teachings of the sacred scriptures, and acts under his own whims; lives not the harmonious life, does not find true happiness and fails from attaining the worthwhile.

तस्माच्छास्त्रं प्रमाणं ते , कार्याकार्यव्यवस्थितौ । ज्ञात्वा शास्त्रविधानोक्तम् , कर्म कर्तुम् इहार्हसि ॥ १६.२४

tasmācchāstraṁ pramāṇaṁ te , kāryākāryavyavasthitau I

jñātvā śāstravidhānoktam , karma kartum ihārhasi II 16.24

16.24 Therefore the Guru and the Scripture is your guide in organizing your time and devoting yourself to noble tasks. Having sought true guidance thus live a complete and fulfilling life.

ॐ तत् सत् । इति श्रीमद्भगवद्गीतासु उपनिषत्सु ब्रह्मविद्यायां योगशास्त्रे श्रीकृष्णार्जुनसंवादे

दैवासुर-सम्पद्-विभाग-योगो नाम षोडशोऽध्यायः ॥ १६ ॥

oṁ tat sat I iti śrīmadbhagavadgītāsu upaniṣatsu brahmavidyāyāṁ yogaśāstre śrīkṛṣṇārjunasaṁvāde daivāsura-sampad-vibhāga-yogo nāma ṣoḍaśo'dhyāyaḥ II 16 II

17 Yoga of Sattvic Rajasic Tamasic Worships

Yoga of Three Types of Faith
Yoga of Light Dawn and Dark
Yoga of Body Speech Mind austerity
Yoga of Worship Service Lifestyle
Yoga of Om Tat Sat

Previously in the 14th chapter, we heard about the powerful shakti of the lord trifurcating as the Sattva Rajas and Tamas energies to maintain the balance in creation.
This triple split maintains equilibrium in all facets of life.
- As in our waking-dream-sleep states
- As in the 3 types of matter viz. Living, non-Living and the intermediate Plant Life.
- As in necessity of Work-Play-Rest
- As in Male-Female-Transgender
- As in Bhur-Bhuvah-Suvah
- As in grandparent-parent-child
- As in Summer-Winter-Monsoon

Now in this chapter we hear about the faith, food and modes of worship.

ॐ श्री परमात्मने नमः । अथ सप्तदशोऽध्यायः

oṁ śrī paramātmane namaḥ । atha saptadaśo'dhyāyaḥ

अर्जुन उवाच

ये शास्त्रविधिम् उत्सृज्य , यजन्ते श्रद्धयान्विताः । तेषां निष्ठा तु का कृष्ण , सत्त्वम् आहो रजस् तमः ॥ १७.१

arjuna uvāca

ye śāstravidhim utsṛjya , yajante śraddhayānvitāḥ ।

teṣāṁ niṣṭhā tu kā kṛṣṇa , sattvam āho rajas tamaḥ ॥ 17.1

Arjuna has a catchy query
17.1 What about the people who don't have access to the Guru or the Scripture? How may they be categorized and what may their fate be O Krishna?

श्री भगवान् उवाच

त्रिविधा भवति श्रद्धा , देहिनां सा स्वभावजा । सात्त्विकी राजसी चैव , तामसी चेति तां शृणु ॥ १७.२

śrī bhagavān uvāca

trividhā bhavati śraddhā , dehināṁ sā svabhāvajā ।

sāttvikī rājasī caiva , tāmasī ceti tāṁ śṛṇu ॥ 17.2

The benevolent Lord supplies

17.2 Threefold is the lifestyle followed and temperament endowed of the individuals, namely Sattvic Rajasic Tamasic. Listen to the same.

सत्त्वानुरूपा सर्वस्य , श्रद्धा भवति भारत । श्रद्धामयोऽयं पुरुषः , यो यच्छ्रद्धस् स एव सः ॥ १७.३

sattvānurūpā sarvasya , śraddhā bhavati bhārata ।

śraddhāmayo'yaṁ puruṣaḥ , yo yacchraddhas sa eva saḥ ॥ 17.3

17.3 Faith and Conviction of each is according to his personality. A man is governed by his conviction. Verily character determines him.

यजन्ते सात्त्विका देवान् , यक्षरक्षांसि राजसाः । प्रेतान् भूतगणांश्चान्ये , यजन्ते तामसा जनाः ॥ १७.४

yajante sāttvikā devān , yakṣarakṣāṁsi rājasāḥ ।

pretān bhūtagaṇāṁścānye , yajante tāmasā janāḥ ॥ 17.4

17.4 The Sattvic people believe in the word of god. The Rajasic ones lay store by the rich and famous. The remaining Tamasic dregs of society are fascinated by the bizarre and the grotesque.

अशास्त्रविहितं घोरम् , तप्यन्ते ये तपो जनाः । दम्भाहङ्कारसंयुक्ताः , कामरागबलान्विताः ॥ १७.५

aśāstravihitaṁ ghoram , tapyante ye tapo janāḥ ।

dambhāhaṅkārasaṁyuktāḥ , kāmarāgabalānvitāḥ ॥ 17.5

17.5 Those men who practice black magic and terrible rituals not enjoined by Guru or Scripture, drunk with madness and egotism, possessed by lust and attachment...

कर्शयन्तश् शरीरस्थम् ,भूतग्रामम् अचेतसः । मां चैवान्तःशरीरस्थम् ,तान् विद्ध्यासुरनिश्चयान्॥ १७.६

karśayantaś śarīrastham , bhūtagrāmam acetasaḥ ।

māṁ caivāntaḥśarīrastham , tān viddhyāsuraniścayān ॥ 17.6

17.6 Torturing themselves senselessly, mutilating their organs and blackening their soul, know them to be of demented temperament.

आहारस् त्वपि सर्वस्य , त्रिविधो भवति प्रियः । यज्ञस् तपस् तथा दानम् , तेषां भेदम् इमं शृणु ॥ १७.७

āhāras tvapi sarvasya , trividho bhavati priyaḥ I

yajñas tapas tathā dānam , teṣāṁ bhedam imaṁ śṛṇu II 17.7

17.7 Now hear also regarding the three types of food eaten. And the distinction in ritual, lifestyle and service.

आयुःसत्त्वबलारोग्यसुखप्रीतिविवर्धनाः । रस्यास् स्निग्धास् स्थिरा हृद्याः ,आहारास् सात्त्विकप्रियाः ॥ १७.८

āyuḥsattvabalārogyasukhaprītivivardhanāḥ I

rasyās snigdhās sthirā hṛdyāḥ , āhārās sāttvikapriyāḥ II 17.8

17.8 Diet that fosters longevity, sincerity, strength, health, joy and cheer; which is savoury and buttery, substantial and agreeable is liked by Sattvic people.

कट्वम्ललवणात्युष्णतीक्ष्णरूक्षविदाहिनः । आहारा राजसस्येष्टाः , दुःखशोकामयप्रदाः ॥ १७.९

kaṭvamlalavaṇātyuṣṇa-tīkṣṇarūkṣavidāhinaḥ I

āhārā rājasasyeṣṭāḥ , duḥkhaśokāmayapradāḥ II 17.9

17.9 Foods tasting very - bitter, sour, salty, hot in temperature, pungent, dry and chilli burning; that over time result in pain, numbness and disease are relished by Rajasic people.

यातयामं गतरसम् , पूति पर्युषितं च यत् । उच्छिष्टम् अपि चामेध्यम् , भोजनं तामसप्रियम् ॥ १७.१०

yātayāmaṁ gatarasam , pūti paryuṣitaṁ ca yat I

ucchiṣṭam api cāmedhyam , bhojanaṁ tāmasapriyam II 17.10

17.10 Meals improperly cooked, lacking nourishment, putrid evil smelling, stale; and leftovers and soiled groceries are fancied by Tamasic people.

अफलाकाङ्क्षिभिर् यज्ञः , विधिदृष्टो य इज्यते । यष्टव्यम् एवेति मनः , समाधाय स सात्त्विकः ॥ १७.११

aphalākāṅkṣibhir yajñaḥ , vidhidṛṣṭo ya ijyate I

yaṣṭavyam eveti manaḥ , samādhāya sa sāttvikaḥ II 17.11

17.11 Ceremonies and Rituals and Yagyas performed cheerfully and reverently as per local traditions and scriptures, without being feverish of the fruits are Sattvic worship.

अभिसन्धाय तु फलम् , दम्भार्थम् अपि चैव यत् । इज्यते भरतश्रेष्ठ , तं यज्ञं विद्धि राजसम् ॥ १७.१२

abhisandhāya tu phalam , dambhārtham api caiva yat ।

ijyate bharataśreṣṭha , taṁ yajñaṁ viddhi rājasam ॥ 17.12

17.12 Likewise the puja done with a strong expectation of fruit and merit and also seeking popularity and acclaim, comes under Rajasic worship.

विधिहीनम् असृष्टान्नम् , मन्त्रहीनम् अदक्षिणम् । श्रद्धाविरहितं यज्ञम् , तामसं परिचक्षते ॥ १७.१३

vidhihīnam asṛṣṭānnam , mantrahīnam adakṣiṇam ।

śraddhāvirahitaṁ yajñam , tāmasaṁ paricakṣate ॥ 17.13

17.13 Tamasic worship is that done hurriedly, not respecting the tradition, without any decoration nor any seating or distribution of prasad for guests. Neither are the pundits compensated nor is there any devotional ambience.

देवद्विजगुरुप्राज्ञपूजनं शौचम् आर्जवम् । ब्रह्मचर्यम् अहिंसा च , शारीरं तप उच्यते ॥ १७.१४

devadvijaguruprājñapūjanaṁ śaucam ārjavam ।

brahmacaryam ahiṁsā ca , śārīraṁ tapa ucyate ॥ 17.14

17.14 A lifestyle wherein elders are honoured, pillars of society are strengthened, the Guru is eagerly sought for and served, and satsang company of the wise is a regular feature. A life lived handsomely, wholesomely, within one's resources, and not depleting the ecosystem. Such are the parameters and disciplines for maintaining sacredness of body.

अनुद्वेगकरं वाक्यम् , सत्यं प्रियहितं च यत् । स्वाध्यायाभ्यसनं चैव , वाङ्मयं तप उच्यते ॥ १७.१५

anudvegakaraṁ vākyam , satyaṁ priyahitaṁ ca yat ।

svadhyayabhyasanam caiva , vaṅmayaṁ tapa ucyate ॥ 17.15

17.15 Speech without hysteria, speech that combines truthfulness, sweetness and common welfare, and the practice of chanting aloud mantras and sacred verses, are the attributes for maintaining purity of tongue.

मनः प्रसादस् सौम्यत्वम् , मौनम् आत्मविनिग्रहः । भावसंशुद्धिर् इत्येतत् , तपो मानसम् उच्यते ॥ १७.१६

mana× prasādas saumyatvam , maunam ātmavinigrahaḥ ।

bhāvasaṁśuddhir ityetat , tapo mānasam ucyate ॥ 17.16

17.16 Keeping the mind pleasant and cheerful; keeping the temperament gentle, reserved and thoughtful; and striving for emotional purity are the essential guidelines for fitness of mind.

श्रद्धया परया तप्तम् , तपस् तत् त्रिविधं नरैः । अफलाकाङ्क्षिभिर् युक्तैः , सात्त्विकं परिचक्षते ॥ १७.१७

śraddhayā parayā taptam , tapas tat trividhaṁ naraiḥ I

aphalākāṅkṣibhir yuktaiḥ , sāttvikaṁ paricakṣate II 17.17

17.17 Such threefold austerity of body-tongue-mind, adhered to with a high degree of faith and commitment by men of integrity and grit is declared to be a Sattvic lifestyle.

सत्कारमानपूजार्थम् , तपो दम्भेन चैव यत् । क्रियते तद् इह प्रोक्तम् , राजसं चलम् अध्रुवम् ॥ १७.१८

satkāramānapūjārtham , tapo dambhena caiva yat I

kriyate tad iha proktam , rājasaṁ calam adhruvam II 17.18

17.18 Likewise attempting the same discipline of body-tongue-mind with a heart seeking rewards, riches, gains and popularity is called Rajasic living. Such a lifestyle turns unstable and short-lived.

(as seen in the phrase - pride goes before a fall - and in reports of well established celebrities and figures falling flat at some point, being ground into the dust, and spat on by history to come).

मूढग्राहेणात्मनो यत् , पीडया क्रियते तपः । परस्योत्सादनार्थं वा , तत् तामसम् उदाहृतम् ॥ १७.१९

mūḍhagrāheṇātmano yat , pīḍayā kriyate tapaḥ I

parasyotsādanārthaṁ vā , tat tāmasam udāhṛtam II 17.19

17.19 A life lived with stupidity, lacking vision or discipline, injuring oneself by various accidents and illnesses, and causing harm and danger to society is an example of Tamasic personality.

दातव्यम् इति यद् दानम् , दीयतेऽनुपकारिणे । देशे काले च पात्रे च , तद् दानं सात्त्विकं स्मृतम् ॥ १७.२०

dātavyam iti yad dānam , dīyate'nupakāriṇe I

deśe kāle ca pātre ca , tad dānaṁ sāttvikaṁ smṛtam II 17.20

17.20 Service done as a sense of duty, without causing obligation in the mind of the served, and done in time of need, with due regard to the prevailing situation; such service is a Sattvic gift.

यत् तु प्रत्युपकारार्थम् , फलम् उद्दिश्य वा पुनः । दीयते च परिक्लिष्टम् , तद् दानं राजसं स्मृतम् ॥ १७.२१

yat tu pratyupakārārtham , phalam uddiśya vā punaḥ ।

dīyate ca parikliṣṭam , tad dānaṁ rājasaṁ smṛtam ॥ 17.21

17.21 Indeed the Service done with agitation, as a business transaction expecting profit, and with a degree of doubt and reluctance is considered a Rajasic gift.

अदेशकाले यद् दानम् , अपात्रेभ्यश्च दीयते । असत्कृतम् अवज्ञातम् , तत् तामसम् उदाहृतम् ॥ १७.२२

adeśakāle yad dānam , apātrebhyaśca dīyate ।

asatkṛtam avajñātam , tat tāmasam udāhṛtam ॥ 17.22

17.22 Service that is actually not a service but a burden and strain, done when time and place are repressive and guilt causing, to someone not at all needing it, and haughtily and insultingly; qualifies as a Tamasic gift.

(like calling someone for dinner and feeding them forcefully beyond their capacity and even noticing their squirming and suffocation).

or

(throwing a party where harmful liqueurs and drugs are served).

or

(fixing an official meeting during lunch break or after duty hours, causing the invitees to feel imprisoned and repressed).

ॐ तत् सद् इति निर्देशः , ब्रह्मणस् त्रिविधस् स्मृतः । ब्राह्मणास् तेन वेदाश्च ,यज्ञाश्च विहिताः पुरा ॥ १७.२३

oṁ tat sad iti nirdeśaḥ , brahmaṇas trividhas smṛtaḥ ।

brāhmaṇās tena vedāśca , yajñāśca vihitāḥ purā ॥ 17.23

17.23 "Om Tat Sat" - this statement is contemplated upon as the threefold designation for Brahman, the supreme reality. Such Meditation created the initial wise men, the sacred scriptures, and the righteous works and worthwhile occupations.

तस्माद् ॐ इत्युदाहृत्य , यज्ञदानतपःक्रियाः । प्रवर्तन्ते विधानोक्ताः , सततं ब्रह्मवादिनाम् ॥ १७.२४

tasmād oṁ ityudāhṛtya , yajñadānatapaḥkriyāḥ ।

pravartante vidhānoktāḥ , satataṁ brahmavādinām ॥ 17.24

17.24 Therefore the ardent seekers for the ultimate goal of a human life begin their day, their chores, their worship and service after uttering the sacred syllable "Om".

तद् इत्यनभिसन्धाय , फलं यज्ञतपःक्रियाः । दानक्रियाश्च विविधाः , क्रियन्ते मोक्षकाङ्क्षिभिः ॥ १७.२५

tad ityanabhisandhāya , phalaṁ yajñatapaḥkriyāḥ ।

dānakriyāśca vividhāḥ , kriyante mokṣakāṅkṣibhiḥ ॥ 17.25

17.25 Yoked with discrimination and dispassion, the Seeker after Liberation lives his life of worship and service, maintaining a pure lifestyle, being aware of the eternal principle "That".

सद्भावे साधुभावे च , सद् इत्येतत् प्रयुज्यते । प्रशस्ते कर्मणि तथा , सच्छब्द× पार्थ युज्यते ॥ १७.२६

sadbhāve sādhubhāve ca , sad ityetat prayujyate ।

praśaste karmaṇi tathā , sacchabda× pārtha yujyate ॥ 17.26

17.26 All that is Real is referred to by the word "Sat". All that is Good is "Sat". So also is all Auspicious action "Sat".

यज्ञे तपसि दाने च , स्थितिस् सदिति चोच्यते । कर्म चैव तदर्थीयम् , सद् इत्येवाभिधीयते ॥ १७.२७

yajñe tapasi dāne ca , sthitis saditi cocyate ।

karma caiva tadarthīyam , sad ityevābhidhīyate ॥ 17.27

17.27 Again Sincerity in Worship, Lifestyle and Service is "Sat". Even any thought-word-deed endowed with "That" purity, divinity, cheerfulness is "Sat".

अश्रद्धया हुतं दत्तम् , तपस् तप्तं कृतं च यत् । असदित्युच्यते पार्थ , न च तत् प्रेत्य नो इह ॥ १७.२८

aśraddhayā hutaṁ dattam , tapas taptaṁ kr̥taṁ ca yat ।

asadityucyate pārtha , na ca tat pretya no iha ॥ 17.28

17.28 O Partha! Whatever worship, service or lifestyle lacks faith-commitment-devotion, it never yields the optimum result, is an unfounded and unreliable practice and a big zero, null and void.

ॐ तत् सत् । इति श्रीमद्भगवद्गीतासु उपनिषत्सु ब्रह्मविद्यायां योगशास्त्रे श्रीकृष्णार्जुनसंवादे

श्रद्धा-त्रय-विभाग-योगो नाम सप्तदशोऽध्यायः ॥ १७ ॥

oṁ tat sat । iti śrīmadbhagavadgītāsu upaniṣatsu brahmavidyāyāṁ yogaśāstre śrīkr̥ṣṇārjunasaṁvāde śraddhā-traya-vibhāga-yogo nāma saptadaśo'dhyāyaḥ ॥ 17 ॥

18 Yoga of Liberation by letting go

Yoga of Renunciation Tyaga
Yoga of Attainment of Success
Yoga of God Realization
Yoga of Karma Bhakti Jnana

ॐ श्री परमात्मने नमः । अथ अष्टादशोऽध्यायः

oṁ śrī paramātmane namaḥ । atha aṣṭādaśo'dhyāyaḥ

अर्जुन उवाच

सन्न्यासस्य महाबाहो , तत्त्वम् इच्छामि वेदितुम् । त्यागस्य च हृषीकेश , पृथक् केशिनिषूदन ॥ १८.१

arjuna uvāca

sannyāsasya mahābāho , tattvam icchāmi veditum ।

tyāgasya ca hṛṣīkeśa , pṛthak keśiniṣūdana ॥ 18.1

Arjuna has the ultimate query
18.1 O Mahabaho! Kindly enlighten me. O Hrishikesha! convincingly elucidate the sublime truth of Sannyasa and Tyaga, O Keshinisudana!

(the free use of first name in addressing signifies the trust, closeness and intimacy; most essential in teaching and learning).

श्री भगवान् उवाच

काम्यानां कर्मणां न्यासम् , सन्न्यासं कवयो विदुः । सर्वकर्मफलत्यागम् , प्राहुस् त्यागं विचक्षणाः ॥ १८.२

śrī bhagavān uvāca

kāmyānāṁ karmaṇāṁ nyāsam , sannyāsaṁ kavayo viduḥ ।

sarvakarmaphalatyāgam , prāhus tyāgaṁ vicakṣaṇāḥ ॥ 18.2

Instantly the Lord satisfies
18.2 Sages understand sannyasa as a way of life that involves work and action without expectation. Scholars declare tyaga to be unflustered by the results of work and action.

(in other words tyaga is only possible for a sannyasi, or tyaga is only possible in the rare moment when one already has abundant contentment).

त्याज्यं दोषवदित्येके , कर्म प्राहुर् मनीषिणः । यज्ञदानतपःकर्म , न त्याज्यम् इति चापरे ॥ १८.३

tyājyaṁ doṣavadityeke , karma prāhur manīṣiṇaḥ I

yajñadānatapa×karma , na tyājyam iti cāpare II 18.3

18.3 Some philosophers declare any action to be tinged with hope of reward. Others opine that desire should be strong for righteous worship, service and lifestyle.

निश्चयं श्रृणु मे तत्र , त्यागे भरतसत्तम । त्यागो हि पुरुषव्याघ्र , त्रिविधस् सम्प्रकीर्तितः ॥ १८.४

niścayaṁ śr̥ṇu me tatra , tyāge bharatasattama I

tyāgo hi puruṣavyāghra , trividhas samprakīrtitaḥ II 18.4

18.4 Regarding such statements, hear about tyaga-renunciation with an open mind O Bharatasattama. Verily tyaga has been declared to be of three types O Purushavyaghra.

यज्ञदानतपःकर्म , न त्याज्यं कार्यमेव तत् । यज्ञो दानं तपश्चैव , पावनानि मनीषिणाम् ॥ १८.५

yajñadānatapa×karma , na tyājyaṁ kāryameva tat I

yajño dānaṁ tapaścaiva , pāvanāni manīṣiṇām II 18.5

18.5 Righteous worship, service and lifestyle should at no cost be forsaken or neglected. These are highly worth performing for human beings as they alone purify and support life.

एतान्यपि तु कर्माणि , सङ्गं त्यक्त्वा फलानि च । कर्तव्यानीति मे पार्थ , निश्चितं मतम् उत्तमम् ॥ १८.६

etānyapi tu karmāṇi , saṅgaṁ tyaktvā phalāni ca I

kartavyānīti me pārtha , niścitaṁ matam uttamam II 18.6

18.6 Perform worship and service and live righteously without getting feverish of the fruits or rewards thereof. This not becoming entangled to the payoffs while living righteously is decidedly the noblest lifestyle O Partha, in the eyes of the Lord.

नियतस्य तु सन्न्यासः , कर्मणो नोपपद्यते । मोहात् तस्य परित्यागः , तामसः परिकीर्तितः ॥ १८.७

niyatasya tu sannyāsaḥ , karmaṇo nopapadyate I

mohāt tasya parityāgaḥ , tāmasa× parikīrtitaḥ II 18.7

18.7 Verily neglect of responsibility is a serious error. Escaping from duty is due to delusion and such tyaga-abandonment is called tamasic.

दुःखम् इत्येव यत् कर्म , कायक्लेशभयात् त्यजेत् । स कृत्वा राजसं त्यागम् , नैव त्यागफलं लभेत् ॥ १८.८

duḥkham ityeva yat karma , kāyakleśabhayāt tyajet ।

sa kṛtvā rājasaṁ tyāgam , naiva tyāgaphalaṁ labhet ॥ 18.8

18.8 Indeed shirking primary responsibility due to it being challenging, laborious or physically demanding and engaging elsewhere is a form of Rajasic tyaga. It will never bring success.

कार्यम् इत्येव यत् कर्म , नियतं क्रियतेऽर्जुन । सङ्गं त्यक्त्वा फलं चैव , स त्यागस् सात्त्विको मतः ॥ १८.९

kāryam ityeva yat karma , niyataṁ kriyate'rjuna ।

saṅgaṁ tyaktvā phalaṁ caiva , sa tyāgas sāttviko mataḥ ॥ 18.9

18.9 Letting go of the claims of performing one's duty, and also being unconcerned regarding the fruits accrued thereof is regarded as sattvic tyaga.

न द्वेष्ट्यकुशलं कर्म , कुशले नानुषज्जते । त्यागी सत्त्वसमाविष्टः , मेधावी छिन्नसंशयः ॥ १८.१०

na dveṣṭyakuśalaṁ karma , kuśale nānuṣajjate ।

tyāgī sattvasamāviṣṭaḥ , medhāvī chinnasaṁśayaḥ ॥ 18.10

18.10 The true tyagi does not shirk unpleasant or difficult responsibility, nor is he seduced in the performance of agreeable and delightful jobs. His work demonstrates lightness, intelligence and confidence.

न हि देहभृता शक्यम् , त्यक्तुं कर्माण्यशेषतः । यस्तु कर्मफलत्यागी , स त्यागीत्यभिधीयते ॥ १८.११

na hi dehabhṛtā śakyam , tyaktuṁ karmāṇyaśeṣataḥ ।

yastu karmaphalatyāgī , sa tyāgītyabhidhīyate ॥ 18.11

18.11 Recognize that just to maintain body and live, one cannot stop doing work. However working without being agitated and caught up in the remuneration and appreciation received is the correct application of tyaga-the highest renunciation.

अनिष्टम् इष्टं मिश्रं च , त्रिविधं कर्मण× फलम् । भवत्यत्यागिनां प्रेत्य , न तु सन्न्यासिनां क्वचित् ॥ १८.१२

aniṣṭam iṣṭaṁ miśraṁ ca , trividhaṁ karmaṇa× phalam ।

bhavatyatyāginām pretya , na tu sannyāsinām kvacit ॥ 18.12

18.12 Reward, criticism and repercussion is the three types of merit that accrues to the non-tyagi. No such binding force applies to the tyagi-renunciate.

पञ्चैतानि महाबाहो , कारणानि निबोध मे । साङ्ख्ये कृतान्ते प्रोक्तानि , सिद्धये सर्वकर्मणाम् ॥ १८.१३

pañcaitāni mahābāho , kāraṇāni nibodha me ।

sāṅkhye kr̥tānte proktāni , siddhaye sarvakarmaṇām ॥ 18.13

18.13 Realize the five distinct components, facets or factors in each work or action O Mahabaho, also known as Pancakosha. As enumerated in the teaching that leads to perfection in life.

अधिष्ठानं तथा कर्ता , करणं च पृथग्विधम् । विविधाश्च पृथक् चेष्टाः , दैवं चैवात्र पञ्चमम् ॥ १८.१४

adhiṣṭhānaṁ tathā kartā , karaṇaṁ ca pr̥thagvidham ।

vividhāśca pr̥thak ceṣṭāḥ , daivaṁ caivātra pañcamam ॥ 18.14

18.14 Annamaya kosha-the combined effect of external circumstances and one's own bodily strength, Pranamaya kosha-the vitality of breath that keeps one alive and kicking, Manomaya kosha-the keen instruments in the form of one's senses and mind and usage of resources, Vigyanmaya kosha-the deep emotions and experiences that make significant contribution to any action, and finally the fifth in the form of Grace. Grace or Divinity is the backbone for each deed.

शरीरवाङ्मनोभिर् यत् , कर्म प्रारभते नरः । न्याय्यं वा विपरीतं वा , पञ्चैते तस्य हेतवः ॥ १८.१५

śarīravāṅmanobhir yat , karma prārabhate naraḥ ।

nyāyyaṁ vā viparītaṁ vā , pañcaite tasya hetavaḥ ॥ 18.15

18.15 All expressions of body-speech-mind that translate to thought-word-action, any right or otherwise decision and deed, is influenced by these five factors.

तत्रैवं सति कर्तारम् , आत्मानं केवलं तु यः । पश्यत्यकृतबुद्धित्वात् , न स पश्यति दुर्मतिः ॥ १८.१६

tatraivaṁ sati kartāram , ātmānaṁ kevalaṁ tu yaḥ ।

paśyatyakr̥tabuddhitvāt , na sa paśyati durmatiḥ ॥ 18.16

18.16 Such being the case, only a fool takes full credit for an act, faulty is his judgment and it is the cause of ruin.

यस्य नाहङ्कृतो भावः , बुद्धिर् यस्य न लिप्यते । हत्वापि स इमाँल्लोकान् , न हन्ति न निबध्यते ॥ १८.१७

yasya nāhaṅkr̥to bhāvaḥ , buddhir yasya na lipyate ।

hatvāpi sa imām̐llokān , na hanti na nibadhyate ॥ 18.17

18.17 Action free of egotism executed by intellect that is unclouded is the sort of action that liberates and proves successful.

ज्ञानं ज्ञेयं परिज्ञाता , त्रिविधा कर्मचोदना । करणं कर्म कर्तेति , त्रिविधः कर्मसङ्ग्रहः ॥ १८.१८

jñānaṁ jñeyaṁ parijñātā , trividhā karmacodanā ।

karaṇaṁ karma karteti , trividhaḥ karmasaṅgrahaḥ ॥ 18.18

18.18 Another way to understand any deed is to realize the involved trinity in the form of knowledge-known-knower, process-object-subject and instrumentation-feedback-control.

ज्ञानं कर्म च कर्ता च , त्रिधैव गुणभेदतः । प्रोच्यते गुणसङ्ख्याने , यथावच्छृणु तान्यपि ॥ १८.१९

jñānaṁ karma ca kartā ca , tridhaiva guṇabhedataḥ ।

procyate guṇasaṅkhyāne , yathāvacchr̥ṇu tānyapi ॥ 18.19

18.19 Process, Object and Subject are further threefold categorized as per their traits. Hear too this enumeration attentively.

सर्वभूतेषु येनैकम् , भावम् अव्ययम् ईक्षते । अविभक्तं विभक्तेषु , तज्ज्ञानं विद्धि सात्त्विकम् ॥ १८.२०

sarvabhūteṣu yenaikam , bhāvam avyayam īkṣate ।

avibhaktaṁ vibhakteṣu , tajjñānaṁ viddhi sāttvikam ॥ 18.20

18.20 Process that is understood to contain the quality of Grace, that is inherent in all processes, underlying the inseparateness in all creation, know that process to be Sattvic.

पृथक्त्वेन तु यज्ज्ञानम् , नानाभावान् पृथग्विधान् । वेत्ति सर्वेषु भूतेषु , तज्ज्ञानं विद्धि राजसम् ॥ १८.२१

pr̥thaktvena tu yajjñānam , nānābhāvān pr̥thagvidhān ।

vetti sarveṣu bhūteṣu , tajjñānaṁ viddhi rājasam ॥ 18.21

18.21 Process that is but understood to be distinct from other processes without any underlying divinity, by which one separates each science arbitrarily, know that process to be Rajasic.

यत् तु कृत्स्नवदेकस्मिन् , कार्ये सक्तम् अहैतुकम् । अतत्त्वार्थवदल्पं च , तत् तामसम् उदाहृतम् ॥ १८.२२

yat tu kr̥tsnavadekasmin , kārye saktam ahaitukam ।

atattvārthavadalpaṁ ca , tat tāmasam udāhr̥tam ॥ 18.22

18.22 Process that is limited and without reference, without deliberation, without real foundation and superfluous, know that process to be Tamasic.

नियतं सङ्गरहितम् , अरागद्वेषतः कृतम् । अफलप्रेप्सुना कर्म , यत् तत् सात्त्विकम् उच्यते ॥ १८.२३

niyataṁ saṅgarahitam , arāgadveṣataḥ kr̥tam ।

aphalaprepsunā karma , yat tat sāttvikam ucyate ॥ 18.23

18.23 Object that is weighed at face value free from bias and excitement becomes Sattvic.

यत् तु कामेप्सुना कर्म , साहङ्कारेण वा पुनः । क्रियते बहुलायासम् , तद् राजसम् उदाहृतम् ॥ १८.२४

yat tu kāmepsunā karma , sāhaṅkāreṇa vā punaḥ ।

kriyate bahulāyāsam , tad rājasam udāhr̥tam ॥ 18.24

18.24 Object that is weighed with ulterior motive, strong ego, bias and much struggle turns Rajasic.

अनुबन्धं क्षयं हिंसाम् , अनवेक्ष्य च पौरुषम् । मोहाद् आरभ्यते कर्म , यत् तत् तामसम् उच्यते ॥ १८.२५

anubandhaṁ kṣayaṁ hiṁsām , anavekṣya ca pauruṣam ।

mohād ārabhyate karma , yat tat tāmasam ucyate ॥ 18.25

18.25 Object that is illusory, defective, inconsequential, injury prone and lossy is Tamasic.

मुक्तसङ्गोऽनहंवादी ,धृत्युत्साहसमन्वितः । सिद्ध्यसिद्ध्योर् निर्विकारः , कर्ता सात्त्विक उच्यते ॥ १८.२६

muktasaṅgo'nahaṁvādī , dhr̥tyutsāhasamanvitaḥ ।

siddhyasiddhyor nirvikāraḥ , kartā sāttvika ucyate ॥ 18.26

18.26 Subject that works freely, displays humility yet is firm, enthusiastic and upright in success as well as unsuccess is Sattvic.

रागी कर्मफलप्रेप्सुः , लुब्धो हिंसात्मकोऽशुचिः । हर्षशोकान्वितः कर्ता , राजसः परिकीर्तितः ॥ १८.२७

rāgī karmaphalaprepsuḥ , lubdho hiṁsātmako'śuciḥ ।

harṣaśokānvitaḥ kartā , rājasaḥ parikīrtitaḥ ॥ 18.27

18.27 Subject filled with bias, feverish for results, greedy, unrelenting, with an attitude of by hook or crook, and tossed about by success and failure is Rajasic.

अयुक्तः प्राकृतस् स्तब्धः , शठो नैष्कृतिकोऽलसः । विषादी दीर्घसूत्री च , कर्ता तामस उच्यते ॥ १८.२८

ayuktaḥ prākr̥tas stabdhaḥ , śaṭho naiṣkr̥tiko'lasaḥ ।

viṣādī dīrghasūtrī ca , kartā tāmasa ucyate ॥ 18.28

18.28 Subject who is a scatterbrain, vulgar, fanatic, fraudulent, malicious, lethargic, despondent and given to postponing is Tamasic.

बुद्धेर् भेदं धृतेश् चैव , गुणतस् त्रिविधं श्रृणु । प्रोच्यमानम् अशेषेण , पृथक्त्वेन धनञ्जय ॥ १८.२९

buddher bhedaṁ dhr̥teś caiva , guṇatas trividhaṁ śr̥ṇu ।

procyamānam aśeṣeṇa , pr̥thaktvena dhanañjaya ॥ 18.29

18.29 Now listen to the threefold categorization of Intelligence and Grit. This is told completely covering all aspects O Dhananjaya!

प्रवृत्तिं च निवृत्तिं च , कार्याकार्ये भयाभये । बन्धं मोक्षं च या वेत्ति , बुद्धिस् सा पार्थ सात्त्विकी ॥ १८.३०

pravr̥ttiṁ ca nivr̥ttiṁ ca , kāryākārye bhayābhaye ।

bandhaṁ mokṣaṁ ca yā vetti , buddhis sā pārtha sāttvikī ॥ 18.30

18.30 Intelligence that recognizes when to act and when to surrender, that knows what ought to be done and what ought not, that displays humility as well as courage, fraternity and also individuality, that O Partha is Sattvic.

यया धर्मम् अधर्मं च , कार्यं चाकार्यमेव च । अयथावत् प्रजानाति , बुद्धिस् सा पार्थ राजसी ॥ १८.३१

yayā dharmam adharmaṁ ca , kāryaṁ cākāryameva ca ।

ayathāvat prajānāti , buddhis sā pārtha rājasī ॥ 18.31

18.31 Intelligence that is unable to distinguish righteousness from unrighteousness, and falters when facinq dilemma is Rajasic.

अधर्मं धर्मम् इति या , मन्यते तमसावृता । सर्वार्थान् विपरीतांश्च , बुद्धिस् सा पार्थ तामसी ॥ १८.३२

adharmaṁ dharmam iti yā , manyate tamasāvr̥tā ।

sarvārthān viparītāṁśca , buddhis sā pārtha tāmasī ॥ 18.32

18.32 Intelligence that is shrouded, blocked, perverted and mixes up good and evil is Tamasic.

धृत्या यया धारयते , मनःप्राणेन्द्रियक्रियाः । योगेनाव्यभिचारिण्या , धृतिस् सा पार्थ सात्त्विकी ॥ १८.३३

dhr̥tyā yayā dhārayate , manaḥprāṇendriyakriyāḥ I

yogenāvyabhicāriṇyā , dhr̥tis sā pārtha sāttvikī II 18.33

18.33 Grit that boldly conducts business, infuses stamina in sports, and enjoys in moderation with an integration of personality O Partha is Sattvic.

यया तु धर्मकामार्थान् , धृत्या धारयतेऽर्जुन । प्रसङ्गेन फलाकाङ्क्षी , धृतिस् सा पार्थ राजसी ॥ १८.३४

yayā tu dharmakāmārthān , dhr̥tyā dhārayate'rjuna I

prasaṅgena phalākāṅkṣī , dhr̥tis sā pārtha rājasī II 18.34

18.34 Grit but that causes friction in duty, makes earning a source of discontentment, and free time a burden; due to unreasonable likes and dislikes, and undue stress on outcome O Partha is Rajasic.

यया स्वप्नं भयं शोकम् , विषादं मदम् एव च । न विमुञ्चति दुर्मेधाः , धृतिस् सा पार्थ तामसी ॥ १८.३५

yayā svapnaṁ bhayaṁ śokam , viṣādaṁ madam eva ca I

na vimuñcati durmedhāḥ , dhr̥tis sā pārtha tāmasī II 18.35

18.35 Grit that is no grit at all, rather a deluded mix of day dreaming, fear, regret, despair, opinionated; being bound by such harmful notions O Partha is Tamasic.

सुखं त्विदानीं त्रिविधम् , शृणु मे भरतर्षभ । अभ्यासाद् रमते यत्र , दुःखान्तं च निगच्छति ॥ १८.३६

sukhaṁ tvidānīṁ trividham , śr̥ṇu me bharatarṣabha I

abhyāsād ramate yatra , duḥkhāntaṁ ca nigacchati II 18.36

18.36 Now listen attentively to the colours of joy O Bharatarshabha! The clarity of which delivers all joys, cloudiness of which ends in sorrow.

यत् तद् अग्रे विषम् इव , परिणामेऽमृतोपमम् । तत् सुखं सात्त्विकं प्रोक्तम् , आत्मबुद्धिप्रसादजम् ॥ १८.३७

yat tad agre viṣam iva , pariṇāme'mr̥topamam I

tat sukhaṁ sāttvikaṁ proktam , ātmabuddhiprasādajam II 18.37

18.37 Joy that presents as a big challenge initially and gradually dissolves to provide the nectar of bliss, being persistent in that by force of clear vision is Sattvic.

(getting up at 4am to do padmasadhana and sudarshan kriya is very challenging and equally rewarding in all aspects of life).

विषयेन्द्रियसंयोगात् , यत् तद् अग्रेऽमृतोपमम् । परिणामे विषम् इव , तत् सुखं राजसं स्मृतम् ॥ १८.३८

viṣayendriyasaṁyogāt , yat tad agre'mṛtopamam ।

pariṇāme viṣam iva , tat sukhaṁ rājasaṁ smṛtam ॥ 18.38

18.38 Joy that titillates the senses and is alluring initially and fades away to reveal its bristles and thorns by and by is Rajasic.

(pain-killers, cold water, fried morsels, spicy viands are sure to damage the organs and destroy the intellect).

यद् अग्रे चानुबन्धे च , सुखं मोहनम् आत्मनः । निद्रालस्यप्रमादोत्थम् , तत् तामसम् उदाहृतम् ॥ १८.३९

yad agre cānubandhe ca , sukhaṁ mohanam ātmanaḥ ।

nidrālasyapramādottham , tat tāmasam udāhṛtam ॥ 18.39

18.39 Joy that completely paralyses the system sooner or later, caused by intoxicants, laziness and heedlessness is Tamasic.

न तद् अस्ति पृथिव्यां वा,दिवि देवेषु वा पुनः । सत्त्वं प्रकृतिजैर् मुक्तम् ,यदेभिस् स्यात् त्रिभिर् गुणैः॥ १८.४०

na tad asti pṛthivyāṁ vā , divi deveṣu vā punaḥ ।

sattvaṁ prakṛtijair muktam , yadebhis syāt tribhir guṇaiḥ ॥ 18.40

18.40 Again ponder on these three forces operating in nature, since these energies are universal and prevalent in both developed and under developed nations.

ब्राह्मणक्षत्रियविशाम् , शूद्राणां च परन्तप । कर्माणि प्रविभक्तानि , स्वभावप्रभवैर् गुणैः ॥ १८.४१

brāhmaṇakṣatriyaviśām , śūdrāṇāṁ ca parantapa ।

karmāṇi pravibhaktāni , svabhāvaprabhavair guṇaiḥ ॥ 18.41

18.41 Deeds of Brahmanas-the learned, Kshatriyas-the valorous, Vaishyas-those with business acumen and Sudras-the lay workers O Parantapa; are well differentiated due to genes and the upbringing.

(this is an intrinsic classification for all human beings, irrespective of race, culture or nationality. As seen in world history over the past and current century, a wrong match of profession with intrinsic temperament plays havoc and destroys, whereas a correct fit produces charming success.

Notice that judging someone by resume, biodata and forms filling has very little to no gains. This is intuitive as the qualities of Strength, Endurance, Patience, Uprightness and Integrity are not at all related to oratory, intellect or skillset. Hence the so called developed nations have witnessed untold misery and depression and emotional breakups.

Only an intuitive administrator can select the right man for the right job, it has NOTHING to do with education as it currently stands. This was the brilliant deduction of ancient sages and it is still in use by Ashrams and Gurukuls - so their advice needs to be seriously sought for and implemented).

शमो दमस् तपश् शौचम् , क्षान्तिर् आर्जवम् एव च । ज्ञानं विज्ञानम् आस्तिक्यम् , ब्रह्मकर्म स्वभावजम् ॥ १८.४२

śamo damas tapaś śaucam , kṣāntir ārjavam eva ca ।

jñānaṁ vijñānam āstikyam , brahmakarma svabhāvajam ॥ 18.42

18.42 Brahmanas are the ones who display long term calmness, restraint, forbearance, purity, forgiveness and sincerity in all their expressions. Strong memory, a scientific temperament and high degree of faith are built into their genes itself.

शौर्यं तेजो धृतिर् दाक्ष्यम् , युद्धे चाप्यपलायनम् । दानम् ईश्वरभावश् च , क्षात्रं कर्म स्वभावजम् ॥ १८.४३

śauryaṁ tejo dhr̥tir dākṣyam , yuddhe cāpyapalāyanam ।

dānam īśvarabhāvaś ca , kṣātraṁ karma svabhāvajam ॥ 18.43

18.43 Kshatriyas display gallantry, splendour, grit, dexterity, also not fleeing from confrontation, generosity and a majestic outlook. These again are inborn qualities.

कृषिगौरक्ष्यवाणिज्यम् , वैश्यकर्म स्वभावजम् । परिचर्यात्मकं कर्म , शूद्रस्यापि स्वभावजम् ॥ १८.४४

kr̥ṣigaurakṣyavāṇijyam , vaiśyakarma svabhāvajam ।

paricaryātmakaṁ karma , śūdrasyāpi svabhāvajam ॥ 18.44

18.44 Vaishyas are great farmers, cattle and livestock rearers, entrepreneurs, manufacturers and traders. It is in their blood.
Sudras suit well in all and sundry jobs, and perform best under supervision, being service oriented by birth.

स्वे स्वे कर्मण्यभिरतः , संसिद्धिं लभते नरः । स्वकर्मनिरतस् सिद्धिम् , यथा विन्दति तच्छृणु ॥ १८.४५

sve sve karmaṇyabhirataḥ , saṁsiddhiṁ labhate naraḥ ।

svakarmaniratas siddhim , yathā vindati tacchr̥ṇu ॥ 18.45

18.45 Thus engaged in and devoted to the correct profession according to his temperament, each man attains the highest glory. Now listen attentively to how success showers on the one dedicated and steadfast in his befitting role.

यतः प्रवृत्तिर् भूतानाम् , येन सर्वम् इदं ततम् । स्वकर्मणा तमभ्यर्च्य , सिद्धिं विन्दति मानवः ॥ १८.४६

yataḥ pravṛttir bhūtānām , yena sarvam idaṁ tatam I

svakarmaṇā tamabhyarcya , siddhiṁ vindati mānavaḥ II 18.46

18.46 Work is worship that being the core motto, Honouring divinity that underlies all action, Seeing the one lord supervising all tasks, such a vision grants success.
(eat food with reverence, breath with gratefulness, sleep like a baby, noticing that there is something common in all individuals that sustains this life, the seasons and the sunsets).

श्रेयान् स्वधर्मो विगुणः , परधर्मात् स्वनुष्ठितात् । स्वभावनियतं कर्म , कुर्वन् नाप्नोति किल्बिषम् ॥ १८.४७

śreyān svadharmo viguṇaḥ , paradharmāt svanuṣṭhitāt I

svabhāvaniyataṁ karma , kurvan nāpnoti kilbiṣam II 18.47

18.47 Best it is to be duly engaged in an occupation in accordance with one's own nature and conscience, even though the remuneration might be lesser, than to secure a top paying job that goes against one's grain. Such a choice augurs well in the long run.

सहजं कर्म कौन्तेय , सदोषम् अपि न त्यजेत् । सर्वारम्भा हि दोषेण , धूमेनाग्निर् इवावृताः ॥ १८.४८

sahajaṁ karma kaunteya , sadoṣam api na tyajet I

sarvārambhā hi doṣeṇa , dhūmenāgnir ivāvṛtāḥ II 18.48

18.48 Work that is harmonious to one's well-being, even though lacking in comforts, is not to be forsaken at any cost; recognize that even the most plushy job cannot be without sting, headache or tax burden.

असक्तबुद्धिस् सर्वत्र , जितात्मा विगतस्पृहः । नैष्कर्म्यसिद्धिं परमाम् , सन्न्यासेनाधिगच्छति ॥ १८.४९

asaktabuddhis sarvatra , jitātmā vigataspṛhaḥ I

naiṣkarmyasiddhiṁ paramām , sannyāsenādhigacchati II 18.49

18.49 Intellect and decision making that is not coloured by bias, not run over by galloping senses, free from lust, delivers the ideal conducive for supreme bliss, being guided by one's sane temper.

सिद्धिं प्राप्तो यथा ब्रह्म , तथा आप्नोति निबोध मे । समासेनैव कौन्तेय , निष्ठा ज्ञानस्य या परा ॥ १८.५०

siddhiṁ prāpto yathā brahma , tathā āpnoti nibodha me ।

samāsenaiva kaunteya , niṣṭhā jñānasya yā parā ॥ 18.50

18.50 Now listen attentively O Kaunteya, how one who has tuned and perfected himself, attains Brahman-the state of all knowing undecaying contentment.

(knowledge is power is an accepted saying, that talent which is wholesome, unsullied and well used is the real power to be attained).

बुद्ध्या विशुद्धया युक्तः ,धृत्यात्मानं नियम्य च । शब्दादीन् विषयांस्त्यक्त्वा ,रागद्वेषौ व्युदस्य च ॥ १८.५१

buddhyā viśuddhayā yuktaḥ , dhṛtyātmānaṁ niyamya ca ।

śabdādīn viṣayāṁstyaktvā , rāgadveṣau vyudasya ca ॥ 18.51

18.51 Endowed with a well-rounded intelligence, utilizing one's moods and memories to advantage, directing one's senses capably without being thwarted by thunder and storm, overcoming one's limited vision and broadening one's comfort zone...

विविक्तसेवी लघ्वाशी , यतवाक्कायमानसः । ध्यानयोगपरो नित्यम् , वैराग्यं समुपाश्रितः ॥ १८.५२

viviktasevī laghvāśī , yatavākkāyamānasaḥ ।

dhyānayogaparo nityam , vairāgyaṁ samupāśritaḥ ॥ 18.52

18.52 Resorting to a secluded place, eating to satisfy hunger, keeping speech unsullied, body in shape, mind pleasant, sparing enough time and money for yogic practices and meditation, and taking refuge in detachment and dispassion...

अहङ्कारं बलं दर्पम् , कामं क्रोधं परिग्रहम् । विमुच्य निर्ममश् शान्तः , ब्रह्मभूयाय कल्पते ॥ १८.५३

ahaṅkāraṁ balaṁ darpam , kāmaṁ krodhaṁ parigraham ।

vimucya nirmamaś śāntaḥ , brahmabhūyāya kalpate ॥ 18.53

18.53 Abandoning false pretenses, letting go of rash use of power, keeping arrogance at bay, maintaining lust-anger-covetousness to a minimum, not falling prey to influence or bribery; such a state of sustained peacefulness when one achieves, one becomes fit for sainthood or lordship.

ब्रह्मभूत× प्रसन्नात्मा , न शोचति न काङ्क्षति । समस् सर्वेषु भूतेषु , मद्भक्तिं लभते पराम् ॥ १८.५४

brahmabhūta× prasannātmā , na śocati na kāṅkṣati ।

samas sarveṣu bhūteṣu , madbhaktiṁ labhate parām ॥ 18.54

18.54 Saintliness or lordliness having been attained, anxiety and expectation both vanquished, he rests in devotion that surpasses all.

भक्त्या माम् अभिजानाति ,यावान् यश् चास्मि तत्त्वतः । ततो मां तत्त्वतो ज्ञात्वा , विशते तद् अनन्तरम् ॥ १८.५५

bhaktyā mām abhijānāti , yāvān yaś cāsmi tattvataḥ ।

tato māṁ tattvato jñātvā , viśate tad anantaram ॥ 18.55

18.55 Bhakti Yoga - Devotion-a composite mix of faith, focus, humility and the attitude of selfless service - leads to oneness with this creation, oneness with nature, and that is the summum bonum of divinity.

सर्वकर्माण्यपि सदा , कुर्वाणो मद्व्यपाश्रयः । मत्प्रसादाद् अवाप्नोति , शाश्वतं पदम् अव्ययम् ॥ १८.५६

sarvakarmāṇyapi sadā , kurvāṇo madvyapāśrayaḥ ।

matprasādād avāpnoti , śāśvataṁ padam avyayam ॥ 18.56

18.56 Karma Yoga - Working with a sense of being supported, sheltered and protected by the divine, performing deeds with a sense of reverential offering; bestows grace that is eternal, indestructible and all blissful.

चेतसा सर्वकर्माणि , मयि सन्न्यस्य मत्परः । बुद्धियोगम् उपाश्रित्य , मच्चित्तस् सततं भव ॥ १८.५७

cetasā sarvakarmāṇi , mayi sannyasya matparaḥ ।

buddhiyogam upāśritya , maccittas satataṁ bhava ॥ 18.57

18.57 Jnana Yoga - willingly and cheerfully acknowledging the supreme divinity while working, playing and resting, and seeing the unity and oneness in creation, the gyani is ever absorbed in the lord.

मच्चित्तस् सर्वदुर्गाणि , मत्प्रसादात् तरिष्यसि । अथ चेत् त्वम् अहङ्कारात् ,न श्रोष्यसि विनङ्क्ष्यसि ॥ १८.५८

maccittas sarvadurgāṇi , matprasādāt tariṣyasi ।

atha cet tvam ahaṅkārāt , na śroṣyasi vinaṅkṣyasi ॥ 18.58

18.58 Thus resorting to Bhakti, or Karma, or Jnana, allow the divine grace to clear all obstacles and attain success. The one who misses this priceless instruction or avoids it due to egotism is doomed.

यद् अहङ्कारम् आश्रित्य , न योत्स्य इति मन्यसे । मिथ्यैष व्यवसायस् ते , प्रकृतिस् त्वां नियोक्ष्यति ॥ १८.५९

yad ahaṅkāram āśritya , na yotsya iti manyase ।

mithyaiṣa vyavasāyas te , prakṛtis tvāṁ niyokṣyati ॥ 18.59

18.59 Egotism is your foremost enemy, it clouds thinking, prevents righteous action and proves futile.

स्वभावजेन कौन्तेय , निबद्धस् स्वेन कर्मणा । कर्तुं नेच्छसि यन्मोहात् , करिष्यस्यवशोऽपि तत् ॥ १८.६०

svabhāvajena kaunteya , nibaddhas svena karmaṇā I

kartuṁ necchasi yanmohāt , kariṣyasyavaśo'pi tat II 18.60

18.60 Your basic drive and temper is geared towards shouldering responsibility, so shed any nagging doubts forthwith, else time and tide shall have their say.

ईश्वरस् सर्वभूतानाम् , हृद्देशेऽर्जुन तिष्ठति । भ्रामयन् सर्वभूतानि , यन्त्रारूढानि मायया ॥ १८.६१

īśvaras sarvabhūtānām , hr̥ddeśe'rjuna tiṣṭhati I

bhrāmayan sarvabhūtāni , yantrārūḍhāni māyayā II 18.61

18.61 The great lord is the innate witness in each heart, each instinct is chiselled to perform work and maintain the body.

तमेव शरणं गच्छ , सर्वभावेन भारत । तत्प्रसादात् परां शान्तिम् , स्थानं प्राप्स्यसि शाश्वतम् ॥ १८.६२

tameva śaraṇaṁ gaccha , sarvabhāvena bhārata I

tatprasādāt parāṁ śāntim , sthānaṁ prāpsyasi śāśvatam II 18.62

18.62 Surrender to Him alone with your entire being O Bharata, by His grace you shall attain supreme felicity, the eternal fortune.

इति ते ज्ञानम् आख्यातम् , गुह्याद् गुह्यतरं मया । विमृश्यैतद् अशेषेण , यथेच्छसि तथा कुरु ॥ १८.६३

iti te jñānam ākhyātam , guhyād guhyataraṁ mayā I

vimr̥śyaitad aśeṣeṇa , yathecchasi tathā kuru II 18.63

18.63 Thus completely and in adequate detail has the hardest to grasp science been explained and taught to you by the divine. Contemplate and reflect, digest and assimilate to your heart's content, then choose your path, embark on your mission with conviction and confidence.

सर्वगुह्यतमं भूयः , श्रृणु मे परमं वचः । इष्टोऽसि मे दृढम् इति , ततो वक्ष्यामि ते हितम् ॥ १८.६४

sarvaguhyatamaṁ bhūyaḥ , śr̥ṇu me paramaṁ vacaḥ I

iṣṭo'si me dr̥ḍham iti , tato vakṣyāmi te hitam II 18.64

18.64 Listen again and again to the highest teaching O beloved seeker. It is most profound and hard to incorporate, yet most beneficial, salutary and significant.

(notice that in ashram Sri Sri gives darshan again and again. He waits till each is addressed, guided and fulfilled. He conducts a plethora of satsangs, meditations, discourses, programs, courses and events for each taste and for everyone's benefit).

मन्मना भव मद्भक्तः , मद्याजी मां नमस्कुरु । मामेवैष्यसि सत्यं ते , प्रतिजाने प्रियोऽसि मे ॥ १८.६५

manmanā bhava madbhaktaḥ , madyājī māṁ namaskuru I

māmevaiṣyasi satyaṁ te , pratijāne priyo'si me II 18.65

18.65 Focus yourself on the highest goal, be devoted and committed, perform actions and deeds of common welfare including fire oblations ordained in the scriptures, glorify the divinity and heed the injunctions of the wise. The divine loves you truly, that is a solemn promise.

सर्वधर्मान् परित्यज्य , माम् एकं शरणं व्रज । अहं त्वा सर्वपापेभ्यः , मोक्षयिष्यामि मा शुचः ॥ १८.६६

sarvadharmān parityajya , mām ekaṁ śaraṇaṁ vraja I

ahaṁ tvā sarvapāpebhyaḥ , mokṣayiṣyāmi mā śucaḥ II 18.66

18.66 Do not dither, be not scattered nor fickle; collect your wits and pull yourself together, and come straight and sure to the divine. To the sacred and pure in your vicinity. To the saint in your village. Pour your heart out; surely help is yours, guidance is yours, support is yours and victory is yours.

इदं ते नातपस्काय , नाभक्ताय कदाचन । न चाशुश्रूषवे वाच्यम् , न च मां योऽभ्यसूयति ॥ १८.६७

idaṁ te nātapaskāya , nābhaktāya kadācana I

na cāśuśrūṣave vācyam , na ca māṁ yo'bhyasūyati II 18.67

18.67 This pristine, sacred, wondrous and all powerful science demands supreme commitment, heightened awareness, total reverence and requisite qualification. It is not meant for the casual shopper or the profane doubter.

य इमं परमं गुह्यम् , मद्भक्तेष्वभिधास्यति । भक्तिं मयि परां कृत्वा , मामेवैष्यत्यसंशयः ॥ १८.६८

ya imaṁ paramaṁ guhyam , madbhakteṣvabhidhāsyati I

bhaktiṁ mayi parāṁ kr̥tvā , māmevaiṣyatyasaṁśayaḥ II 18.68

18.68 He who assimilates this paramount teaching and imparts it further to sincere devotees, sharing willingly with the ardent disciple, shall unquestionably attain salvation.

न च तस्मान्मनुष्येषु , कश्चिन्मे प्रियकृत्तमः । भविता न च मे तस्मात् , अन्यः प्रियतरो भुवि ॥ १८.६९

na ca tasmānmanuṣyeṣu , kaścinme priyakṛttamaḥ ।

bhavitā na ca me tasmāt , anyaḥ priyataro bhuvi ॥ 18.69

18.69 Sharing and spreading of the purest science to those qualified and longing is the highest service to mankind. Such a one is very dear, most laudable, and essentially one with the divine.

अध्येष्यते च य इमम् , धर्म्यं संवादमावयोः । ज्ञानयज्ञेन तेनाहम् , इष्टस् स्याम् इति मे मतिः ॥ १८.७०

adhyeṣyate ca ya imam , dharmyaṁ saṁvādamāvayoḥ ।

jñānayajñena tenāham , iṣṭas syām iti me matiḥ ॥ 18.70

18.70 And he who listens, ponders and meditates on this sacred teaching of the Gita in the form of a dialogue; to him accrues the benefits and rewards of Jnana Yoga or Karma Yoga; such is the divine conviction.

श्रद्धावान् अनसूयश् च , श्रृणुयाद् अपि यो नरः । सोऽपि मुक्तश् शुभाँल्लोकान् , प्राप्नुयात् पुण्यकर्मणाम् ॥ १८.७१

śraddhāvān anasūyaś ca , śṛṇuyād api yo naraḥ ।

so'pi muktaś śubhām̐llokān , prāpnuyāt puṇyakarmaṇām ॥ 18.71

18.71 Also he who hears the Gita chanted or its essence in his native language, imbued with faith and devoid of criticism, he gets absolved of guilt and blame. He too shall correct his course and strive for perfection.

कच्चिद् एतच्छ्रुतं पार्थ , त्वयैकाग्रेण चेतसा । कच्चिद् अज्ञानसम्मोहः , प्रनष्टस् ते धनञ्जय ॥ १८.७२

kaccid etacchrutaṁ pārtha , tvayaikāgreṇa cetasā ।

kaccid ajñānasammohaḥ , pranaṣṭas te dhanañjaya ॥ 18.72

18.72 Has this Gita discourse been heard by you sincerely O Partha? Has the storm of emotion and cloud of doubt been obliterated O Dhananjaya?

अर्जुन उवाच

नष्टो मोहस् स्मृतिर् लब्धा , त्वत्प्रसादान् मयाच्युत । स्थितोऽस्मि गतसन्देहः , करिष्ये वचनं तव ॥ १८.७३

arjuna uvāca

naṣṭo mohas smṛtir labdhā , tvatprasādān mayācyuta ।

sthito'smi gatasandehaḥ , kariṣye vacanaṁ tava ॥ 18.73

Arjuna bursts forth convincingly

18.73 My deception has gone, my wits are restored and my intelligence is functioning again, thanks to your blessing O Achyuta! I am firmly convinced and my path shines clearly, boldly shall i make headway.

सञ्जय उवाच

इत्यहं वासुदेवस्य , पार्थस्य च महात्मनः । संवादम् इमम् अश्रौषम् , अद्भुतं रोमहर्षणम् ॥ १८.७४

sañjaya uvāca

ityahaṁ vāsudevasya , pārthasya ca mahātmanaḥ ।

saṁvādam imam aśrauṣam , adbhutaṁ romaharṣaṇam ॥ 18.74

Sanjaya's comments after the game

18.74 Thus have i heard this most enlightening dialogue between Vasudeva - the indwelling soul in us all, and Partha - palm of the hand signifying a true Karma Yogi, practical, pragmatic and brilliant. The wonder and enigma of that thrilling conversation makes my hair stand on end and my entire body tingle with divine energy.

व्यासप्रसादाच्छ्रुतवान् , एतद् गुह्यम् अहं परम् । (इमं गुह्यतमं परम्)

योगं योगेश्वरात् कृष्णात् , साक्षात् कथयतस् स्वयम् ॥ १८.७५

vyāsaprasādācchrutavān,etad guhyam ahaṁ param।(imaṁ guhyatamaṁ param)

yogaṁ yogeśvarāt kṛṣṇāt , sākṣāt kathayatas svayam ॥ 18.75

18.75 Sage Vyasa was pleased and granted me the supersensory perception to hear the same. Directly from the supreme Lord - from Sri Krishna himself - from the master of Yoga and Yoga personified have i heard this ultimate science.

राजन् संस्मृत्य संस्मृत्य , संवादम् इमम् अद्भुतम् । केशवार्जुनयोः पुण्यम् , हृष्यामि च मुहुर् मुहुः ॥ १८.७६

rājan saṁsmṛtya saṁsmṛtya , saṁvādam imam adbhutam ।

keśavārjunayoḥ puṇyam , hṛṣyāmi ca muhur muhuḥ ॥ 18.76

18.76 O King, playing this discourse again and again, recalling the wondrous marvel that is the pair Kesava and Arjuna, this soul uplifting satsang makes me rejoice again and again.

तच्च संस्मृत्य संस्मृत्य , रूपम् अत्यद्भुतं हरेः । विस्मयो मे महान् राजन् , हृष्यामि च पुनः पुनः ॥ १८.७७

tacca saṁsmr̥tya saṁsmr̥tya ,rūpam atyadbhutaṁ hareḥ ।

vismayo me mahān rājan , hr̥ṣyāmi ca punaḥ punaḥ ॥ 18.77

18.77 Remembering again and again the cosmic immense grand spectacle of Hari's marvellous form, phenomenal is my wonder O King, i exult again and again.

यत्र योगेश्वरः कृष्णः , यत्र पार्थो धनुर्धरः । तत्र श्रीर् विजयो भूतिः , ध्रुवा नीतिर् मतिर् मम ॥ १८.७८

yatra yogeśvaraḥ kr̥ṣṇaḥ , yatra pārtho dhanurdharaḥ ।

tatra śrīr vijayo bhūtiḥ , dhruvā nītir matir mama ॥ 18.78

18.78 Krishna the master of yoga and Partha the bow wielding karma yogi, their twin presence is the harbinger of abundant good fortune, triumph, exaltation and cutting edge strategy. This is the common conviction and an enduring principle.

ॐ तत् सत् । इति श्रीमद्भगवद्गीतासु उपनिषत्सु ब्रह्मविद्यायां योगशास्त्रे श्रीकृष्णार्जुनसंवादे
मोक्ष-सन्न्यास-योगो नाम अष्टादशोऽध्यायः ॥ १८॥

oṁ tat sat । iti śrīmadbhagavadgītāsu upaniṣatsu brahmavidyāyāṁ yogaśāstre śrīkr̥ṣṇārjunasaṁvāde mokṣa-sannyāsa-yogo nāma aṣṭādaśo'dhyāyaḥ ॥ 18 ॥

Thus ends the 18th chapter titled Yoga of Liberation through letting go
In the form of a dialogue
between the Master and Disciple,
between the Mother and Child,
between the Soul and Being,
between Friends.

Ending Prayer

गुरुर् ब्रह्मा गुरुर् विष्णुः गुरुर् देवो महेश्वरः । गुरुस् साक्षात् परब्रह्म तस्मै श्रीगुरवे नमः ॥

श्री गुरुभ्यो नमः हरिः ॐ । श्री कृष्णार्पणमस्तु ॥

gurur brahmā gurur viṣṇuḥ gurur devo maheśvaraḥ ।

gurus sākṣāt parabrahma tasmai śrīgurave namaḥ ॥

śrī gurubhyo namaḥ hariḥ oṁ । śrī kr̥ṣṇārpaṇamastu ॥

Pardon Shlokas

आवाहनं न जानामि नैव जानामि पूजनम् । विसर्जनं न जानामि क्षमस्व परमेश्वर ॥

अन्यथा शरणं नास्ति त्वमेव शरणं मम । तस्मात्कारुण्यभावेन रक्ष रक्ष महेश्वर ॥

मन्त्रहीनं क्रियाहीनं भक्तिहीनं जनार्दन । यत्पूजितं मया देव परिपूर्णं तदस्तु ते ॥

The peoples of Bharata have this humility of asking for pardon in case of a mistake during chanting!

Gita Mahatmyam

गीताशास्त्रम् इदं पुण्यं यᳶ पठेत् प्रयतᳶ पुमान् । विष्णोः पदमवाप्नोति भयशोकादिवर्जितः ॥ १
गीताध्ययनशीलस्य प्राणायामपरस्य च । नैव सन्ति हि पापानि पूर्वजन्मकृतानि च ॥ २
मलनिर्मोचनं पुंसां जलस्नानं दिने दिने । सकृद् गीताम्भसि स्नानं संसारमलनाशनम् ॥ ३
गीता सुगीता कर्तव्या किमन्यैः शास्त्रविस्तरैः । या स्वयं पद्मनाभस्य मुखपद्माद्विनिःसृता ॥ ४
भारतामृतसर्वस्यं विष्णोर्वक्त्राद्विनिःसृतम् । गीतागङ्गोदकं पीत्वा पुनर्जन्म न विद्यते ॥ ५
सर्वोपनिषदो गावो दोग्धा गोपालनन्दनः । पार्थो वत्सः सुधीर्भोक्ता दुग्धं गीतामृतं महत् ॥ ६
एकं शास्त्रं देवकीपुत्रगीतमेको देवो देवकीपुत्र एव ।एको मन्त्रस्तस्य नामानि यानि कर्माप्येकं तस्य देवस्य सेवा ॥ ७ ॥

End the Gita with shlokas that glorify and list the benefits of recital.

Devanagari Latin Velthuis Transliteration Chart

अ	आ	इ	ई	उ	ऊ	ऋ	ॠ	ऌ	
a	aa	i	ii	u	uu	.r	.rr	.l	
ए	ऐ	ओ	औ	◌ं	◌ः		◌ँ	ॐ	
e	ai	o	au	.m	.h (or ×)		/m	.o	
क	ka	च	ca	ट	.ta	त	ta	प	pa
ख	kha	छ	cha	ठ	.tha	थ	tha	फ	pha
ग	ga	ज	ja	ड	.da	द	da	ब	ba
घ	gha	झ	jha	ढ	.dha	ध	dha	भ	bha
ङ	”na	ञ	~na	ण	.na	न	na	म	ma
य	र	ल	व		ळ	ऽ	◌्		
ya	ra	la	va		La	.a	&		
श	ष	स	ह		क्ष	ज्ञ	श्र	त्र	
”sa	.sa	sa	ha		k.sa	j~na	”sra	tra	

Note: Herein the ॐ has been transliterated as ॐ = ओम् = o.m

Om Jai Jagadish Hare

ॐ जय जगदीश हरे स्वामी जय जगदीश हरे ।

भक्त जनों के संकट । दास जनों के संकट क्षण मे दूर करे ॥ ॐ जय जगदीश..

जो ध्यावे फल पावे दुःख बिनसे मन का । स्वामी दुःख बिनसे मन का ।

सुख सम्पति घर आवे कष्ट मिटे तन का ॥ ॐ जय जगदीश ...

मात पिता तुम मेरे शरण गहूँ मैं किसकी । स्वामी शरण पडूँ मैं किसकी ।

तुम बिन और न दूजा आस करुँ मैं जिसकी ॥ ॐ जय जगदीश .....

तुम पूरण परमात्मा तुम अन्तर्यामी । स्वामी तुम अन्तरयामी ।

पार ब्रह्म परमेश्वर तुम सबके स्वामी ॥ ॐ जय जगदीश .....

तुम करुणा के सागर तुम पालन कर्ता । स्वामी तुम रक्षा कर्ता ।

मैं सेवक तुम स्वामी कृपा करो भर्ता ॥ ॐ जय जगदीश .....

तुम हो एक अगोचर सब के प्राणपति । स्वामी सब के प्राणपति ।

किस विध मिलूँ दयालु किस विध मिलूँ कृपालु तुम को मैं कुमति ॥ ॐ जय जगदीश..

दीनबन्धु दुःखहर्ता ठाकुर तुम मेरे । स्वामी रक्षक तुम मेरे ।

अपने हाथ बढाओ अपने शरणि लगाओ द्वार खडा मैं तेरे ॥ ॐ जय जगदीश..

विषय विकार मिटाओ पाप हरो देवा । स्वामी कष्ट हरो देवा ।

श्रद्धा भक्ति बढाओ सन्तन की सेवा ॥ ॐ जय जगदीश..

तन मन धन सब कुछ है तेरा । स्वामी सब कुछ है तेरा ।

तेरा तुझ को अर्पण क्या लागे मेरा ॥ ॐ जय जगदीश..

Epilogue

each verse is complete. each of the 700 verses is fully capable of delivering, of winning, of giving the direct and full answer.
just as a smartphone has tons of apps, all different, all unique yet wholly complete in themselves. just as a wardrobe has so many clothes and shoes, all different, yet each befitting. as you have facebook friends & contacts, each unique yet capable.
just as Guruji answers someone's query in Satsang. It is a specific question. It is a specific answer. Yet it weaves its magic on all. Satisfies many. each of Sri Sri's answers as if meant for one, yet enlightens all.

So it is with the Gita

the verses are weaved together by a magician. they are placed by a divine hand. Gita verses are interspersed and knitted and dyed and woven. Are made up of cottons & silks, nylons and polyester, wool & acrylic, and every yarn under the sun.

the weaving is so deft, smooth, and soft, so cozy, nice and comfortable.
that one may miss the hues shades nuances emotions events and truths.
But one cannot miss the impact! So one may ask; Who is the Gita for? Who benefits? How benefits? The Bhagavad Gita is spoken by the Lord.

Who doth the Lord address?

The entire creation of course.
He addresses every single man woman and child.
He addresses every single plant herb and tree.
Every piece of matter animate or inanimate.
Every bit of energy, no matter whether it is in the visible spectrum or beyond.

The Gita is about Life.

It is about Dinacharya. About Ritucharya. About what to do when.
How to live, how to LOVE. How to be well. How to plan and how to act. What to think and what to speak. About what qualities talents hobbies to nourish. what goals to achieve. About how to meet deadlines and targets.
perhaps you get the drift.
It applies not only to mankind. It also applies to machines and electronics.
It applies also to the Natural Laws and to the life-forms we know and do not know.
It is a complete textbook. A finely detailed user manual. Help book and recipe book.

The Bhagavad Gita is a friend.

सर्वे भवन्तु सुखिनः । सर्वे सन्तु निरामयाः । सर्वे भद्राणि पश्यन्तु । मा कश्चिद् दुःख भाग्भवेत् ॥

ॐ शान्तिः शान्तिः शान्तिः ॥

When faith has blossomed in life, Every step is led by the Divine.
Sri Sri Ravi Shankar

Printed in Great Britain
by Amazon

46025588R00104